Shame on you

Shame on you

A literary perspective on shame and guilt

Gorm Larsen and René Rasmussen (eds.)

UNIVERSITY PRESS OF
SOUTHERN DENMARK

Shame on you

© The authors and University Press of Southern Denmark 2022

University of Southern Denmark Studies in Literature, vol. 74

All rights reserved. No part of this publication may be reproduced, distributed, or transmitted in any form or by any means, without the prior written permission of the publisher, except in the case of brief quotations embodied in critical reviews and certain other non-commercial uses permitted by copyright law.

ISBN 978-87-408-3217-4

Printed by Narayana Press

Cover design by Tessa Rasmussen

The publication is supported by the research group Communication Dynamics, Department of Communication and Psychology, Aalborg University, and Department of Nordic Studies and Linguistics, University of Copenhagen.

Distribution in the United States and Canada:
Independent Publishers Group
www.ipgbook.com

Distribution in the United Kingdom and Ireland:
Gazelle Book Services
www.gazellebookservices.co.uk

University Press of Southern Denmark
Campusvej 55
DK-5230 Odense M
www.universitypress.dk

Contents

1.
Shame and guilt. Introduction 7
Gorm Larsen & René Rasmussen

2.
Freedom, anxiety and shame in the performance society 33
Gorm Larsen

3.
A few paradoxes of guilt and shame in psychoanalysis and
anthropology 53
François Sauvagnat

4.
Mapping shame and guilt
Inner and outer landscapes in *The Adventures of Pinocchio and The
Wonderful Adventures of Nils* 73
Anna Smedberg Bondesson

5.
When we dead awaken: To die of shame 91
Kjell R. Soleim

6.
A short reflection on some scenes of shame 103
Carin Franzén

7.
Friendship as the friend of thought: Franz Kafka and
the gesture of shame 121
Alexander Carnera

8.
Poetics of shame and guilt
Freud and Woolf on shame and guilt in creative writing and the
pleasures and pains of reading 137
Anna-Klara Bojö

9.
Where being and thinking is the s(h)ame: Nightwood,
sub specie ruboris 155
Magnus Bøe Michelsen

10.
Sweet November: Desire and shame in the age of serial monogamy ... 179
Lars Nylander

11.
To write with the arsehole: Abject voices in contemporary literature ... 195
Lone Elmstedt Bild

12.
Shame in Hassan's and Llambías' poetry 205
René Rasmussen

Personal information 225

1.
Shame and guilt. Introduction

Gorm Larsen & René Rasmussen

In recent years, a number of events have made shame the central and topical theme on the international political scene – most conspicuously in the European refugee crisis, the guise of Trump, MeToo, the climate crisis and, most recently, reactions to the Covid-19 pandemic.

When Trump, very surprisingly, was elected president of the United States in 2016, one of the analyses explained that he succeeded in presenting an approach to the management of shame for white workers and middle-class voters, who have felt like social outcasts. He rehabilitated them and put the blame on erroneous globalization, trade agreements and illegal immigration (Williams 2020 [2016], Burgo 2016): They were simply the victims of a failed policy – not losers. His hate speeches and debasement of immigrants and Mexicans etc. were shameless in the ears of many, but at the same time he removed social humiliation for others.

Since then, shame has often been linked to Trump, his non-presidential twitter activities and the policy he stands for. For example, the entry ban aimed at citizens from six Muslim countries, the US weapons legislation and Trump's support of the US weapon lobby National Rifle Association (NRA). After the school shooting in Florida in February 2018, the NRA has given rise to demonstrations and the young Emma

González became known for her indignant speech. "To every politician taking donations from the NRA, shame on you," González said.[1]

In Scandinavia and most of (Northern) Europe, the welfare state is more expanded, and conflicts do not have the same character as in the United States. Here, the states have developed a social security network, which also provides for the sick, disabled, unemployed and poor people. The system for instance recognizes these citizens as equal, and, as a result, it can be argued that these groups do not experience the same level of identity-related vulnerability as in the United States. Even so, the conflict axes of Europe and the United States have similarities: globalization, refugees and the polarization of metropolis vs countryside. The European refugee crisis showed us this. One group is accused of not defending the people and the nation, the other of conducting an inhumane and unworthy policy. These are two various principal forms of shame, two different shame matrices.

When the MeToo movement went viral in October 2017, a series of powerful and famous people, from Harvey Weinstein to Kevin Spacey, were shamed and dishonoured. Some of them were later convicted in court, but (almost) all of them were convicted by the people's court: Ashamed. However, the second part of this conflict is more striking: Women who stand up and say, "Me too". It is well known that victims of sexual assaults feel shame – in the sense of unbearable humiliation and disgrace – towards themselves and others. To say "Me too" requires great courage and overcoming. Therefore, MeToo involves shame for all parties – to be shamed vs to overcome shame. MeToo has spread throughout the Western world with a series of consequences following from it – private companies have been hit as have well-established institutions, such as the Swedish Academy of the Nobel Prize in Literature, which as an effect was not awarded in 2018.

During the corona-pandemic, the citizens as well as the leaders of the world have been put into a hitherto unknown situation: How

---

[1] See e.g. https://www.youtube.com/watch?v=ZxD30-9H1lY

should one react on the unknown and how should one react in relation to the national leaders' injunctions and prohibitions? In the United Kingdom, Boris Johnson initially ridiculed the fear of corona, but later, after being admitted to intensive care having contracted Covid-19, he changed his strategy. Was this a shameful realization? And what about those who had loyally supported Johnson? Trump suffered the same fate, but did not change his course (so as not to lose face). In Sweden, known for always steering a rational course, it was the health authorities who laid out the frame for the corona policy that was adopted. The authorities followed an alternative strategy, which calculated with deaths, albeit not as many as was actually the case. For a long period, Swedish citizens were confronted with living in the country with the highest death rate per capita. The Swedish journalist Göran Rosenberg talked at that time about the corona crisis threatening to crack the varnish of civilization: Corona management in Sweden revealed a society with a poorly functioning crisis alert system, with a poorly functioning crisis responsibility and with a poorly functioning care of the elderly. But even though it was clear that Sweden did not live up to the ideal of being the world's best organized welfare state, this truth could not be spoken out loud because of the damage this would cause to Sweden's self-image (Rosenberg 2020).

In Denmark, the prime minister, who immediately introduced and maintained a strict precautionary course and was able to ensure a low infection rate, attained a certain notoriety for including a handwritten addition in her speech: "Shame on those who have not been sensible". Those who behaved badly should be ashamed. The opposition was in revolt: This was not the way to address the public. No one was to be ashamed. This was in itself nothing new or controversial, what was new was that the shame strategy came to the public's attention and became an explicitly stated policy.

Every civilization has a culture of shame in the form of expressions of the values and norms in society, what is right and what is wrong. Political power also goes hand in hand with setting the agenda for cultural values. This means that what may be the subject of shame can also be a political struggle. This becomes apparent when shame is no longer seen as a hidden norm, in line with most of our culture's values, but is put up for discussion. The counterculture of the 1960s focused on dismantling the authoritarian norms and patriarchal family patterns as well as the strict sexual morality, and they succeeded in shifting the boundaries of shame in a number of areas. But they were not lacking shame. In the hippie commune, there were norms for right and wrong, too, even though focus was on conventions that were broken. There was a focus on equality, human rights, respect for all people, environmental awareness etc. Their successors are perhaps the generation who is most conscious of where the line of shame should be drawn. "How dare you?" were Greta Thunberg's words spoken to the leaders of the world at *The United Nations* in New York City in December 2019, with reference both to the culmination of the climate changes as well as to her stolen childhood and dreams: "This is all wrong. I shouldn't be up here. I should be back in school, on the other side of the ocean. Yet you all come to us young people for hope. How dare you! ... we'll be watching you."[2] And the commandments of today are spoken out loud: Don't travel by air or drive a gas-guzzler, don't eat meat, buy organic etc.

    At the same time, this moralism, which is sometimes referred to negatively as *political correctness*, has created a backlash in the shape of protests against the power of shame. The shamelessness – which Trump, if anything, incarnates – can, by some, be experienced as a liberation. A liberation from shame and the loss of value. When the countercultural movement of the 1960s rebelled, it was against the patriarchal white man, his social order and code of shame. The most striking symbol, so far, of his defeat is the fall of Weinstein. Our time of shamelessness can be seen as an attempt at re-establishing the white man, who could not keep up with the changing times. Jordan

---

2   See e.g. https://www.youtube.com/watch?v=TMrtLsQbaok

Peterson (2018) has presented an intellectual defence of past family patterns and the white man.

Although it can be pointed out that shame is now a topical theme in the Western world, it has been emerging for a long time. The traditional claim is that we, in the West, live in a culture of guilt – unlike the Arabic culture of shame – but it can also be pointed out that the West has moved from being dominated by guilt to a situation where shame, too, has a central position. Literature from the past 100-150 years, from naturalism and modernism to contemporary literature, testifies to this.

Already in 1933, the Danish-Norwegian author Aksel Sandemose formulated the so-called Jantelov (in *A refugee crossing his track*), where the shame regime is put into words. In recent times, especially Lars Såbye Christensen (in for example *The Model*, 2006) and Karl Ove Knausgård (*My Struggle* 1-6, 2009-2011) focus on shame – not to mention the Norwegian television series *SKAM* (*SHAME*) (2015-17) for adolescents, which was subsequently broadcast in a number of new national contexts (American, French, etc.) during 2018-2019. Where *SKAM* focuses on the uncertainty of adolescence in the transition from childhood to adulthood, *My struggle* treats shame individualistically and existentially, but both revolve around uncertainty and the experience of having failed. In *SKAM*, fragility and shame are linked to finding one's inner compass; this is exposed by having a trans- and cross-media mode of presentation: The viewer witnesses a multimodal communication where what is said to friends in physical space often is in contrast to what is communicated over messenger or other media. In Knausgård's novel, there is an identity overlap between the author and the novel's main character. The great wave of other confession novels that have appeared in recent years spurred the discussions about autofiction or reality literature; texts in which writers emerge and report from their private worlds – without beautification.

Literature reflects our society's development away from a bourgeois culture where no one is allowed to break the forms and norms of contemporary time, to one where values and norms have been internalized and the individual is solely responsible for his or her own self-realization, happiness and achievements. This book wishes to demonstrate the relationship between shame and guilt, as reflected in literature from the last 150 years, using it as a prism through which we can understand the mental state of our modern-day society. But first, we want briefly in to explore what shame and guilt are.

Shame and guilt

Shame and guilt are some of the quintessential human emotions. They affect our feelings about ourselves and our social behaviour. They affect us at different levels, as individuals and as a collective culture. That is, they are reflective emotions and what we may call social feelings. Shame and guilt are similar in that they both reveal a failure of the self in regard to common norms. But where shame is about the self—in general—and concerns a person's self-identity as a matter of being, guilt is linked to a specific action toward others. Guilt can be punished, or one can react to it. Shame is a punishment in itself. Shame and guilt are closely related to each other and are often woven together, although they are different feelings. Both are related to norms and standards and both are connected to identity and self-understanding. Shame and guilt are the core principles of the self. Because they are reflections of the self, they are also expressions of cultural norms and codices and may be called feelings of socialization. The things we are ashamed of or feel guilty about are not fixed entities, but change as the culture changes. In this way, these feelings constitute a prism of cultural conventions and norms. It is essential here to underline that shame and guilt are, on the one hand, deeply grounded psychological dynamics that form the self and, on the other hand, are simultaneously conditioned by the sociocultural standards and environment. It may be difficult to draw this distinction since the two dimensions are interwoven. Nonetheless, in the following we will try to do this: firstly, we will examine shame and guilt as emotions from a psychological, mainly psychoanalytical, perspective; secondly, we will investigate the social and historical dynamics of shame and guilt.

Shame as affect

Shame is an affect that strikes the subject, making him or her feel reduced to a worthless object and a social outcast. In this sense, shame is related to anxiety and enjoyment, which are two other important bodily affects; but while enjoyment gives rise to a certain pleasure (although a pleasure mixed with pain), anxiety and shame are negative affects. Let us expand on this from a psychoanalytic point of view. As an affect, shame differs from a bad consciousness, which stems from the superego and the voice connected to it, as Jacques Lacan underlines. Affect is not something that the subject himself can think—it is not present as a thought—but it imposes itself on the subject. Guilt, which emerges in the subject when facing the voice of the Other, is a way of negotiating the Other's judgement (which may be articulated in language). Affects are positioned prior to the Other who judges or values, and yet affects are positioned in regard to the Other's gaze (which is not initially grasped in language).

Shame does not seem capable of the same powerful pathogenic role as guilt, which is not only the recognition of having done wrong, but can, more puzzling perhaps, arise from a mere wish (cf. Grigg, 2015). Guilt can be the result of wishes—particularly subconscious wishes—that the person would never actually act on. Thus, the superego censures and punishes the subject for sins s/he commits, using voice; but since the superego is also an internal agency, it likewise punishes the subject for the sins that s/he does not commit. The subject is not only guilty of his or her acts, but also of his or her secret thoughts. While anxiety manifests itself as an affect influencing the ego, the feeling of guilt is subconscious and concerns wishes.

In the following, shame will be distinguished from guilt. It is linked to the notion of the Other, but it arises even before any Other is there to pass judgement: an Other that is attached to sight and that which can be seen. We may hence see shame as a prior affect, while guilt comes to the subject later. It does not only stem from the subject, but can also depend on the behaviour of the Other. When, for example, a child sees his/her mother naked and feels ashamed, this is caused by the exposure of the Other's nudity and is independent of any misdeed, harm or transgression that the person feeling shame has carried out (Freud, 2010). The subject is absorbed in the scene and, in watching or in being seen, he is absorbed by the spectacle.

Shame is therefore not only the subject's own behaviour, which within each individual can be a source of shame, it is also the behaviour of others, for instance when another person crosses the limits of decency and modesty. We can be affected when we witness the shameful actions of others (for example, the nakedness of our mother or when we experience someone looking through the keyhole). The symbolic distance of judgement is lacking here. The Other's gaze touches the most intimate core of the subject. When we are hit, it is the subject's desire that is affected. The subject cannot hold back the Other's gaze, which underlines the close relationship between shame and the gaze.

Shame is also connected to a fundamental fantasy where the person harbours his own most intimate secrets (cf. Bernard, 2011, p.61). He may even think that he is the only one who has such fantasies. (In the following, we discuss only the neurotic subject, as the perspective is rather different for a psychosis or perversion, and the logic of shame associated with neurosis seems to be more common; for the perverted or psychotic subject, see Bernard, 2011). His fundamental fantasy is not universal, which explains why it is much easier to confess to faults or flaws connected to guilt. True shame seems to be connected to secret fantasy and that which is most intimate to the individual—to that which makes him or her unique. The fundamental fantasy sustains the subject in his very existence and desires, although this fantasy is also more or less unknown to him. This secret fantasy pertains to what is 'more' in the subject than s/he is aware of; it is an unknown 'more'. Shame is in this way connected to what has to be hidden from the Other. The shameful subject is caught in his/her own desires. The subject wants to hide his (unknown) fantasy from the Other's gaze, whereas admitting guilt is much easier.

To be struck by shame does not mean that the subject is an object in a social context (for example, the sexual object of someone else), but that he experiences himself as an object outside of such a context, in a state of nothingness (cf. Bernhard, 2011, p.85ff). He is reduced to being a useless object: s/he has nothing more to say, s/he is seen and sees him/herself as seen—by the Other—as a worthless object. At the moment of the Other's gaze, at the moment when he is seen, he is mortalized, becomes a frozen statue, which explains the importance of the gaze of the Other. The subject is nothing for the Other, or just an object for its disgust. His inner secrets have been laid open, which constitutes an ontological crisis for the neurotic subject. But not only have his inner secrets been revealed to others: they are no longer hidden to himself; they are exposed. With shame, there is therefore a moment of destitution for the subject, because the subject is confronted with a fantasy whose form he barely knows.

Language and social bonds assure a certain distance from the experience of being nobody or of being an outcast. That sense of nothingness, however, is essential at the moment when the subject is struck by shame, which explains why this moment constitutes an ontological crisis; as Giorgio Agamben (2003, p.115) says, "shame is a sort of an ontological emotion, whose proper place is the meeting between man and being." It is a meeting outside language. Jacques Lacan prefers to talk about the shame of living as a sign of the pain of existing, the emotion of being nobody in life and of the non-sense of life.

Shame manifests itself at the moment when the subject (of language) disappears or appears only as an object banished from any social context. Hence, with shame, the subject is momentarily placed outside of the language (Lacan: the symbolic) and momentarily outside of his/her own image of him/herself (outside the imaginary, as Lacan understands it). S/he is reduced to something, which is at one and the same time the most intimate part of him/herself and the one most foreign to him/her, or s/he is frozen in the image of a fallen object (in stark contrast to his/her sublime narcissistic self-image in the imaginary): a waste in space and time. Agamben (2003, p.114) talks about subjectivation and de-subjectivation both of which occur at the same time, because the subject experiences his own loss as a subject.

Shame has to do with the experience of being reduced to a fallen object, but it is also connected to death. Shame, Lacan claims, is an effect of (linguistic) death, as the position of the subject in language vanishes in shame. Dying of shame has a long history in various cultures—for example, in Søren Kierkegaard's understanding: "... the individual can die of shame..." (1997 [1842], p.372). It is an effect of death, because the subject can no longer represent himself in language. Shame is connected to the failure of language, which stresses why it is an affect that arises by means of spoken words. We cannot feel shame as long as we are still deciding whether our death is justified or not, as seems to be the case for 'honest' people—"an honest man cannot die of shame" (Lacan, 1991, p.210). Honour excludes shame: "He does not deserve to die for that". This exclusion of shame is a way of producing an "hontology" [*honte* = shame], as Lacan says (1991, p.209), because this is a way of bringing everything to pointlessness, as we will never feel shameful if we reject the notion that death can be deserved or that a person may wish to die because of shame (e.g. commit suicide).

Reducing everything to pointlessness, which is what happens if the overriding focus is on honour, devalues life: "When honor retains its value, life does not prevail over honor. Where there is honor, life is pure and simple devalued" (Miller, 2006, p.18). When honour reigns, it is not possible to question whether or not life has any value, whereas doing so is important when shame prevails. In opposition to weighing of death's justification, which is incorporated in the idea of honour, leaning towards death presents the path which manifests what is involved in shame: that death is always deserved (we die for something) prior to any question regarding the circumstances of its justification.

On the other hand, in 1970, Lacan underlined that it is unusual to die of shame these days (1991 [1970], p.209ff). But what is lost, or gained, when dying of shame is no longer an option? The disappearance of the possibility of dying from shame is what we should worry about today: shame tends to be displayed and it is talked about shamelessly, although it is a relative of impurity—so to say, of enjoyment. One cannot forget the effects of enjoyment, even if one is no longer ashamed of them.

But let us focus a little on shamelessness. This is marked by a change in the position of the gaze, which was previously placed with the Other. Now it has a new place, for example the spectator's gaze: the gaze that watches reality TV is a gaze deprived of its ability to feel shame. Such a gaze does not bring shame to the subject, because it is not placed in the Other; instead, it is a gaze that is an element in the enjoyment of the subject: it is a gaze that enjoys without shame. "What is transmitted in this shameful universal practice is the demonstration that your gaze, far from conveying shame, is nothing other than a gaze that enjoys as well. It is the 'Look at them enjoying so as to enjoy!'" (Miller, 2006, p.15).

In another context, we also see that shame has become shameless, namely in the domain of contemporary biologically dominated psychiatry (as developed by, for example, the American Psychiatric Association in its Diagnostic and Statistical Manual IV/V), where the subject can rid itself of shame, which is regarded as a phenomenon caused and determined by the mind. And if a cure is necessary, one such can be found by prescribing medicine. Such a prescription permits the subject to approximate a means and moreover to experience an 'ordinary life', which nowadays is the experiential frame of our civilization (Laurent, 2015). It is from this perspective that a true appreciation of self-worth (the ordinary life), or of depression if things go wrong, can be established. Guilt and shame are now useless virtues. Whatever the feelings of shame might be, there is always the hope of treatment in the form of medicine. In such a biologically dominated psychiatry, both shame and depression are determined by failures of the mind; and, from that point of view, shame and guilt are indistinguishable and there is no need to talk about them. The term 'depression' can cover both of them, although from a psychoanalytical point of view they are separate.

In addition to this shamelessness, shame has to do with a common discourse, which is dominated by the idea of satisfaction. Nowadays, we have to enjoy ourselves, and this discourse promotes the notion of limitless enjoyment, although such enjoyment does not exist insofar as it would undermine the subject's place in language. Lacan named such a discourse a capitalistic discourse (2007, p.49) which promotes unrestricted enjoyment. This discourse endorses the notion that there should be no limits to our enjoyment. The discourse is dominated by consumerism and greed: "Greed is good", as the American expression says. While certain aspects of pleasure were previously connected to shame, many of those aspects are today openly flaunted. We live in a system, which promotes shamelessness and annuls shame. It is demanded of the subject not to feel shame regarding his enjoyment, but feel shame regarding his desire, which, with help from the fundamental fantasy, should sustain the subject in his very existence (living)—because desire otherwise breaks enjoyment or constitutes a certain defence against it.

However, shame still seems to be there, albeit not so much associated with what is (or once was) forbidden or what the subject does (or did) not want to share wit7herh others (his/her innermost secrets). Shame seems to be associated with not enjoying enough or not in the right way, and this shameless shame is connected to the subject's very existence, his living of life, because the subject is expected to 'realize' his/her vision (of enjoyment) and give up his/her desire; to enjoy fully is to give up desire. It is no longer a question of being reduced to a despised object, but of giving up one's place in language as well as one's desire, or becoming the object of enjoyment demanded by the capitalistic discourse. Life has lost its dignity; it has become a life which the subject does not believe in. Its shameless shame is the shame of living without having a life: a life you do not believe in anymore (Bernard, 2011, p.196).

The subject is guilty of not satisfying himself through the offers of enjoyment and pleasure, which the capitalist discourse imposes. He is guilty of enjoying (not enjoying enough) and of living (not living according to all the offers), as Bernard expresses it (2011, p.203). Hence, the subject is delivered to his drives or to an absolute de-subjectivation (Agamben, 2003): the subject closes his eyes to his own empty living, while the shame he feels is determined by the continuous offers and constant enjoyment.

Shame and guilt in a social and historical context

A characteristic trait of Homo sapiens is that individuals depend on one another. To be a self is a social matter. Often, we think of ourselves as individuals and of a self as an isolated and independent entity, but to be is to exist among others, in relation to others, just as the self itself is a relation. As Kierkegaard puts it in *The Sickness Unto Death (1849), talking about the self*:

> The self is a relation which relates itself to itself, or that in the relation which is its relating itself. The self is not the relation but is the relation's relating to itself. A human being is a synthesis of the infinite and the finite, of the temporal and the eternal, of freedom and necessity. In short a

> synthesis. A synthesis is a relation between two terms. Looked at in this way a human being is not yet a self.
>
> In a relation between two things the relation is the third term in the form of a negative unity, and the two relate to the relation, and in the relation to that relation; this is what it is from the point of view of soul for soul and body to be in relation. If, on the other hand, the relation relates to itself, then this relation is the positive third, and this is the self.
> (Kierkegaard 2004 [1849], p.43 [Kierkegaard 2006, p.217])

The self is not just a synthesis of related elements that have come together as a static entity. It is founded in the activity, in the relation's relating. The complexity in Kierkegaard's description of the self as a relation and a relation's relating is based on his understanding of the human as spirit and his idea that "the relation which relates to itself has been established by something else" (*Kierkegaard, 2004, p.43*)—in other words, that the self is determined and established by another. According to Kierkegaard, this determining other must be God. The more common conception today is that this determination arises from the self-relation. This kind of anatomy of the self finds a less reflective, but more energetic, expression in Meads' theory of the self, especially in *Mind, Self, and Society* (1934). Here, Mead points out that the self appropriates itself as a self through the acquisition of a special life practice. The "I" and the consciousness occur within a social process. The idea of an isolated self is a romantic conception: Only the body as an object can be properly regarded as a separate entity. The other forms the self in a social process; the self integrates the other's attitude toward itself and acts on this. In Mead's terminology, "I" is a re-reply to the other's attitude or the idea of the other's attitude, called "Me", the social self.

Although there are crucial differences between Mead's understanding of the self and Lacan's understanding of the subject, the dialogical constitution of the subject as the fundamental principle is present in both. According to Mead, the dialectical relation between I and Me forms the self, where Me represents the idea of the other's attitudes and points of view; according to Lacan, the Other is the radical alterity, otherness in both the concrete and abstract understanding—that is, the Other is embedded in the symbolic order related to language and the law.

Through the other—Me and/or the Other—sociality is embedded within the subject. Emotions such as shame and guilt may, as we have seen, have more or less fixed structures, but the substance of the emotions will change through time and from one cultural situation to another. The historical and cultural dimension in the shame-guilt-subject relation is long and complicated. Shame can be defined in relation to specific events, such as rape, the Holocaust, child abuse, etc., which are (hopefully and) ordinarily not part of people's everyday life; or shame can be defined in relation to gender, social class, age, national culture, history, etc. From a generic perspective, we can distinguish between at least four intermixed and overlapping domains from which shame can arise: conformity, sexual behaviour, prosocial behaviour and status (see Greenwald & Harder, 1998, p.229ff). Conformity shame concerns dress (code), food consumption, language usage, rituals etc. Shame related to the body is undoubtedly the strongest domain—that is, bodily exposure, nudity, sex and so on. Shame connected to prosocial behaviour are linked to the extent that helpfulness and sharing are qualities that are both desired and intertwined with one another. The question about status is complex; there are many ways in which status can be acquired and different aspects of status can support each other (cf. Bourdieu's concept of capital). Fear of acting in the wrong way within domains such as these four makes shame a powerful regulator. Shame—and guilt—are social mechanisms that function between people as a behavioural adjustment. But, at the same time, these feelings are internalized and—as an important effect of this—shame especially is a measure of what is considered standard behaviour. Shame works as an internal control, a potentially ongoing self-reflective scanning.

Shame and guilt are closely related to what is prohibited and allowed during a person's upbringing—do this, don't do that. However, what matters is not just what is explicitly said in words, but also what is imposed on each individual through (hidden) expectations. This means that shame and guilt are products of socialization, and it is far from certain that every reaction involving shame—or guilt—is conscious. There is not necessarily any awareness of these regulatory prohibitions and requirements on the part of the individual. They can be difficult to conceptualize although there are cases of obvious rules, too. Therefore, it is simpler to see shame and guilt as only social emotions, relationships that are regulated socially; shame and guilt are in equal measure inscribed in the body and the individual's self-perception.

One of the most important breakthrough studies to express a connection between the state of society and the subject's mental state is Norbert Elias' *Über den Prozess der Zivilisation* (1939) where Elias, among other things, has studied books on etiquette through the ages. Elias finds that there is a close relationship between the social organization and the individual behaviour, between the power relation in society and the psychic structures, and finally between the change in power and the change in the psychical processes of civilization. Shame especially plays a central role in understanding the changes in habits in Western culture throughout history. It is Elias' assertion that the Middle Ages represent a "barbaric" and uncivilized time seen through contemporary eyes. Since that medieval innocence, the contexts and circumstances of man's life have become progressively more complex and subject to greater regulation of his comings and goings. It is this gradual increase in the rules and norms of behaviour and coexistence that Elias calls the process of civilization. Placing the starting point in the Middle Ages does not necessarily mean that civilization begins with this, but only from a defined point in the past can a historical line be drawn up and progress measured (2000 [1978/1939], p.48).

Historically speaking, Europeans have understood themselves as civilized, although they have at the same time exhibited a quite barbaric cruelty in their behaviour. Elias explains this self-understanding with the formation of a mental structure, which is the product of a long evolution, and which has characterized the last centuries of European society.

As habits and manners in relation to bodily secretions, hygiene, nudity, sex, eating, conversations and violence change and are governed by new norms, a new kind of shame consciousness emerges: It is easier to become ashamed—even in areas not previously associated with shame. Elias describes medieval society as characterized by a very low degree of self-control and having few manners. From here, an emotional upheaval takes place: from being able to indulge in the enjoyment of everything from violence to body secretions, the subject imposed self-control and consideration for the other.

Although we cannot detect a strictly linear development, Elias sees a clear trend that points to a still greater regulation of emotions, and he talks about a rationalization of human behaviour and a mechanism of monopolization. As an ever-greater centralization of power occurs, a progressively greater mutual dependence arises between the agencies that possess power; this implies that the person who holds power is dependent on others who dominate in other areas and that these persons therefore mutually regulate one another. This means that the process of European state formation is intertwined with the individual's growing self-control and behavioural control.

Standards and codes from the upper layers of society trickle down and are absorbed by all who want to become part of the elite or strive for more influence, and this has an educational effect beyond that of the family.

> Stricter control of impulses and emotions is first imposed by those of high social rank on their social inferiors or, at most, their social equals. It is only comparatively late, when bourgeois classes comprising a large number of social equals have become the upper, ruling class, that the family becomes

the only—or, more exactly, the primary and dominant—institution with the function of installing drive control. (Elias 2000 [1978/1939], p.116)

Thus, Elias points to the fact that the act of restricting one's instincts is at first only applied in the relationship to others. Simultaneously, the subject learns to control himself and show his immediate needs, and learns to be ashamed of his failed behaviour. The point for Elias is to show that we cannot understand the relationship between the social and the mental if not we do not perceive the mental as a process.

Shame and guilt are means of exercising control. Given that external control is replaced with an internal control in (late) modern society, shame has moved away from being a public disgrace on the individual level, where the subject himself functions as his own judge and shame is internalized. Maybe in recent decades, we have witnessed a turning point: what is happening now is not that we have new and distinct codes and rules of conduct, but, on the contrary, that conventions and restrictions are withdrawn and reduced and that the norms of social groups are individualized and move towards instead of away from each other—and this development is new. On the surface, it seems that shamelessness here has found a new, rich and lucrative space for itself. But, behind this surface, the shameless shame is lurking.

An overview of the volume

The following 11 chapters explore shame and guilt in a Western and especially Scandinavian context, focusing on literature from the past one hundred years, ranging from Carlo Collodi's *The Adventures of Pinocchio* (1880) and Henrik Ibsen's *When We Dead Awaken* (1899) through high modernism and authors such as Frans Kafka, Virginia Woolf, Djuna Barnes and Marguerite Duras, to contemporary literature such as Elizabeth Gilbert's *Eat, Pray, Love* (2006), Charlotte Roche's *Wetlands* (2009) and the much discussed Danish poet Yahya Hassan.

The individual chapters focus on the cultural alteration of shame and guilt – an alteration that is indicated for example by pointing out the contrast between the repression of sexuality that has historically been prevalent and the demand for enjoyment today. This particular development that shame has undergone has hardly in a literary context been examined previously and this examination outlines the changed position of the subject. Hence, our focus on shame also reveals an alteration in the subject's relation to him- or herself.

In spite of the mainly literary perspective, the first two chapters open the book with a theoretical and historical assessment. In the opening chapter, "Freedom, anxiety and shame in the performance society", Gorm Larsen poses questions about how shame and guilt have evolved between modern and late modern society, from disciplinary society to performance society. Sociologists such as Anthony Giddens, Charles Taylor and Byung-Chul Han characterize our age as an unprecedented space of possibilities, but also as defined by the requirement to seize these possibilities and realize oneself. This does not entail following a predestined course of life; on the contrary, the responsibility for self-realization lies, obviously, with the individual, and freedom comes with an obligation. Larsen investigates how freedom is related to anxiety (via Søren Kierkegaard who defines anxiety as the dizziness of freedom) and contains the risk of stumbling or not living up to the ideal image, and also how it is connected to shame. This points to a switch from guilt to shame in the dominant social feelings.

In the last century, notions of shame and guilt, as well as the relationship between the two, have been understood through important modifications in the fields of social anthropology and psychoanalysis. François Sauvagnat attempts to describe and disentangle some of these paradoxes in "A few paradoxes of guilt and shame in psychoanalysis and anthropology". Shame and guilt have repeatedly been considered as opposed to one another, even contradictory, with guilt being seen as more 'noble', 'civilized', 'occidental' than shame—the notion of a lack of empathy in the 'shame culture' is still quite popular in mass media. Later emerged the articulation about a connection between both notions and the idea that they should not be seen as separate entities; ultimately, several authors have promoted the idea that shame is perhaps a more significant notion than guilt, but their opinions regarding this matter are, indeed, very disparate.

In "Mapping shame and guilt. Inner and outer landscapes in *The Adventures of Pinocchio* and *The Wonderful Adventures of Nils*", Anna Smedberg Bondesson focuses on different figures of shame. In Carlo Collodi's *The Adventures of Pinocchio* (1880), the main character experiences several aspects of shame and finally becomes human exactly because he experiences shame until he can no longer bear it and therefore desires to adapt to the norms and be accepted. This is what turns him into "a proper boy". In contrast, Selma Lagerlöf's *The Wonderful Adventures of Nils* (1906-1907) is the story of the spoilt boy, Nils, who is literally cut down to the size of a thumb and travels on the back of a goose all across the length and breadth of Sweden before he returns home, reformed and well-adjusted. While Pinocchio is driven by shame, Nils Holgersson experiences a growing sense of guilt and responsibility. From a historical perspective, the figures of Pinocchio and Nils embody two very different national selves, but also two different roads to take in modernity; and yet, on the surface, the two stories have much in common. However, Nils manages to grow up in one piece, whereas Pinocchio, by contrast, embodies the fundamental division of the modern self, both while he is a puppet without strings, and, in the end, as a boy with metaphorical strings.

In his article, "When we dead awaken: To die of shame", Kjell R. Soleim tries to demonstrate how Henrik Ibsen's final play, *When We Dead Awaken* (1899), can be used to investigate how shame may emerge as a fatal affect resulting from a chance encounter. Jacques Lacan's discourse theory is used as the main analytical tool in this investigation. In Ibsen's play, the two protagonists, the artist and his model, meet accidentally several years after the artist discovers that his use of the model had been exhausted. This break between them leaves the artist socially successful but artistically barren, while the model goes mad. Their final encounter produces a truth event: they see how each of them, in their own peculiar way, has chosen to enjoy the status of a victim rather than assuming responsibility for their acts. It is a shame event.

In "Short reflection on some scenes of shame", Carin Franzén reflects on some of the appearances of shame in European literature and philosophy. By way of different examples taken from Plato through the French moralists to modernity, different historical configurations of shame are assessed using the idea that shame is related to seeing, and more exactly to the experience of being exposed to the gaze of others in a specific context. The main argument is that, even though shame can be seen as an innate and basic affect, its forms and effects are intimately related to a given period's hegemonic discourse. Thus, the chapter traces the movement from the external gaze of the other—i.e. God, the king, public opinion, the father in ancient and early modern cultures—to an internalized other within the current neoliberal order.

In "Friendship as the friend of thought: Franz Kafka and the gesture of shame", Alexander Carnera argues that shame has become part of the performance culture in modern work life and of the individualization of the modern self in late capitalism. The first part of the article discusses how shame in literature and philosophy operate as an immanent strategy for critical thinking. The paper locates shame as a gesture of pure means (Agamben), a particular praxis on the border between body and language. The second part discusses shame as a mode of existence that leads to a special mode of thinking. This potential of shame is revealed as a central theme in the writings of Franz Kafka. In addressing the language of animals and the powerlessness of humans, the problem of shame is placed at the border between human and animal. The powerlessness that shame produces thus becomes an active strategy for creativity in writing and in a critical ethos.

The concept of creativity and its affects has remained an interesting topic in terms of the theories attached to it, even long after the demise of the romantic genius. Looking at Freud's 1908 seminar "Creative Writers and Daydreaming" and Woolf's speech of January 21, 1931, Anna-Klara Bojö, in "Poetics of shame and guilt. Freud and Woolf on shame and guilt in creative writing and the pleasures and pains of reading", outlines and discusses two ways of approaching the concept of creativity, focusing on the concepts of shame and guilt. The Freudian poetics draw on theoretical insights from *The Interpretation of Dreams*, focusing on the writer's overcoming of shame and the subsequent pleasure this brings to the reader. According to Freud, daydreaming and literary creativity may be understood as the subject's way of reorganizing a disturbing reality, thus relegating writing to an act of fulfillment of wishes. Woolf, on the other hand, is preoccupied with the female writer's need to overcome sensations of guilt while also giving a more detailed and elaborate theory of the pleasures and pains of reading. Dismissing Freud's central thesis of creativity as a way of escaping dissatisfactory aspects of real life, Woolf forefronts the pleasures and dangers involved in singing as yet unheard songs.

In "Where being and thinking is the s(h)ame: *Nightwood*, sub specie ruboris", Magnus Bøe Michelsen offers a reading of the function of shame in Djuna Barnes' novel *Nightwood* through the lens of Lacanian psychoanalysis, in particular Lacan's concept of 'l'hontologie'. By way of two different readings of this concept, one by David Bernard and the other by Alain Badiou, Michelsen examines the paradoxical way in which the character of Doctor O'Connor relates to and tentatively treats the shame that follows in the trail of the main character, Robin Vote. On the one hand, the Doctor addresses the real cause of shame as being that of imaginary castration, of being exposed as inherently lacking the object of desire, who is also the supposed object of satisfaction. As Robin, in leaving her partners reveals to them that they do not possess neither her nor her wishes, she also reveals their potent egos to be frauds covering their inherent lacks, thereby causing them shame. On the other hand, the Doctor himself contributes to the covering up of these inherent lacks by his own incessant talk. Michelsen reads the novel as an experience of the impotence and impossibilities universally implied in being human tout court.

In *"Sweet November: Desire and shame in the age of serial monogamy"*, Lars Nylander discusses narrative strategies used to thematize (and downplay) shame in relation to the convention of serial monogamy which, in Western cultures from the 1970s onward, has replaced the older, bourgeois ideal of marriage for life. In this new convention, a sense of shame often tends to appear in the transition from one relationship to another, when the logic of serial monogamy comes into proximity with the more problematic logic of promiscuity. This is exemplified with Elizabeth Gilbert's first-person novel *Eat, Pray, Love* from 2006, where the protagonist's need for love and sex conflicts with her need of self-realization. After this, the article adopts a more unusual, head-on manner of presenting the practice of serial monogamy, which appears in Robert Ellis Miller's film comedy *Sweet November* from 1968. Here, we meet a woman who has established a convention of one-month marriage-like relationships, which combine the ideal of a love that never grows old with notions of personal growth. Today, the film stands as an ironic reflection of the convention of serial monogamy.

Lone Elmstedt Bild's "To write with the arsehole: Abject voices in contemporary literature" investigates the suggestion of "writing with the asshole" presented in the Danish novel, The Skin Is the Elastic Covering That Encases the Entire Body by Bjørn Rasmussen (transl. 2019, orig. 2011). This suggestion is also implicitly present in the German novel *Wetlands* by Charlotte Roche (2009). Through close readings of these two novels, the article suggests that "writing with the arsehole" can be understood as a poetic invitation to give the abject self a voice in Julia Kristeva's psychoanalytic sense of the word. By means of abject voices, the novels examine some of the identity challenges the modern subject faces today. *Wetlands* uses the abject voice to set new standards for the existing ideal of the woman but ends up confirming another female ideal: "to enjoy". *The Skin is the Elastic*

Cover Surrounding the Whole Body struggles with identity categories as such. In other words, the former points out the boundaries of certain female identity categories, whereas the latter struggles to find a way to live with a deep ambivalence towards all identity categories.

Shame seems to have acquired a new place in literature, at least if we look at some of poems by the Danish poets Yahya Hassan and Pablo Llambías. Llambías' main character assumes shameless shame, while the shame in Hassan's poetry is projected onto the main character's father, whereas the main character himself seems to escape it. This has to do with the fact that the shame of enjoyment (especially enjoying something that was previously regarded as shameful) is more or less replaced by shame of not being able to enjoy it enough. But shame of not enjoying enough leads to anxiety, since the subject succumbs to the infinite enjoyment that is demanded of him. In "Shame in Hassan's and Llambías' poetry", René Rasmussen tries to locate some of the historical reasons for this development and to show how shame and anxiety are configured in the two authors' poems.

References

Agamben, G. (2003). *Ce qui reste d'Auschwitz*. Paris: Rivages.

Bernard, D. (2011). *Lacan et la honte. De la honte à l'hontologie*. Paris: Éditions du Champ Lacanien.

Burgo, J. (2016). Shame Management and the Trump Supporter. In *Psychology Today*. Posted Nov 13, 2016, retrieved from https://www.psychologytoday.com/us/blog/shame/201611/shame-management-and-the-trump-supporter" \l "comments_bottom

Elias, N. (2000 [1978/1939]). *The civilizing process*. Second edition. Oxford: Blackwell.

Freud, S. (2010 [1900]). *Interpretation of dreams*. New York: Basic Books.

Greenwald, D. F., & Harder, D. W. (1998). Domains of shame: Evolutionary, cultural, and psychotherapeutic aspects. In P. Gilbert & B. Andrews (Eds.)

Shame. Interpersonal behavior, psychopathology, and culture. (P.225-244). New York/Oxford: Oxford University Press.

Grigg, R. (2015). *Shame and guilt*. Retrieved from http://recil.grupolusofona.pt/ bitstream/ handle/10437/40/nr1Shame%2520and%2520Guilt.pdf?sequence=1 Retrieved from http://recil.grupolusofona.pt/bitstream/handle/10437/40/ nr1Shame %2520and%2520Guilt.pdf?sequence=1. Consulated 1.09.2016

Kierkegaard, S. (1997 [1842]). *Begrebet Angest* [*The concept of anxiety*]. In *Søren Kierkegaards Skrifter* [*Writings of Søren Kierkegaard*], V.4. Copenhagen: Gads Forlag.

Kierkegaard, S. (2004 [1849]). *The Sickness Unto death*. Trans. Alastair Hannay. N.Y./London: Penguin Books. [*Sygdommen til Døden* (2006 [1849]). In *Søren Kierkegaards Skrifter* [*Writings of Søren Kierkegaard*], V.11. Copenhagen: Gads Forlag].

Lacan, J. (1991). *L'envers de la psychanalyse*. Paris: Seuil.

Lacan, J. (2007). *D'un discours qui ne serait pas du semblant*. Paris: Seuil.

Laurent, E. (2015). *Symptom, discourse: In/out*. Retrieved from http://www.lacancircle.net/LaurentSymptomDiscourseinOut.pdf

Mead, H. G. (2005 [1934]). *Mind, self, and society* Chicago: University of Chicago.

Miller, J.-A. (2006). On shame. In J. Clemens & R. Grigg (Eds.), *Jacques Lacan and the other side of psychoanalysis*. Durham and London: Duke University Press.

Peterson, J. B. (2018). *12 Rules for Life: An Antidote to Chaos*. New York: Penguin Random House.

Williams, J. C. 2017. *White Working Class: Overcoming Class Cluelessness in America*. Boston, Massachusetts: Harvard Business Review Press.

2.
Freedom, anxiety and shame in the performance society

Gorm Larsen

Several sociologists, from Anthony Giddens through Charles Taylor to Byung-Chul Han, not only characterise our age as an unprecedented space of possibilities, but also as differentiated by a requirement to seize these possibilities and realise oneself. This does not entail following a predetermined course of life; the responsibility for self-realisation lies with the individual. Paradoxically, then, freedom comes with an obligation. How this relates to the concept of shame is an open question, which I will now seek to answer.

Introduction: shame and shamelessness

In *The Culture of Narcissism* (1979), Christopher Lasch announced the decay of Western culture; it is now almost 40 years since Lasch's statement. Lasch refers to a culture characterised by egotism, a culture which has entered an era that can be described as the era of narcissism. However, according to Lasch, man has always been selfish, and ethnocentric groups have always existed. Lasch examines various new tendencies in society, such as consumerism, public and private bureaucracy, identity created through image, the therapeutic market, rationalisation of the inner life and, in the end, changes to family life.

He shows how all of these societal tendencies constitute new forms of socialisation that ultimately create a new personality structure. In a metaphorical sense, this personality may be described as egotistic, although it contains an element of personality disorder in the form of a psychological complex involving the rejection (or merely a lack) of love, which then turns into self-hatred.

Fourteen years later, in *The Revolts of the Elites and the Betrayal of Democracy* (1993), Lasch wrote about the ousting of shame as a social pathology: outwardly, shame is associated with the standard codes of behaviour in a given culture, and inwardly, shame prevents us from taking ourselves too seriously. Shame is a defence mechanism which causes us to lower our eyes and hide what cannot bear to see the light of day. Or, as Donald Nathanson (1992) writes, shame is an essential part of our ""basic behavioural pattern", which protects the organism "from its growing avidity for positive affect. By forcing us to recognise and remember our mistakes" it takes on the role of a "teacher"" (cited in Lasch, 1993, p.177).

Shamelessness is a familiar reaction to shame. For example, in *No Place to Hide* (1991), Michael Nichols describes shamelessness as a manic attempt to deny and overcome a deeply rooted inner fear of weakness. However, Lasch does not seek to explain shamelessness as an expression of shame; instead, he focuses on how an amoral ideology of acceptance is dominant in a culture in which there are no boundaries and where the emphasis is on eliminating any notion of failure and defeat. This being the case, it is the attempts to heal the shame that constitute the actual socio-pathological problem (Lasch, 1993, p.181). Still, the question is whether postmodern shame may be reduced to the display of shamelessness.

The subject-generating roots of shame

According to Sartre, feeling shame is an essential part of being human, since the awareness and experience of being merely an object in the eyes of the Other is embedded in shame. This is fundamental to the self: suddenly finding yourself in a social room and realising that not only are you the subject of the gaze of the Other, but you are also intertwined with it. The essence of shame is the manner in which the subject embraces the image of him- or herself as perceived by the Other and accepts this image as true. Or rather, the subject accepts the image as s/he believes it is perceived by the Other. This way, an uncertainty arises in the subject: s/he does not know what the Other is seeing and thinking, and the possibility of shame becomes an essential matter. Thus, shame is the personal experience that something worth feeling ashamed of actually exists. Shame illustrates an intimate relationship with the ego and shows how things might not always be the way we want them to be.

The way in which Sartre regards both shame and the gaze of the Other as fundamental features of the subject is not far from how Lacan establishes the Other as a subject presumed to possess knowledge in the genesis of the subject. This knowledge of the ego of the subject belongs to the Other; however, the subject can only presume to know the content of the knowledge. In other words, the attention of the ego is directed towards the gaze of the Other, and this is established as a malaise—the notion of a stranger's supervision and perspicacity from which the ego can never escape. We can only form our own views about this. Sartre's view of the Other is predominantly that of a particular and concrete Other, whereas Lacan is more abstract and merely focuses on the notion of the Other.

In traditional psychology, shame is regarded as a self-reflexive emotion. Along with emotions such as embarrassment and pride, both shame and guilt are evaluative feelings of self-awareness as opposed to primary emotions, such as joy, delight, fear, anxiety, sorrow, sadness, disgust and surprise. These are all emotions which direct the attention of the subject towards himself.

Shame revolves around the self, around identity, and around the degradation and devaluation inflicted by self-awareness and self-perception, whether these derive from within the individual or from outside influences. In contrast to this, guilt is attached to an act that has been inflicted on others.

According to Tomkins (1963), Izard (1977) and Lewis (1971), a mix of both subjective and objective conditions applies. In other words, he who is shameful acts as an object of shame as well as a subject of shame; he views himself as the one being watched.

Whereas no emotion constitutes a direct contrast to guilt, honour is the positive antipole to shame. Shame and honour are intertwined as negations of one another: he who is deprived of his honour will experience shame. However, the opposite is not the case—not feeling shameful is not automatically awarded with the attainment of honour. Shame and honour are connected, and the sense of honour is "a passion for the social form in itself" (Hansen, 2007, p.27; my translation). If honour is the positive antipole to shame, embarrassment must be the negative antipole, with the apparently unfair appraisal and the vast amount of attention that is suddenly bestowed upon the subject.

Originally, the concept of shame seemed to be associated with the body, with sexuality and with exposure of the body. Later on, shame was associated with apparel and compliance with dress code. In more general terms, shame concerns the transgression of the norms of behavioural and moral codes; in other words, shame is not necessarily connected to legal matters.

Whereas guilt is specific and local in the sense that it is linked to a particular act and concerns a single aspect of the subject, shame is global and concerns the identity of a person as well as the person per se; it is thus a more extensive concept. Guilt defines the subject by directing his attention to the self and the actions for which he is responsible. Guilt can be atoned for. Shame, on the other hand, cannot be atoned for. Shame is connected to the existence of the subject; it forms the self (Kjellquist, 1994). Where shame, as we have learned, is evoked by the gaze, which is the gaze of the Other, guilt is (metaphorically) connected to hearing; namely, as the stuff which is disclaimed by the subject, that which makes the subject close his ears.

This must be the reason why shame exists in two moods, as pointed out by Peer Hultberg (2005 [1993]) and Else-Britt Kjellquist (1994). The emotion of shame that is associated with embarrassment and shyness causes the shy person to turn his eyes away, whereas deep shame will eventually paralyse the self and prevent the subject from responding. The first of these is regulatory and forms a safeguard around private and intimate matters, but the second type of shame is both invasive and destructive. Both are fashioned out of the social norms of being a subject and thus also subject to the law.

The concept of shame (and guilt) has gained relevance in a modern context. This may be a result of how the framework for the first type of shame has been radically altered over the past few decades; apparently, it has become minimalised and individualised and is connected to the fact that, now, shame is seemingly something you have to confess. This means that the deep sense of shame has now been given greater latitude. Thus, when Lasch refers to the current narcissistic era from which shame has been banished, he is referring to the 'red shame', which is the first type of shame—the type associated with blushing and regulative behaviour based on (the notion of) a judgemental sociality. Naturally, the manner in which we act within the social space is still regulated and limited, and we refrain from actions that may lead to humiliation. However, emancipation has occurred in almost all areas of social practice, and, as a result, norms have become more casual. The boundaries of shyness are more liberal, the norms relating to social class are shifting, classic authorities are degenerating and institutions such as family and church have lost a great deal of status. Consequently, the act of not complying with prohibitions no longer provokes the same sense of shame, and the prohibitions have become less rigid.

The second type of shame is referred to here as 'white shame'. White shame concerns the identity of the subject and causes the individual to stiffen. This variant is not likely to have disappeared. On the contrary, it seems more present than ever: following the reduction of protective shame and the exposure of the subject, white shame is becoming more visible and present.

Nevertheless, there is reason to be vigilant with this somewhat schematic categorisation of shame. The two moods are obviously interrelated and must be regarded as merely graduations of shame.

If we are to examine the conditions for and the nature of this configuration of shame, we must be able to comprehend the sociocultural relations that form the basis of the dynamics of shame. Thus, Lasch's cultural analysis, with its attention to consumerism, image creation, etc., may well point to essential conditions of our age; however, the analysis does not take into account the circumstances regarding the aspects of shame that form the subject.

The performance society

A few years prior to the release of Lasch's diagnosis, Michel Foucault's *Surveiller et Punir* (1975) (*Discipline and Punish* (1975)) used the idea of discipline in the characterisation of modernity. In doing so, Foucault sought to emphasise the particularly privileged position discipline had in the process of individualisation. The postmodern subject was corrected by means of fear inflicted by the authorities. This fear was related to the human body through the use of corporal punishment or by entertaining the crowds with the torture of criminals and rivals of power, making the permanent marking of the body serve as proof that justice had been done. In opposition to this, the soul of the modern subject must be adjusted to the norms of society by means of a humanistic upbringing in the home, the school and the workplace. In short, now that the responsibility for mental self-discipline lies with the subject, the authorities no longer oppress the subject. Instead, the mechanisms of discipline produce oppressing subjectivities.

Through surveillance, manipulation and the employment of procedures for punishment and discipline, the disciplinary state forms a subject in whom the question of guilt is ever present. The subject cannot be penalised as such, but will, to a greater extent, take the blame himself. The disciplined subject is an obedient, responsible and guilt-oriented subject.

Whereas characteristic elements of the society described by Foucault were schools, madhouses, prisons and factories, the buildings symptomatic of the twenty-first century are fitness centres, office blocks, airports, shopping centres and genetics laboratories.

In this performance society, as described by Alain Ehrenberg (1998) and Byung-Chul Han (2012), the negativity of the disciplinary society has been abandoned and is instead replaced by positivity. The new mantra is the word 'can' and, symbolically, this is reinforced. by Obama's very optimistic 'Yes, we can' campaign of 2008. "The prohibition, directions or permissions of the disciplinary society are substituted by projects, the initiatives and the motivation" (Han, 2012, p.22; my translation). This is an unconscious social reorganisation from 'must' to 'can'.

The problem today is that this positivity has no counterbalance; the dialectic has vanished completely, and we are left with more of the same: more work and more consumption. The disciplinary society was characterised by negativity and prohibitions. In contrast, the performance society renders ordinance and the negativity of prohibitions obstructive to further optimisation. "The positivity of *can* proves all the more effective than the negativity of *must*" (Han, 2012, p.23; my translation).

On a general level, the change from disciplinary society to performance society presents continuity; a radical break with this society never occurred, and the agendas of the disciplinary society are still predominantly employed in many fields and environments. "The performance subject is still disciplined" (Han, 2012, p.23; m.t.); however, the performance subject has left the disciplinary phase and is now intensifying the current level of production.

In *The Human Condition* (1958), or *Vita Activa oder Vom tätigen Leben* (1960) as the German edition in named, Hannah Arendt analyses the active life involving work, actions and production—that is, the things we do. Based on John Locke's distinction between "the work of our bodies and the work of our hands" (Locke, *Second Treatise of Civil Government*, sec. 26 in Arendt 1958, p.79), Arendt employs a distinction between those who produce by the work of their hands (homo faber), and those who perform a task predetermined by continuous repetition (animal laborans). The farmer cultivates his farmland in order to ensure his own survival, whereas the workman produces objects that will outlive him. Production serves as a means for creating a material world of durability, an artificial world of objects. Homo faber is the manufacturing being who changes the present through his calculating and transforming actions before it becomes part of a cultivated material world. Arendt's prescient main point is that modern society with its (assembly line) production technologies is characterised by the manufacture of non-durable products—predominantly perishable consumer goods. Homo faber has lost his domain and has evolved into animal laborans, a working animal. The modern individual is surrendered to an anonymous life process in which "all kinds of vita activa—to act as well as to create—sinks to the plane of work" (Han, 2012, p.35 m.t., see also Arendt, 1958, p.88f).

However, Han believes that this analysis is no longer an accurate description of the social development caused by the performance society. This is because the late modern animal laborans has become individualised and equipped with an ego which is anything but passive. This is, Han writes, "on reflection, anything but animalistic. It is hyperactive and hyperneurotic" (Han, 2012, p.37 m.t.). In other words, the explanation why all activities are taking place at work level must be found elsewhere, and Han finds this in the very same book—towards the end of *Vita Activa*, Arendt points out that what has suffered least in this negative social development is the act of thinking. Using Cato's words, Arendt concludes by stating that "never is [a person] more active than when he does nothing, never is he more alone than when he is by himself" (Arendt, 1958 p.345).

Though Arendt considers thinking as one of the different activities of the vita activa, she has not included this in her analysis. Han makes a point of this and claims that thinking belongs to a different domain than the vita activa.

It is through the vita contemplativa and not through an active lifestyle that the individual becomes the person he was meant to be and that the individual is formed psychologically into who he shall be. At the same time, "the [very] loss of the contemplative ability, which is not least linked to the rendering absolute of the vita activa, is the reason for the hysteria and anxiety of the modern active society" (Han, 2012, p.42 m.t.). In the performance society, there is no time or energy to be inactive, to pause; everything is concerned with more of the same, with positivity and activity—but activity without being. There is no constancy. Hyperactivity only manifests transitoriness and renders impossible any attachment relations, such as family attachment. Existence is not characterised by hiding behind anonymity, but by being exposed as a "hero".

However, it is still difficult to imagine what the vita activa would be devoid of thinking. Thinking belongs to activity. But it seems indisputable that the character of thinking has changed. How to characterise this thinking in greater detail within the performance society will be studied in the following, including the ideas of Anthony Giddens, who focused on the self-reflective subject and in whose theories on shame and guilt as reflective emotions are attached to social-historical conditions.

Fear and the self-reflective subject

According to Anthony Giddens (1991), the relationship between the individual and society takes on a new character in modern society. He describes modernity in terms of the interplay between three conditions: the separation of time and space, the disembedding mechanisms and the reflexivity of modernity.

1) Firstly, modernity is characterised by the fact that social articulations and exchanges are not bound by unity in time and space; on the contrary, they have become empty entities of which media technologies have become the catalysts, a situation that is increasingly revealed to have consequences.

2) Secondly, social institutions have become embedded in abstract systems; in other words, social relations have become detached from their local contexts. Here, Giddens is preoccupied with two systems, one of which he calls symbolic tokens (such as money, exam grades, Facebook likes, etc.) and one of which he terms expert systems. This refers to the fact that our society is characterised by a large number of different specialised domains, ranging from the construction of a metro system to our health system. Both abstract tokens and expert systems are based on trust and commitment. For instance, all trade and economic systems are only functional because we all have confidence in the value of money, and because we are trustful of credit card transfers; at the same time, however, we are also obliged to rely on money, on the doctor or on the expert. Nevertheless, this does not exclude risk and danger; a factory building might actually collapse, or a doctor might diagnose his or her patient wrongly, etc.

3) Thirdly, the separation and transformation of time and space combined with the disembedding mechanisms constitute the contexts of reflexivity, in which knowledge of the conditions of our social life processes re-constitute the very same life and its conditions. Life practices are continually revised on the basis of new information and new knowledge. This means that many of the expert systems en-

countered by modern individuals are repeatedly questioned. We can hardly hear about a psychiatric treatment or an assessment of the global environmental situation without also encountering statements that contradict these experts' announcements. This methodological doubt, which calls into question and undermines all certainty, is the condition of late modernity.

> The reflexivity of modernity has to be distinguished from the reflexive monitoring of action intrinsic to all human activity [...] to chronic revision in the light of new information or knowledge. [...] the reflexivity of modernity turns out to confound the expectations of Enlightenment—although it is the very product of that thought. (Giddens, 1991, pp.20-21)

This means that the reflexivity of modernity undermines any certain knowledge. Knowledge can no longer be restricted to science; it becomes an existential mode that permeates all human activity. Unlike pre-modern forms, modern expert systems generate reflexive orientation. Thus, dialectics exist between the reflexivity of modernity and changes in the identity of the self. Homo sapiens has become a reflecting, sceptical subject.

These dynamics in the human world are characterised by a post-traditional order in which the self becomes a "reflexive project" (Giddens, 1991, p.32). In modernity, the self must be explored and constructed, thus becoming an expression of the "reflexive mobilisation of the identity of the self". This is evident in times of break-up and crisis (such as divorces and psychological crises), but it is also a common feature of modern existence where the subject has to invent himself. As the Canadian sociologist and philosopher Charles Taylor (1991) explains, the artist as an autonomous and constantly innovative and creative character is the ideal of our time:

> Artistic creation becomes the paradigm mode in which people can come to self-definition. The artist becomes in some way the paradigm case of the human being, as agent of original self-definition. (Taylor 1991, p.62)

The space of opportunity which is thus allocated to the individual and the expectation that each person should shape his own life and be responsible for his own success and happiness (or failure) places the modern identity of the self in relation to anxiety. In particular, Søren Kierkegaard's, or rather the pseudonymous author Vigilius Haufniensis', definition of anxiety is a recurring theme—as it is for Giddens—because it is defined in relation to human freedom: "Anxiety is freedom's actuality as the opportunity of opportunity" (Kierkegaard, 2014 [1844], p.51, [1997, p.348]). However, Kierkegaard's thinking concerning anxiety occurs in the context of the spirit. Spirit is related to the creation of a self. The human being as spirit is a synthesis of the psychical and the physical. It is in this connection that the ontogenesis of anxiety (i.e. how anxiety emerges) must be understood:

> Innocence is ignorance. In innocence the human being is not characterized as spirit but is psychically characterized in immediate unity with its natural condition. Spirit is dreaming in the human being. [...] In this state there is peace and repose, but at the same time there is something else, something that is not dissension and strife, for there is nothing against which to strive. What, then, is it? Nothing. But what effect does nothing have? It begets anxiety. This is the profound secret of innocence, that at the same time it is anxiety. (Kierkegaard, 2014 [1844], p.50, [1997, p.347])

Thus, Kierkegaard not only links anxiety to a difference between soul and spirit, as a difference between the state of innocence (the state of childhood) and the domain of the guilt of the knowledgeable (the state of adulthood); anxiety is constituted as a force which always already exists but which lies hidden as an indefinite force, and which is therefore best characterised as "nothing". Although anxiety is linked to the synthesis of the spirit and to freedom, it will always be present as the entirely unknown, i.e. as that which does not yet have any form. The first object of anxiety is nothing. The spirit lies dreaming within the human being, i.e. the spirit is latently present in the budding subject. The spirit is that which allows and synchronises the psychical and the physical. When we become self-conscious, however, and relate to ourselves, our self-relation generates both opportunities and anxieties; the self transcends the naïve and carefree existence.

The transition from innocence and ignorance to guilt and knowledge involves anxiety because it directs the subject's attention to the possibilities. Not to choose and not to show the world who you are is to remain in the state of nothingness. Here is peace, repose and lack of strife. To be in this open field of possibilities creates anxiety and activates the necessity of choosing. This, in turn, gives rise to anxiety. Anxiety is therefore constantly hidden, as something that might arise at any given time.

The field of ignorance is characterised by prejudices, thresholds and prohibitions—you can only go so far, but no further: "But of the tree of the knowledge of good and evil thou shalt not eat of it" (Genesis 2:17). At the same time, however, this prohibition kindles a desire, it points towards the possibility of violation and indirectly calls attention to the freedom of acting on that desire. In the Garden of Eden, Adam lives in a state of innocence, but through God's prohibition – which, according to Kierkegaard, Adam does not really understand – the imagination of possibilities is aroused and the drives awakened. The prohibition indicates the possibility of freedom. The prohibition tempts, while the possibility scares. Anxiety and the transition from innocence to guilt is determined by Kierkegaard as a dialectical relation between attraction and avoidance, between "a sympathetic antipathy and an antipathetic sympathy" (Kierkegaard, 2014 [1844], p.51 (1997, p.348)), as the child's ambivalence between attraction and repulsion of the adventurous, mysterious and uncanny. In the first place, the possibility of acting is essential. When man can do wrong, this is merely an option enabled by freedom. As a result, Kierkegaard is free to compare anxiety to dizziness:

> He whose eye happens to look down the yawning abyss becomes dizzy. But what is the reason for this? It is just as much in his own eye as in the abyss, for suppose he had not looked down. Hence, anxiety is the dizziness of freedom, which emerges when the spirit wants to posit the synthesis and freedom looks down into its own possibility, laying hold of finiteness to support itself. Freedom succumbs to dizziness. (Kierkegaard, 2014 [1844], p.72, [1997, p.365])

Anxiety is the dizziness of freedom. However, it is a dizziness associated with reflection and thus with the subject relating to himself and to his choices. Anxiety is the sign that the subject cannot escape from himself, and with this the absolute freedom ceases. This dizziness is caused by the disappearance of the protecting prohibition; in this case, too, the subject is left to himself. Anxiety as the possibility of freedom reveals the uncertainty of existence.

In late modernism, where the normative and protecting hands of family, social class and God have been greatly weakened, the subject experiences an escalating dizziness of freedom. Where Kierkegaard will point to anxiety as a condition for being, or rather becoming, a subject, then today, in the performance society, the possibility of freedom is quite different from Kierkegaard's context. Kierkegaard wrote in a religious age, and *The Concept of Anxiety* has an explicitly Christian agenda. Anxiety suggests that there is something higher than the perishable world. Anxiety about nothing belongs to the realm of paganism and the non-religious wherein the eternal is not understandable. Anxiety as a religious theme relates to a reconciliation with the eternal as a reality, but above all, anxiety takes on the consequences of the original sin; that is, it leads to being independent in relation to what follows from the family, and herein to realize one's own responsibility for the sin of one's own family.

While this religious context has less meaning today, anxiety has become a more crucial concept than it was one hundred and seventy years ago. The nothingness and the eternality with which freedom is faced are more present, because life is felt to be meaningless at the same time as choices are needed on all levels of existence. During such anxiety-provoking times, it is no wonder that working life and vita activa represent a way of escaping. One way to try to anticipate and manage freedom and eternality is to continuously act. At the same time, this is a way to avoid a more contemplative life, the vita contemplativa.

Giddens takes up Kierkegaard's description of anxiety as the possibility of freedom. Anxiety is free flowing because it is devoid of any object; it can be understood as opposed to habits, routines, familiar social interactions, etc. The unknown and uncertain potentially gives rise to insecurity and anxiety, as the individual choices can end in the uncertain, unforeseeable, untested, etc. Anxiety and freedom are related to the identity of the subject and the life story that the single person conveys. Anxiety expresses a struggle between being and non-being to which the category of possibilities is associated: it is through a reality-accept and a realised life-praxis that the subject fulfils itself as being.

In the premodern society, the traditions had a central position and were not only agents of organising the social life, but also essential to transitions, which often was ritualised in the shape of *rites de passage*, as Giddens writes. The transition situation of the subject has always been psychically challenging; but in such pre-modern cultures,

> where things stayed more or less the same from generation to generation on the level of the collectivity, the changed identity was clearly staked out – as when an individual moved from adolescence into adulthood. In the settings of modernity, by contrast, the altered self has to be explored and constructed as part of a reflexive process of connecting personal and social change. (Giddens 1991, p.33)

In the era of late modernity, the self-identity is not given by an unspoken contract with society, but is part of an active process that can be both challenging and full of anxiety.

On the basis of the reflection of modernity and anxiety as the possibility of freedom, Giddens associates shame and guilt with the social-psychological situation of ultra-modernity. He emphasises the emotion of shame as particularly significant because it revolves around the question of being and of existence (i.e. what is embedded in anxiety), whereas guilt was previously a predominant part of the inhibitions preventing the individual from being the person he believed himself to be.

Thus, guilt is related to the disciplinary society and shame is associated with the performance society.

Shame in the field of positivity

Shame is the embodiment of dialectics, a dialectic between who you are—flaws and imperfections included—and who you wish to be; it involves the ideal image that inevitably proves unattainable. In a way, the occurrence of shame seems to disappear; blushing evoked by shame is rare in a performance society in which anything seems to be possible. Freedom and possibilities are endless and there is apparently little to feel ashamed of.

Christopher Lasch had an eye for the shamelessness of shame, that hides behind the abyss of anxiety and freedom, which must be associated with the identity and the being of the subject; accordingly, it is a matter of the subject's constitution of shame. In the performance society, the subject is faced with an apparently infinite freedom, which involves a claim for self-realisation; the positivity transcends the space of possibilities and institutes a requirement to act. The Other in Lacan's term is no longer an agent of prohibition. This does not merely set the stage for the paradox of freedom in the classical sense, as in Kierkegaard's thinking; it is also a command to capture freedom and make a choice. On the one hand, it is a requirement to exist within the choices as something positive, to enjoy all the choices: Positivity, more of the same, the absence of negativity is the formula for pleasure and enjoyment. To be in tune with the performance society is to enjoy the possibilities and get new energy from one's doings. On the other hand, it is a choice associated with responsibility and it is inextricably linked to the fear of defeat and the worry that freedom is perhaps misused—in other words, that the wrong choices are made. Defeat and shame are always lurking.

Within the logic of the command lies the 'surveillance' of the subject and the subject's awareness of being watched by others. Consequently, the performance society is a metaphorical theatre. The Other does not lose the ability to maintain surveillance, but by the shift from prohibition to injunction, the self is subject to the requirement to perform and self-realise as an acting character. Han and Ehrenberg describe, not surprisingly, the pathological type of subject in performance society as the depressive subject—a subject who voluntarily allows himself to be exploited without any external coercion and who is both victim and perpetrator. However, we may suggest that this is a subject who is experiencing shame. At stake are the identity and the being of the subject, not in relation to specific sets of norms, but in relation to a principle of creation: perform, select, be free. The subject is torn between his continuous reflexiveness on the self-identity and his manic efforts to take part in the hyperactivity of the performance society. As the modest, red shame diminishes, the subject cannot hide. He has to expose himself—with the danger of recognising that his self is inadequate. The white shame is always lurking in the background. Moving away from or transgressing the shame is the only way of ensuring a secure self-identity.

The essence is that we cannot merely regard modern shame as a concept of the individual psychology: shame also captures a socio-pathological situation in which a free, choosing subject meets the detached, self-projecting, judgemental gaze.

References

Arendt, H. (1958). *The Human Condition.* Chicago & London: The University of Chicago. [*Vita Activa oder Vom tätigen Leben* (1960). Stuttgart: W. Kohlhammer].

Ehrenberg, A. (1998). *La Fatigue d'être soi. Dépression et société.* Paris: Odile Jacob. [*The Weariness of the Self: Diagnosing the history of Depression in the Contemporary Age* (2010). Montreal & Kingston: McGill-Queen's University Press].

Foucault, M. (1975). *Surveiller et punir: Naissance de la prison.* Paris: Gallimard. [*Discipline and Punish: the Birth of the Prison*, (1975). New York: Random House].

Giddens, A. (1991). *Modernity and self-identity.* Cambridge: Polity Press.

Izard, C. E. (1977). *Human emotions.* New York: Plenum Press.

Han, B.-C. (2012). *Træthedssamfundet.* Copenhagen: Møller. [*Müdigkeitsgesellschaft* (2010). Berlin: Matthes & Seitz].

Hansen, N-G. (2007). Ufine handlemåder, som måske ingen har lagt mærke til. Skamfølelsen i sociologien, fænomenologien og hos Peter Seeberg. [Unfair practices, that nobody may have noticed. The shame feeling in sociology, phenomenology, and with Peter Seeberg]. *Kritik,* 183. April 2007. Copenhagen: Gyldendahl.

Holy Bible. (2013). Genesis. *King James Version.* Utah: The Church of Jesus Christ of Latter-day Saints Salt Lake City.

Hultberg, P. (2005 [1993]). Om Freud, om skam, om Dora [On Freud, on shame, on Dora]. In *Min verden – Bogstaveligt talt.* Copenhagen: Lindhardt og Ringhof.

Kierkegaard, S. (2014 [1844]). *The concept of anxiety: a simple psychologically oriented deliberation in view of the dogmatic problem of hereditary sin.* (Translated by A. Hannay). New York: W.W. Norton. [*Begrebet Angst* (1997 [1844]). In *Sørens Kierkegaards Skrifter* [*Writings of Søren Kierkegaard*], V.4. Copenhagen: Gads Forlag].

Kjellquist, E.-B. (1994). *Rött och vitt. Om skam og skamlöshet.* [*Red and white. On shame and shamelessness*]. Stockholm: Carlsson bokförlag.

Lasch, C. (1979). *The culture of narcissism.* New York: W.W. Norton & Co.

Lasch, C. (1993). *The revolt of the elites and the betrayal of democracy.* New York: W.W. Norton & Co.

Lewis, H. B. (1971). *Shame and guilt in neurosis*. New York: International University Press.

Nathanson, D. (1992). *Shame and Pride. Affect, Sex, and the Birth of the Self.* New York: W.W. Norton & Co.

Nichols, M. (1991). *No Place to Hide*. New York: Simon & Schuster.

Taylor, C. (1991). *The malaise of modernity*. Toronto: House of Anansi Press.

Tomkins, S. S. (1963). *Affect imagery consciousness. Volume II, the negative affects.* New York: Springer.

3.
A few paradoxes of guilt and shame in psychoanalysis and anthropology

François Sauvagnat

> *... Scham, die als eine exquisit weibliche Eigenschaft gilt, aber weit mehr konventionell ist, als man denken sollte...* (Shame, which passes as an exquisitely feminine peculiarity, but is much more conventional than one might think). (Freud, 1999 [1931], p.188)

> *Mourir de honte est le seul affect de la mort qui la mérite* (Dying of shame is the only affect of death that deserves it). (Lacan, 2007 [1970], p.209)

Introduction

Even if shame has always been an important theme of literatures and religions, its systematic study has been only recently envisaged by the human sciences, and specifically by two of them, anthropology and psychoanalysis. In both, shame has always been associated in some way with guilt.

In the last hundred years, the relationship between anthropology and psychoanalysis has been through important modifications in these fields. They have been successively regarded as opposed and even contradictory, with guilt being seen as more 'noble', 'civilized', 'occidental' than shame – the notion of the 'lack of empathy' in a 'shame culture' is still quite popular in the mass media.[1] Later, the idea that the two notions should been seen as separate entities came to the fore; most recently, several authors have promoted the idea that shame is perhaps the more significant notion compared to guilt – but their opinions were far more dissenting than they might seem at first sight. We shall attempt to describe and disentangle a few of the paradoxes involved.

Freud's preference for guilt

Quite rightly, the prevalence of the notion of guilt in human sciences has been strongly associated with psychoanalysis. The frequency of occurrence of the term *Schuld* in Freud's *Gesammelte Werke* (Freud, 1999 – indicated in the *Gesamtregister* included in the eighteenth volume (674 occurrences)) dwarfs that of the other notions we will discuss, like *Schande* (only five!) and even its semantic complement *Scham* (54): in German, *Schande* is mainly used as an objective notion (as in *Jemandem Schande machen*, or shaming someone, etc.), and *Scham* as a subjective one (as in "*sich schämen*", to be ashamed). It seemed quite obvious from the start that Freud tended to consider the lexical couple *Scham/Schande* as depicting rather artificial, conventional feelings imposed on individuals by a certain state of social mores.

As Ernest Jones (1953-1957) has rightly put forward, psychoanalysis emerged at the end of Queen Victoria's reign, a puritan era that certainly did not make light of social conventions and heavily insisted on the obligation of moral integrity, especially in women; however, Freud's own liberal inclinations, his support of several feminist move-

---

[1] In most of the recent presentations of 'terrorist mentality', this notion is ubiquitous.

ments (especially Helene Stöker's "*Sexualreform Bewegung*"), of the pro-homosexual Humanitarian Committee (which lobbied to end the criminalization of homosexuality – *Sodomie* – in German and British law and to align them with the French legal system, which made it a crime to inquire about someone's sexual orientations or practices), of the Youth *Wandervogel* movement and, of course, his thesis that most moral values could be secretly supported by not-so-moral instinctual tendencies, tended to lead him into the opinion that a fair proportion of shame feelings were, in fact, "*falsche Scham*" (Freud, 1999 [1895]). This phrase, which apparently is not so frequent in German, may have been an imitation of the extremely common French "*fausse honte*", especially in the French *théâtre de boulevard*, which deeply influenced one of Freud's favourite playwrights, Johann Nepomuk Nestroy (Sauvagnat, 2003). It is derived from the French word "*honte*" – which is of Germanic origin, related to Old High German *Honida* and Middle Dutch *Hoonde*, and phonetically associated with *honneur* (honour).[2] In medieval and baroque times, it used to be a fairly frequently cited motive behind duels and wars, whereas most of its recent usage is negative. Generally, and in comparison to Scandinavian languages, contemporary French is quite poor in phrases and idioms concerning shame. It is a commonly assumed notion in the dominant French secular/republican/egalitarian ideology that one should not make too much of a fuss about one's embarrassment ("*toute honte bue*"), one should avoid exaggerating the importance of social conventions and denounce unnecessary hypocrisy (which would lead a person to exhibit false shame, or *fausse honte*) – even if the practice of duels actually survived into the twentieth century in small segments of society (a handful of journalists and politicians) and even if another contradictory phrase, *mourir de honte* ("dying of shame", albeit often used only in ironic contexts) is also quite frequent.

---

2   Centre National de Resources Textuelles et Lexicales, article Honte. http://www.cnrtl.fr/etymologie/honte

Guilt and symptom formation in Freudian psychoanalysis

The main difference between shame (*Scham/Schande*) and guilt (*Schuld*), and the overwhelming import attributed by Freud to the latter, lies in Freud's claims about psychoneurotic symptom formation: a mere psychological trauma, he contended, is unable to create an enduring symptom unless a sexual signification becomes woven into it. What he calls 'sexual' here is not only the emergence of embarrassment about some innocent game: it has to do with the subject's initiative, be it action, thoughts or desires – no matter how secret the latter may be. Freud had a special word for this: *Urteil* – that is, judgement, understood as a mental act, a decision that did not need to be fully conscious in order to operate and involve the individual's responsibility. A signification could only have an enduring, symptom-building effect if the subject felt that he was somehow, in his fantasies, involved in a guilty sexual activity – i.e. one that could have disastrous consequences for himself, his kin and significant others. That this judgement was repressed, often in a complex way, and that it was not the mere effect of social pressures, but the result of conflicting unconscious mechanisms, was at the core of what Freud was eager to assert. Although he never quite found a satisfactory explanation of the phenomenon – admitting that his evolutionary works, like *Totem and Taboo* (Freud, 1955 [1915]), and his attempts at historical reconstructions, like *Moses and Monotheism* (Freud, 1939), contained many more hypotheses than verified facts – Freud nevertheless stuck to the notion that psychoneurotic symptoms were directly influenced by (mainly unconscious) guilt feelings.

There have been several attempts to explain why such symptom formations were linked to sexuality. The interpretations by Fromm, similar to Horkheimer and Adorno's theory of reification in *The Dialectics of Enlightenment* (2002 [1944]) as a perverse result of the dialectic of reason, seemed to infer, following a Schellingian perspective (Sauvagnat, 2004), that the tragic events of the 30s and 40s were due to a kind of revenge of the myth against rationality. Wilhelm Reich, a famous proponent of the energizing qualities of genitality (the so-called Orgone theory), assumed that there had to be a special link between character defences (constituting a "körperlicher Panzer"), pregenital sado-masochistic fixations and authoritarian social structure (Reich, 1945 [1933]). More modestly, Lacan saw sexuality as a source of irreconcilable misunderstanding. He also saw the prevalence of sexual themes (Fliess, 1906; Swoboda, 1904; Weiniger, 1906) at the turn of the nineteenth century as promoting the new figure of the cheated master, as several of Freud's observations clearly showed: The dream of the father who did not know that he was dead (according to the subject's desire), in Freud's *Formulierungen über den zwei Prinzipien des psychischen Geschehens* (Freud, 1999 [1911]) and the famous Cracow-Lemberg joke in which, Lacan argues, the real subject of enunciation is expressed as "I cheat you" (Freud, 1999 [1901]; Lacan, 1977, p.160).

Compared to the meagre comments he had on shame, Freud's contributions on guilt has been intensely researched and documented. He not only discussed the modification of passive seduction into *nachträglich* trauma (Freud, 1999 [1895]), as well as the way in which active seduction transformed into obsessions, he also commented on the way drives cornered the individual into unbearable paradoxes, with dramatic changes of 'dialect' between the different instinctual stages, starting from the first emotions of the infant. Satisfaction in itself seemed to bestow occasions of guilt, while family history, the guilt of the fathers, the recriminations or humiliations of mothers – as in the case of the Rat-man (Freud, 1955 [1909]) – could bring new occasions of moral affliction and to compensate produce mythomaniac fantasies of *Familieromane*. Finally, drawing on Lamarckian biology, he formulated the hypothesis of a "phylogenic crime" (Freud, 1955 [1915]), which is repressed but attempts to return in every possible manner, utilizing the most discrete circumstances of an individual's life to express the guilt he or she deserved. This notion was quite comparable to the theme of original sin in Jewish and Christian traditions, a theme that has been copiously expanded on by Freud's followers.

One of the closest opponents of this hypothesis during Freud's lifetime was Alfred Adler (1870-1937), a convert to Protestantism with a professed interest in socialism (he was in contact with Leon Trotsky and was the therapist of Adolf Joffe, one of the main redactors of *Pravda*). Adler claimed that neuroses had "biological bases" which determined a sense of humiliation, and that no other significant factor was to be reckoned in the formation of symptoms: a non-sexual inferiority complex based on social or even organic defect, against which the "manly protest" of the individual had failed, was the only relevant factor (Adler, 1921). Although Freud was intensely critical of him, Adler was immensely popular in the United States and probably opened the way for what would become ego-psychology and self-psychology; more generally, one may suppose that his popularity expressed a local aversion towards the detailed study of unconscious guilt mechanisms.

Extreme "primitive shame": Cannon's research on decorticate cats and "sudden voodoo death"

The opposition between guilt and shame was extremely popular in social anthropology from the 1930s on under the form of a purported contradiction between guilt cultures and shame cultures – this was elaborated on by Ruth Benedict (1934) and Margaret Mead (2003 [1935]) – that seems to have simply, in the mind of many of its enthusiasts, continued the less sophisticated opposition between 'modern' and 'primitive' cultures, a distinction that met with very little opposition or even discussion before the 1960s. Its popularity even touched a domain where modern sociology was not necessarily welcome – classical humanities. In a celebrated study of classical Greek culture, *The*

Greeks and the Irrational, Eric R. Dodds (1951) contended that, whereas Hellenic culture is often perceived as the original crucible of Western rational thought, such was hardly the case in Homeric times when a culture of shame was totally predominant: contempt or ridicule were felt to be totally unbearable, and the Athenian philosophers around Socrates mainly sketched the possibility of a rational, autonomous conduct within the framework of a functional democracy. Plato, for instance, never admitted of the notion of inherited guilt: his view of the divinity, no matter how lofty it was, never included a clear notion of responsibility. Politically, he never went farther than conceiving a closed society in which rational agency would be submitted to that of a (hopefully philosophically-minded) tyrant.

If Freud's preference for guilt over shame as an aetiology of psychoneuroses was mainly related to the context of the end of the Victorian era, the notion that Western subjectivity was strongly dominated by feelings of self-conscious guilt, theological disputes on the meaning of atonement and a sense of personal responsibility was also imposing itself in another context, namely that of the colonial conquests on which anthropology was strongly dependent. Even if we feel somewhat awkward about this, we have to admit that colonialist views of the world and the distinction between Western and non-Western populations still dominated the humanities not so long ago, with the notion that "primitive mentalities", especially in non-Christians or partially Christianized populations, were intensely sensitive to shame and mainly immune to guilt. One of the most impressive documents among the huge literature on the subject is probably Walter Cannon's famous article on "voodoo death". Cannon, a physician and researcher, was the first to introduce the notion of "adrenalin discharge in fight or flight situations" (Cannon, 1914) and one of the first specialists of stressful situations. He devoted a paper to cases of "pure shame" in which he compiled cases of "primitive subjects" around the globe who were convinced that they had been cursed by a wizard. His idea was that these populations were so vulnerable to such beliefs that death could occur in no time, once an individual was persuaded that a spell had been cast on him. As the evidence he proposed for this phenomenon was mainly hearsay and even outright fiction, he was keen to show that his laboratory research on stress in "decorticate cats" had proved that such an eventuality was physiologically quite possible. Under stressful circumstances of "sham rage",

> The (cats') hairs stand on end, sweat exudes from the toe pads, the heart rate may rise from about 150 beats per minute to twice that number, the blood pressure is greatly elevated, and the concentration of sugar in the blood soars to five times the normal. This excessive activity of the sympathetic-adrenal system rarely lasts, however, more than three or four hours. By that time, without any loss of blood or any other event to explain the outcome, the decorticate remnant of the animal, in which this acme of emotional display has prevailed, ceases to exist. (Cannon, 1942, p.187)

Suffice it to say that "voodoo death" is considered by today's anthropologists as mainly fictional (Lester, 1972); even if the accusation of having "cast a spell" is frequent in places like Western Africa and the Caribbean, and does provoke various quarrels, instantly dying of this belongs to the domain of mythology – not least because various recourses against spells are traditionally to be found, such as (magical) countermeasures, redirecting the spell and also by referring to other religions. However, the notion that non-Westerners belong to "cultures of shame" has been a very enduring notion, which periodically reappears in the most diverse domains, for instance in psychiatry, along with the (highly controversial) thesis that depression does not exist in non-Western cultures (Pewzner-Apeloig, 1992), in some local variants of psychoanalysis (Wurmser, 2003, on the "shame culture of the terrorists" ignoring "feminine sensitivity") or in applied anthropology and political sciences (with the notion that non-Western cultures are obsessed with the danger of "losing face publicly", whereas Westerners are busy managing their guilt-feelings), and also of course in war propaganda in which populations of coveted oil-rich territories are typically depicted as cruel, immoral and dominated by a "culture of shame". One of the most curious phenomena in this respect is the obsession among researchers on China (Ho, 1974, 1976; Hu, 1944) to document the notion of a local prevalence of "losing face" in traditional Chinese culture, or we might consider the classical study by Marcel Granet (1926) of *Jang* in classical China – a cultural phenomenon, which is precisely the opposite of losing face: it is a series or ritualized situations (and dancing ceremonies) in which the subject shows how humble and self-critical he can be in order to create a new equilibrium into which he could fit as a secret strategy to conquer the highest political posts.

The book that was certainly the most instrumental in popularizing the separation between guilt and shame cultures was Ruth Benedict's *The Chrysanthemum and the Sword* (1948). Benedict (1887-1948), a pupil of Franz Boas and a junior colleague of Margaret Mead, seems to have responded to a demand by the American State Department and Office of War Information to provide a social-anthropological account of Japanese mentality, in order to propose appropriate political decisions now that Japan had been defeated. Under her influence, the hierarchical structure of the country, and especially the imperial administration, was preserved: the occupying power refrained from enforcing a regime change. This was on the basis of the notion of "basic personality" (the notion that a culture could best be grasped as a "personality type" dominating the corresponding society), which was at the time an extremely popular view among anthropologists and psychologists (as evidenced by its use in the Frankfurt School and during the contemporary Nuremberg trials), and which she had tried to systematize in the preceding decade in her preface to *Patterns of Culture* (Benedict, 1934). In this, she contrasted, for instance, the 'Dionysian' Kwakiutl with the 'Apollonian' Zuni, etc. Unable to do field research during the war, Benedict resorted to newspaper articles, interviews with Japanese-Americans, novels, films and histories. Her theoretical framework had been presented in the previous decade; she described a two-fold culture in which poetic sensitivity and aesthetic values – the chrysanthemum culture – were but a disguise of a much more strongly implanted core of "samurai values", a cult of heroism and a total dependence on exterior signs of honour, virtue and commitment to duty (*on* and *giri*), a high sensitivity to humiliation and shame and a quasi-absence of an interiorized sense of guilt, compassion and autonomous responsibility. This is how she sums up her views:

> A society that inculcates absolute standards of morality and relies on developing a conscience is a guilt culture by definition. True shame cultures rely on external sanctions for good behavior, not, as true guilt cultures do, on an internalized conviction of sin. Shame is a reaction to other people's criticism. A man is shamed either by being openly ridiculed and rejected or by fantasying to himself that he has been made ridiculous. In either case it is a potent sanction. But it requires an audience or at least a fantasy of an audience. Guilt does not. In a nation where honor means living up to one's picture of oneself, one may suffer from guilt though no one knows of the misdeed, and a feeling of guilt may actually be relieved by confessing the sin. (Benedict 1948, pp.222-223)

Even if she later admitted that she had underestimated the dimension of "secret guilt" in Japanese conscience, and even if, in a few years' time, the Japanese would overcome their proverbial politeness to point out the high degree of inaccuracy and the lack of nuance in Benedict's account, this bipartition has become a sort of an intellectual stereotype which, by the time it became obvious that sociologists and anthropologists could no longer afford to approve it, had made its way into public relations techniques and propaganda documentaries. The public reception of this book was, at least at first, all the more favourable since both Benedict and her colleague Margaret Mead enjoyed a "liberal" profile and presented themselves as audacious explorers of cultural diversity, anti-racists and implicit supporters of the "liberation movements" that flourished in the 1960s.

Takeo's Doi response: amae as a core Japanese "guilt feeling"

In his famous book *Amae non kozo* (The Anatomy of Dependence), Japanese psychoanalyst Takeo Doi (1920-2009) took issue with Benedict's bipartition between shame and guilt cultures and its application to Japan. He did not deny that a "samurai ideology" had been governing his country, but he insisted that Benedict, who had never set foot on the Nippon archipelago, had failed to understand the presence of deep-rooted mechanisms of guilt in Japanese individuals. He claimed that this mechanism was, of course, difficult to perceive for a foreigner; but to whoever has lived Japanese culture from the inside, the dominant, although sometimes hidden, emotion is that of *amae*, a term derived from the verb *amaeru*, which means to depend on and presume someone's benevolence. In the explanations he provides on *amaeru*, Doi insists on the mother-child relationship. *Amaeru* means struggling to be loved, protected, trying to provoke in the other a protective, loving reaction; it implies being defenceless and anticipating the other's negative reaction; it also implies a deeply internalized sense of dependence on the community and an intense feeling of guilt over whatever inner movement could go against these criteria. In a dialectic typical of the *Nihonjinron* tradition (a local tradition trying to depict what is 'purely Japanese'), Doi asserts that the Japanese language is certainly the one that enjoys the greatest lexical wealth to describe such feelings, which are the true bases of Japanese social bonds, even though he admits that such kinds of bonds clearly exist also in other cultures.

Gerhart Piers and Milton Singer: a new approach to the relationship between guilt and shame

Whereas the approaches heretofore mentioned insisted on the contradictions and even incompatibility between shame and guilt cultures, from the 1950s onwards a number of authors started claiming that this bipartition was wrong and that what ought to be studied was, in fact, the way either notion more or less combined with the other. In fact, one of the first authors who seem to have launched such a notion was Imre Hermann, the main inspirer of the concept of attachment, who claimed to enlighten psychoanalytic practice by drawing on animal ethology, and who provided descriptions of primary shame feelings in apes when the mother-child dyad is perturbed by an angry adult male, producing "Augenleuchten" (fiery eyes) and "Lautwerden" (auditory din) (Hermann, 1941 [1934]). His efforts, however, seem to have remained mostly unnoticed. Piers, a psychoanalyst, and Singer, a social anthropologist (specializing in the study of Indian culture), both residing in Chicago, were particularly instrumental in making the case that guilt cannot be separated from shame. Their little book (of only 86 pages) comprised two parts (Piers & Singer, 1953).

In the first part, "Shame and guilt: a psychoanalytic study", Piers contended that, whereas shame could be defined as the failure to comply with some standards or ideals presented to the ego by the ego ideal, guilt was the transgression of boundaries set by the superego. There is, moreover, a difference in the threat implied (castration in the case of guilt, abandonment in the case of shame). What is particularly insightful (and Dostoyevskian) in Piers' approach is that he subtly infers that, most of the time, there is a dynamic relationship between shame and guilt, revealing a functional signification of masochism. Shame can relieve guilt; conversely, too strong a humiliation can be resolved by a (forbidden) impulse through which the subject proves to himself that he is able to reach his ideal, in which case shame becomes guilt.

Singer's contribution, "Shame cultures and guilt cultures", used Piers' two-fold conception to criticize the notion proposed by Margaret Mead in *Cooperation and Competition*, which was that in guilt cultures social control is internalized, whereas in shame cultures it depends on an exterior agency. Singer tackled the common mantra about non-Western cultures being structured exclusively by internalized control. He used mainly his own field research on Indian industrialists in Madras, who had proved able to move from a very traditional countryside setting to a metropolis and become extremely successful without abandoning their cultural institutions, including a significant proportion of internalized guilt feelings. Although Piers and Singer's contribution has frequently been presented in a simplified manner, there is a general agreement that their little book marks a sort of a "turn of the tide", reshuffling the cards and preparing the way for the notion that the Anglo-Saxon culture might not be univocally a guilt culture after all.

Kohut's mirroring and narcissistic rage

Heinz Kohut (1913-1981), an immigrant from Vienna who became extremely popular in the US after he promoted "self-psychology" and the notion that a grandiose narcissistic self should be considered a normal phenomenon in young children, borrowed the cornerstone of his theory, "mirroring" in the eyes of one's mother, from an article by Donald Wood Winnicott (1971 [1967]), who in turn had borrowed this from Lacan's "mirror stage" theory (Lacan, 2006 [1949]). But whereas Lacan's theory never purported to erase guilt in favour of shame; quite the contrary, Lacan even contended that analysands should confirm their guilt as a means of alleviating their anxiety and limit their death-drives (Lacan, 2001 [1970]). Lacan's theory moreover saw the various imagoes (weaning, fraternal rivalry, mirror stage, Oedipus complex) as a series of moments through which several varieties of guilt could be displayed, while Kohut (1971), on the other hand, understood mirroring as a dependency on the gaze of a significant other through which the subject's narcissism could and should flourish, and which was far more important than the issue of unconscious guilt. One of the most striking examples of this is the notion of "narcissistic rage". Pathological aggressiveness has traditionally been understood as determined by a desire for revenge over a crippling sadistic superego, and more or less linked to death-drives. Kohut claimed that most of it could be better explained by narcissistic frustrations, which could produce "narcissistic rage", a catchphrase that has enjoyed considerable popularity since then. The "conservative leftist" Christopher Lasch (1979) lamented that North American culture has progressively abandoned its puritan roots to the real in the "culture of narcissism", as new versions of capitalism have promoted, via advertisements and mass media, a new "narcissistic personality of our times" (Lasch 1979, p.11). Heinz Kohut has probably been one of the main instruments of this in the domain of psychoanalysis.

Lacan: dying of shame and the seamy side of contemporary history

As we have already mentioned, Lacan, in most of his research, seems to have mainly continued the Freudian prevalence of guilt over shame. He was originally known as a theoretician of guilt feelings, of the sadistic superego, and even his theory of enunciation owes quite a lot to these (Sauvagnat, 2005). In fact, the term "shame" hardly appears at all in his seminars and published texts, except in two seminars, 'The other side of psychoanalysis', and 'Ou pire' ("Or worse"). In his seminar 'The other side of psychoanalysis', Lacan claims that, although he has hardly used the term, the issue of shame lies at the heart of what he has been trying to promote. The reference to H. de Balzac's *L'envers de l'histoire contemporaine* (1848; *The Seamy Side of Contemporary*

History), in which the novelist describes a secret Catholic society whose (religious) role is to save individuals in dire straits, is used as an ethical guideline to illustrate an essential aspect of the discourse: "dying of shame". Transforming the Heideggerian notion of "Sein zum Tode" (Heidegger, 1977 [1929]) in a direction that the German philosopher probably never foresaw, he regarded shame as the only affect indicating directly the "being for death" that characterizes a subject's relationship with "being".

At a conference at the University of Louvain in Belgium in 1972, Lacan was to claim that death was a "matter of faith" insofar that, if one fails to recognize that one's life is bound to end, one's existence becomes unreal. In cases of psychotic melancholia, Cotard's syndrome (Cotard, 1891) shows the incapacity of such subjects to conceptualize, to accept the idea that their life will have an end, and the result is an unlimited, delusional feeling of guilt. Thus, Lacan presented shame as an anticipation of the object included in guilt: the part of guilt that can be articulated through what he calls a discourse. In Balzac's novel, *The Seamy Side of Contemporary History* (Balzac 1848/1855), the secret society of the Brothers of Consolation is informed that a certain man is exhibiting strange conduct and is suspected of planning to commit suicide; he is discreetly followed, and he is found to hide a shameful secret. In spite of the modesty of his trade, he has arranged a secret room with all possible luxury in which his daughter, Vanda, lies in bed suffering from a mysterious disease, the Polish plait. A specialist, who is a Jewish physician, is summoned to the premises by the Brothers of Consolation, only to find that the poor woman is paying for her grandfather's faults: he is a Polish noble who betrayed his country to the Russian Empress Catherine II and permitted it to disappear. On the other side, her father is the prosecutor who has pronounced the death penalty during the French Revolution against the daughter of Mme de la Chanterie, the main leader of the Brothers of Consolation, but who found himself penniless after the restoration of the kingship. Because it is the result of this double shame, Vanda's symptoms can only be cured by persons who have been victims of her father and her grandfather. Thus, the change of discourse, the political transformations in which the victor becomes the vanquished, are measured in terms of unbearable shame. The true subject of discourse, in Lacan's view, is the subject of shame: the subject at the mercy of the master signifier.

Whereas a growing proportion of US psychoanalysts started to abandon the classical notion that guilt was more crucial than shame in symptom formation and increasingly depended on the study of shame and narcissistic mechanisms, relying on concepts that were originally coined by Lacan, Lacan himself described shame as being at the heart of guilt in a new version of the Freudian death-drives.

What if the US culture were in fact… a culture of shame?

In recent years, although there has been some continuation of the classical opposition between the "primitive shame cultures" and the "civilized guilt cultures" in political and war propaganda, there has been an inflation of interest in mechanisms of shame – even to the point that several authors, following Lasch's example, have proclaimed that "US culture is a culture of shame". There is little question that the notion of guilt is not exactly popular in this cultural domain, while "guilt feelings" are considered highly pathological.

Kaufman & Raphael (1984, p.57) and Kaufman (1989, p.93) have argued that the real moral standard in the US was shame, but that this went unrecognized because of a local taboo, according to which "one should not show his shame", one should "proclaim his pride" and that, when unavoidable, shame would be described in more lenient terms, such as "embarrassment". Similarly, Scheff (2003), following Tomkins (1963), finds that shame should be considered as the social emotion *par excellence* – the feeling that social bonds are threatened – while guilt should be seen as a subordinate to this.

Concluding remarks

Although psychoanalysis appeared, until the late 1960s, to be mainly concerned with guilt and to underestimate the importance of shame – and cultural anthropology seemed to endorse this position – a complete reversal of this picture has recently taken place with a number of analytical texts that dealing mainly with shame. One may rejoice that the traditional prejudice concerning the alleged gap between 'shame cultures' and 'guilt cultures' appears to be thus reduced; but this has not happened without some misunderstanding. Whereas it seems clear that the recent notion of a "culture of narcissism" is the source of this curious adoption of shame feelings by the Anglo-Saxon world, one wonders whether this very notion is the best choice if the deepest motives of shame are to be explored. This is where we find the idea that shame should not only be seen in terms of intersubjectivity, but also as the point where the subject, submitted to the master signifier, is confronted with the function of death.

References

Adler, A. (1921). *The neurotic constitution*. New York: Moffat, Yard and Co.
Balzac, H. de (1848/1855). *L'envers de l'histoire contemporaine*. Retrieved from http://beq.ebooksgratuits.com/balzac/Balzac-60.pdf
Benedict, R. (1934). *Patterns of culture*. Boston: Houghton Miflin Harcourt.
Benedict, R. (1948). *The chrysanthemum and the sword*. Boston: Houghton Miflin.
Boas, F., Mead, M., & and Lamphere, L. (1934). Preface, in R. Benedict, *Patterns of culture*. Boston: Houghton Miflin Harcourt.
Cannon, W.B. (1914). The emergency function of the adrenal medulla in pain and the major emotions. *Am J Physiol 33*.
Cannon, W.B. (1942). Voodoo death. *American Anthropologist, 44*.
Cotard, J. (1891). *Etudes sur les maladies cérébrales et mentales*. Paris: Baillière.

Doi, T. (1973). *The anatomy of dependence: the key analysis of Japanese behavior*. Tokyo: Kodansha International.

Dodds, E. R. (1951). *The Greeks and the irrational*. Berkeley, CA: University of California Press.

Fliess, W. (1906). *Der Ablauf des Lebens. Grundlegung zur exakten Biologie*. Wien: Franz Deuticke.

Freud, S. (1939). *Moses and monotheism*. London: Hogarth Press.

Freud S. (1953-1974). *The Standard Edition of the Complete Psychological Works of Sigmund Freud*. Trans. from the German under the general editorship of James Strachey, in collaboration with Anna Freud, assisted by Alix Strachey, Alan Tyson, and Angela Richards. 24 volumes, London: Hogarth Press and the Institute of Psycho-Analysis.

Freud, S. (1955 [1909]). Notes upon a case of obsessional neurosis. In *Standard Edition, X*.

Freud, S. (1955 [1915]). Totem and taboo. *Standard Edition, XIII*.

Freud, S. (1999 [1895]). Die Psychotherapie der Hysterie. In *Studien über Hysterie, Gesammelte Werke, Bd I*.

Freud, S. (1999 [1901]). Der Witz und seine Beziehung zum Unbewussten. In *Gesammelte Werke VI*.

Freud, S. (1999 [1911]). Formulierungen über den zwei Prinzipien des psychischen Geschehens. In *Gesammelte Werke VIII*.

Freud, S. (1999 [1931]). Die Weiblichkeit, in Neue Folge der Vorlesungen zur Einführung in die Psychoanalyse. In *Gesammelte Werke* Bd. X.

Freud, S. (1999). *Gesammelte Werke. Chronologisch geordnet*. 19 Bände, dazu ein Registerband (Bd. 18) und ein Band mit Nachträgen (Bd. 19). Fischer Taschenbuch-Verlag: Frankfurt am Main.

Granet, M. (1926). *Danses et légendes dans la Chine ancienne*. Paris: Presses Universitaires de France.

Heidegger, M. (1977 [1929]). *Sein und Zeit*. Hrsg. von Friedrich-Wilhelm von Herrmann. Frankfurt am Main: Vittorio Klostermann.

Hermann, I. (1934). Urwahrnehmungen, insbesonders Augenleuchten und Lautwerden des Inneren. *Internationale Zeitschrift für Psychoanalyse, 20*.

Hermann, I. (1941). Anklammerung, feuer, schamgefühl. *Internationale Zeitschrift für Psychoanalyse und Imago, 26*.

Ho, D. Y.-F. (1974). Face, social expectations, and conflict avoidance. In J. Dawson & W. Lonner (Eds.), *Readings in cross-cultural psychology: Proceedings of the inaugural meeting of the International Association for Cross-Cultural*

Psychology held in Hong Kong, August 1972. Hong Kong: Hong Kong University Press.

Ho, D. Y.-F. (1976). On the concept of face. *American Journal of Sociology, 81*(4).

Honte. In *Centre National de Resources Textuelles et Lexicales*. Retrieved from http://www.cnrtl.fr/etymologie/honte

Horkheimer, M., & Adorno, T. W. (2002 [1944]). *The dialectics of enlightenment*. Stanford, CA: Stanford University Press.

Hu, H. C. (1944). The Chinese concept of 'face'. *American Anthropologist, 46*(1).

Jones, E. (1953-1957). *The life and work of Sigmund Freud, Vol I & II*. London: Basic Books.

Kaufman, G. (1989). *The psychology of shame*. New York: Springer.

Kohut, H. (1971). *The analysis of the self: a systematic analysis of the treatment of the narcissistic personality disorders*. Chicago: University of Chicago Press.

Lacan, J. (1972). *Louvain conference*. Retrieved from http://www.hksproductions.com/ Jacques-Lacan-Conference-de-Louvain-Video-et-Texte_v146.html

Lacan, J. (1977). *The four fundamental concepts of psychoanalysis, Seminar XI, 1963-64*. Transl. A. Sheridan. London: Hogarth.

Lacan, J. (2001 [1970]). Radiophonie. In *Autres Ecrits*. Paris: Seuil.

Lacan, J. (2006 [1949]). The mirror-stage as formative of the function of the I as revealed in the psychoanalytic experience. In *Ecrits*. New York: W.W. Norton.

Lacan, J. (2007 [1970]). *The other side of psychoanalysis, Seminar 1969-70*. Transl. R. Grigg. New York: Norton.

Lacan, J. (2011). *Ou pire, Seminar 1972-73*. Paris: Seuil.

Lacan, J. (2014). *Anxiety, Seminar X 1962-63*. Transl. A. R. Price. Cambridge: Polity.

Lasch, C. (1979). *The culture of narcissism: American life in an age of diminishing expectations*. New York: Norton.

Lester, D. (1972). Voodoo death: some new thoughts on an old phenomenon. *American Anthropologist, 74*(3).

Mead, M. (2003 [1935]). *Sex and temperament in three primitive societies*. First Perennial edition. New York: Perennial, HarperCollins Publ.

Pewzner-Apeloig, E. (1992). *L'homme coupable: la folie et la faute en occident*. Toulouse: Privat.

Piers, G., & Singer, M. (1953). *Shame and guilt*. Springfield: Charles C. Thomas.

Reich, W. (1945 [1933]). *Character analysis*. Transl. V. Carfagno. New York: Farrar, Straus and Ginoux.

Sauvagnat, F. (2003). Johann Nepomuk Nestroy ou l'envers de l'angoisse freudienne. In *L'inquiétant (Research group) Psychanalyse et Recherches Universitaires*. Renne: Presses Universitaires de Rennes.

Sauvagnat, F. (2004). La psychopathologie saisie par les mythes. In M. Zafiropoulos & M. Boccara (Eds.), *Le mythe: pratique, récit, théorie. Volume IV: Anthropologie et Psychanalyse*. Paris: Anthropos.

Sauvagnat, F. (2005) Hallucinations psychotiques et énonciation. La voix, dans et hors la cure. *Revue Psychologie Clinique, 19*.

Scheff, T. (2003). Shame in self and society. *Symbolic Interaction, 26*.

Swoboda, H. (1904). *Die Perioden des menschlichen Organismus in ihren psychologischen und biologischen Bedeutung*. Leipzig u. Wien: Franz Deuticke.

Tomkins, S. (1963). *Affect, imagery, consciousness. Vol. 2: the negative affects*. New York: Springer.

Weiniger, O. (1906). *Sex and character*. London, New York: N.P. Putnam & Son.

Winnicott, D. W. (1971 [1967]). Mirror-role of mother and family in child development. In *Playing and reality*. London: Tavistock Publ.

Wurmser, L. (2003). Psychoanalytic reflections on 9/11, terrorism, and genocidal prejudice: roots and sequels. *Journal of the American Psychoanalytic Association, 52*(3).

4.
Mapping shame and guilt
Inner and outer landscapes in *The Adventures of Pinocchio* and *The Wonderful Adventures of Nils*[1]

Anna Smedberg Bondesson

Shame as double rejection and guilt as reconciliation

In an interview from 2010 with the Norwegian psychiatrist and writer Finn Skårderud, the Estonian-Finnish writer Sofi Oksanen says:

> There are very few in today's Finland who write cross-culturally and describe what it is like to be a second-generation immigrant, which is what I represent. While I was working on *Stalin's Cows*, it turned out to be more and more a story about a country. I wrote about the country of my mother and my grandmother, I wrote about Finland, and about Russia, which for such a long time has influenced both Estonia and Finland. I wrote to document my life. Without memories there is no identity. And the countries became like a body. The main character is ashamed of

---

1   For a Swedish and slightly extended version (but in two different chapters), see Smedberg Bondesson (2018). The Wonderful Adventures of Nils is the title of the translation of the first book about Nils Holgersson, made by Velma Swanston Howard more than a century ago (Lagerlöf, 1999). The translations cited in this article, though, are all from the recent translation made by Peter Graves (Lagerlöf, 2014).

this body. The eating disorder becomes a silent language for this kind of shame. (Skårderud, 2011, pp.438-439)[2]

This quotation highlights a central paradox regarding the strong emotion of shame: the shame affect is a kind of double rejection, since it has to do with not having access to a certain community, with being rejected and, simultaneously, with not getting away—i.e. being stuck and desperately trying to reject and repulse what stubbornly sticks to the identity. In the case of Oksanen's debut novel from 2003, Finland represents what, in a way is, yearned for in vain as a space to be part of, because it is a community that is not only imagined, but also much desired, while Estonia represents the dark side, which has to be repressed and remain in darkness. Shame as a double rejection—to be rejected and to reject—arises at the border between these two contrasting rejections, which establish the paradox and so produce a lie about happiness and wholeness. This lie, in turn, covers up the very same paradox.

The main difference between shame and guilt, I would suggest, is that guilt, since it has to do with behaviour rather than the self, comes to terms pragmatically with this paradox: it finds a way towards reconciliation. Guilt is not as strong an emotion as shame; guilt is a kind of regulated and already processed shame, while shame as affect is non-processed. It first appears at the age of 2-3 and is productive since it helps us behave in society. But shame can also be destructive and without any actual guilt, as is the case with abuse victims. According to Silvan S. Tomkins affect theory, shame is one of the nine

---

2   My translation: "Det er få i dagens Finland som skriver om det krysskulturelle og om hvordan det er å være en andregenerasjons innvandrer, som jeg er en representant for. Mens jeg skrev på *Stalins kyr*, ble det mer og mer en beretning om et land. Jeg skrev om min mors og min mormors land, jeg skrev om Finland, og om Russland som lenge har påvirket begge. Jeg skrev for å dokumentere mitt liv. Uten minner finnes ingen identitet. Og landene ble som en kropp. Hovedpersonen skammer seg over denne kroppen. Spiseforstyrrelsen blir et taust språk for en slik skam."

primary affects. We are born with the capacity of bodily experiencing the affects, but we have to learn, in interaction with other people, to interpret, translate and understand them in order to regulate them and even to be fully aware of them.[3]

Guilt, on the other hand, is a conscious feeling of responsibility that comes with a mature conscience. It could be the responsibility felt for another person or for a whole, imagined community, from within or from without this community, such as, for example, a nation and its history. It may also be the responsibility felt for the self and the kind of life that the self lives. Guilt incorporates all this.

Nevertheless, guilt can be a big burden, of course, almost a bodily weight or an inner prison. And the stronger the sense of guilt is, the more it could actually redevelop itself into shame, which in turn can cause even more shame, which then loops itself into a feeling about the feeling that goes round and round incessantly. Hence, not only may shame develop into a conscious feeling of guilt, but actual guilt can also cause shame, and shame always carries the risk of turning into a shame-shame loop.[4]

This article will be a journey through the inner and outer landscapes of shame and guilt as bodily transformations and mental metamorphoses in *The Adventures of Pinocchio* (1881) and in *The Wonderful Adventures of Nils* (1906-07). Both stories end with the respective protagonists having finally travelled so far and learnt so much about life and the world that they can take part in the human—and perhaps also national—community and become human beings.

---

[3] See Tomkins (1995); Nathanson (1992); Skårderud (2011).
[4] For a definition of emotion loops, see Scheff (2011).

Shame and guilt in Pinocchio and Nils

The Adventures of Pinocchio starts with a piece of wood that comes alive even before it has been transformed into a puppet. Every time the puppet tells a lie, its wooden nose grows bigger, which is, of course, a figure of shame symbolised by a physical and bodily concretisation; the ultimate metaphor of shame in the story is when the puppet is transformed into a donkey. Finally, though, Pinocchio succeeds in becoming "a proper boy" (Collodi, 1996, p.170).[5]

The Wonderful Adventures of Nils, which also begins with a metamorphosis, is the story of the spoilt and lazy boy Nils, who is—literally—cut down to the size of a thumb by an elf, following which he must travel on the back of a goose along the length and breadth of Sweden until he can finally return home again, reformed and matured. In the end, he regains normal, corporal size and bursts out, proudly and happily: "Mother! Father! I'm big! I'm a human being again!" (Lagerlöf, 2014, p.644).[6] As Louise Vinge puts it, this is the core of the story as a psychological drama. Nils' mission is to become human again (Vinge 1999).

At the beginning of the two stories, shame is what prevents the main characters from returning home and, instead, it causes—or initiates—their long journeys. The extremely complex and interesting figure of Pinocchio makes, then, in comparison to Nils and his tour of Sweden all the way to the very north and then down south again, a very different and more of a vagabond-like trip through a countryside that might be Tuscany, but is never actually situated in geography. Both of them, Pinocchio and Nils, suffer of shame as a result of actual guilt, since they, initially, resist to take responsibility for their acts and their guilt. But from here they develop in quite different ways.

The shame of Nils is not as strong as that of Pinocchio. It is de-

---

5 "un ragazzino perbene" (Collodi, 2002, p.234).
6 "Mor och far, jag är stor, jag är människa igen!" (Lagerlöf, 1907, p.483).

scribed as something which has to do with his transformation into an elf: "No sooner was the boy's belly full than he began to feel ashamed of having eaten something raw. 'That shows that I'm a real elf and not human any more,' he thought" (Lagerlöf, 2014, p.38).[7] Being an elf and no longer a human being is the reason for Nils' hesitation to return home and presenting himself before his parents: "The boy thought it might be a good idea not to face his parents for a while" (Lagerlöf, 2014, p.39).[8]

Pinocchio also avoids presenting himself and facing his "parent", i.e. Joe (Geppetto). And this shame—or actually shamelessness, which makes the shame so much worse, because it offers no turning back—of Pinocchio is a truly severe one. In order to buy a ticket to watch the puppet show instead of going to school, Pinocchio sells his alphabet book, although poor Joe has had to sell his one and only cape in order to buy it:

> So the book was sold then and there. And just think how that poor man, Joe, was trembling with cold at home, in nothing but his shirt-sleeves, because he had been determined to buy the alphabet book for his little boy! (Collodi, 1996, p.26)[9]

This is a real and present guilt that can easily result in a sense of guilt so strong that it almost strangles you. And, naturally, it also causes shame, a shame that makes it impossible for Pinocchio to return home with nothing in his hands. At least, this is what the young reader/listener to

---

[7] "Då pojken väl var mätt, kände han sig allt skamsen över att han hade kunnat äta något rått. 'Det syns, att jag inte är en människa mer, utan en riktig tomte', tänkte han" (Lagerlöf, 1906, p.31).
[8] "Pojken tänkte, att det kunde vara rätt så bra att slippa visa sig för föräldrarna än på en tid" (Lagerlöf, 1906, p.32).
[9] "E il libro fu venduto lì su due piedi. E pensare che quel pover'uomo di Geppetto era rimasto a casa a tremare dal freddo in maniche di camicia, per comprare l'abbecedario al figliolo!" (Collodi, 2002, p.46).

the story is obviously supposed to feel and think. And the suspicion that Pinocchio himself is shameless because he lacks conscience—a faculty totally externalised from him and only represented by the talking cricket, whom Pinocchio brutally kills in the fourth chapter—just makes it even worse. The talking cricket returns in the twelfth chapter as a shadow, but still without any power to convince Pinocchio of his duties as a son.

The donkey metamorphosis is the final result of Pinocchio's shamelessness and lack of conscience. When confronted with the image in the mirroring water in the washbasin, Pinocchio at first experiences only the kind of shame the narrator lets the reading/listening child imagine or project. But then the emotional reaction is described, and this immediately becomes a feeling about the feeling, which loops itself into a sorrow-shame-fear-loop, a process that is concretized metaphorically by the growing ears:

> He went searching for a mirror at once to see what he looked like, but, not finding a mirror, he filled the washbasin with water and looking into it he saw something he would never have wished to see: what he saw was his image adorned with a magnificent pair of ass's ears.
>
> I leave you to imagine poor Pinocchio's misery, shame and anguish!
>
> He began to weep and shriek and bang his head against the wall; but the more distracted he became, the more his ears grew and grew and grew, and now hair sprouted at the ends. (Collodi, 1996, p.130)[10]

---

10 "Andò subito in cerca di uno specchio, per potersi vedere; man non trovando uno specchio, empì d'acqua la catinella del lavamano e, specchiandovisi dentro, vide quel che non avrebbe mai voluto vedere: vide, cioè, la sua immagine abbellita di un magnifico paio di orecchi asinini. / Lascio pensare a voi il dolore, la vergogna a la disperazione del povero Pinocchio. / Cominciò a piangere, a strillare, a battere la testa nel muro; ma quanto più si disperava, e più i suoi orecchi crescevano crescevano e diventavano pelosi verso la cima." (Collodi, 2002, p.186)

Pinocchio does not really change or seem to mature until he eventually gets the opportunity to rescue his "father" Joe (Geppetto) and himself from the stomach of the Shark and thus becomes a hero. However, one could argue that, in fact, he shows this kind of altruism and heroism from the very start—as, for example, when he offers himself to be burned in place of Harlequin: "Tie me up and throw me into the middle of those flames. No, no! It's not right that poor Harlequin, my true friend, should die for me" (Collodi, 1996, p.32).[11] Yet, it is also very clear that Pinocchio here simply uses his skills of melodrama: he knows exactly how to make everybody cry and feel mercy.

Nils Holgersson, on the other hand, gradually, day after day, region by region, learns more and more. From the very beginning of his long journey, he starts taking on a responsibility which is new to him, helping the fainting gander to find water. As Anna Bohlin stresses, in her article "Nils and the Social Mother as a Migrating Goose", Nils helps other individuals, across borders of species, on his journey out of fear (which, by the way, according to Tomkins is another of the nine primary affects). Inspired by Sara Ahmed's theory of 'affective economies', Bohlin investigates "the function of fear in building a nation". Bohlin argues convincingly that in Lagerlöf's affective economy, "the experience of dependence and fear is necessary to achieve a responsible form of independence" (Bohlin, 2018, p.117).

Shame and fear are related in so far as shame entails the social fear of not belonging anywhere and to anyone at all. Even so, the real reason why Nils goes off with the geese is perhaps neither shame nor fear but yet another primary affect: curiosity! A combination of curiosity, a hunger for adventures, laziness and the desire to escape from all social obligations and duties drives both Nils and Pinocchio. In the case of Nils, this is a kind of comfort for the sadness and sorrow

---

11 "Legatemi e gettatemi là fra quelle fiamme. No, non è giusta che il povero Arlecchino, il vero amico mio, debba morire per me." (Collodi, 2002, p.55)

(yet another primary affect) he feels about his lost status as human being now that he has been bewitched:

> Before falling asleep he lay awake thinking that if the geese allowed him to go with them he would no longer have to put up with being scolded for laziness. He would be able to laze around all day and his only worry would be finding things to eat. Not that it was likely to be much trouble since he needed so little these days.
>
> And he imagined all the things he would see and all the adventures he would be part of. Oh, how different it would be from the dreary round of work and drudgery at home!
>
> "If only I can make this journey with the wild geese," he thought, "I won't be in the least bothered about having had a spell put on me."
> (Lagerlöf, 2014, p.66)[12]

There is evidently a kind of double urge in Nils. He wants to escape, but he also wants to see something new—that is, he wants to learn things about his country, and perhaps also about the world as a whole—which means to expand and mature in terms of his learning. Perhaps what he truly longs for is imagination, an inner world, an ability to imagine, which is what enables a person to feel empathy. One could possibly argue that Nils goes from feeling guilt/shame in the form of rejection/repulsion and an urge to escape to increasingly feeling guilt/empathy in the form of an embracement and an urge to return back home.

---

12 "Innan han somnade, låg han och tänkte på att om han finge följa med vildgässen, skulle han slippa alla bannor för att han var lat. Då finge han slå dank hela dagarna, och hans enda bekymmer skulle vara att skaffa sig något att äta. Men han behövde så litet nu för tiden, så det bleve det nog råd för. / Och så målade han ut för sig allt, vad han skulle få se, och så många äventyr han skulle få vara med om. Ja, det skulle bli annat än släpet och slitet därhemma. 'Om jag bara finge följa med vildgässen på deras resa, skulle jag inte sörja över att jag har blivit förvandlad', tänkte pojken." (Lagerlöf, 1906, p.60)

Creating Sweden as a national space

The Wonderful Adventures of Nils evidently has, just like *The Adventures of Pinocchio*, a great deal of imaginative power. This power has made it possible for the story to fly on goose-wings all around the world. But crossing the borders of Sweden in this manner was not at all calculated or even foreseen. When Alfred Dalin, the leading figure in one of the teacher's unions, asked the author Selma Lagerlöf in 1901 if she could undertake the writing of a school reader, she debated with herself whether or not to accept the offer, as can be seen in a letter she wrote to her travel partner, Sophie Elkan:

> It is, you understand, a book that would not really work outside of Sweden, but it is probably more worthwhile to try to reach into every little home within Sweden than to bother about abroad, where success seems so very hard to come by. (Lagerlöf, 1992, p.185)[13]

Some scholars, such as Björn Sundmark and Bjarne Thorup Thomsen, have recently returned to read the book in its original context, demonstrating that, because it was published as a work of instruction in the discipline of geography, it can easily be seen as a calculated move deliberately intended to build both character and nation. Nils' journey is analysed as the production of the Swedish national space and the imagined community in Benedict Anderson's understanding of the term (Anderson, 1991; Sundmark, 2008; Thomsen, 2007).

In producing this national space and imagined community, Selma Lagerlöf actually anticipates the very idea of Sweden as the 'people's home', a *folkhem*. This concept was launched by the social democratic

---

[13] My translation. This letter to Sophie Elkan is without date but was answered 1st November 1901. "Det är ju en bok, som ej kan gå utom Sverige, men det är väl mer värdt att komma in i hvarenda stuga härhemma än att bråka med utlandet, som är så svårt att vinna och som aldrig tycks lyckas."

leader Per Albin Hansson in 1928. In the following years, it gained wide currency and, at least until recently, it remained central to Swedish self-understanding. As Sundmark puts it, also citing Vivi Edström: "Solidarity, good will and an optimistic belief in progress is part of it, and 'the notion that the state ought to function as a good home in which everyone contributes to its growth and development'" (Edström, 1984, p.64; Sundmark, 2008, p.181).

It was Selma Lagerlöf's own idea that her Swedish reader was to be introduced to Swedish geography. Dealing with geography and topography means dealing with different kinds of maps and mapping. *The Wonderful Adventures of Nils* is perhaps the most obvious and literal example of what we today call literary mapping or cartographic writing. Lagerlöf's stated aim with the book was: "to give life to the map" (Lagerlöf, 1967, p.251); and she succeeds by employing, literally, "the bird's eye view convention of modern maps" and the whole "discourse of mapping" (Anderson, 1991, pp.172-175; Sundmark, 2008, p.175).

But mapping is, of course, always also an act of inventing, and *The Wonderful Adventures of Nils* strikes a perfect balance between realism and fantasy: Although the text produces a strong sense of reality and Nils never leaves Sweden, he "enters a magically enhanced version" of the country. The real is made magic and ordinary places become universes of possibility (Sundmark, 2008, p.171).

What happens, then, to the story of Nils when it does exactly what Nils and the geese within the story never do—that is, when it transgresses the geographical and national border of Sweden? Perhaps the Japanese writer Kenzaburo Oe gives us the best answer to that question. When receiving the Nobel Prize for literature in 1994, he was asked what he most enjoyed about this global acknowledgement and appreciation. He answered, "That I could finally come to the land of Nils!"[14] Oe's acquaintance with the story of Nils began when, as a little

---

14 Studentafton (a student evening event), AF (Academic Association Building), Lund. Sweden, 14th December, 1994. I quote from memory.

boy during the Great War, he read for the first time *The Wonderful Adventures of Nils* by Selma Lagerlöf. He then "felt sympathetic [to] and identified with Nils" (Oe, 1994).

Oe's spontaneous answer, and Sofi Oksanen's reflection and description in the interview quoted at the beginning of this article, both highlight the variety of ways in which concepts such as place, space, embodiment/disembodiment, and inclusion in versus exclusion from a certain imagined community can take on meaning in terms of shame/guilt in the form of repulsion or of guilt/empathy in the form of embracement, inside and outside literature, inside and outside your home country, in an inner and an outer landscape.

Pinocchio's Italian passport

Shame has to do with not being seen as a whole and complex person. It consequently also afflicts an individual who neglects itself in its fully potential. If that is the case, the shame remains unprocessed in the body and becomes something which this body wishes to expel, almost like an impulse to vomit. In the beginning of the two adventures, both Nils and Pinocchio experience this urge to expel as they try to deny their guilt or at least not think about it. This kind of shame/denied guilt as repulsion always also has to do with not having access to something that one desires access to. It has to do with rejection, exclusion and with little space for maturing.

On the other hand, if guilt is not denied but instead accepted, it means that the process of being able to be seen—that is, being able to see and handle what others can see in you, without having neither to hide within yourself from nor reduce yourself to that internalized gaze—and the maturation has begun. Instead of rejection there is then a kind of embracement at stake, which is what Nils finally achieves at the end of the story: after first having escaped his obligations he eventually returns home reformed. This kind of guilt/empathy as embracement can function in the opposite way and form both the person and the nation, as in the example of *The Wonderful Adventures of Nils*.

As mentioned, the ultimate metaphor of shame/guilt as repulsion in *The Adventures of Pinocchio* is when the puppet literally is transformed into a donkey. We find yet another trope of shame at the very end, when he rejects his past: "How funny I was when I was a puppet!" (Collodi, 1996, p.170).[15] So, while Nils Holgersson grows hand in hand with a growing sense of guilt, empathy and responsibility, Pinocchio finally becomes human through experiencing what could otherwise have been an endlessly looping shame, which would be unbearable and therefore turn into shamelessness. He ends up longing for adaptation to the norm and acceptance, but this is really his only way out of the shame loop, just as the mouth of the Shark is the only way out of its body; his only escape is to turn into "a proper boy" (Collodi, 1996, p.170).

When the story of *The Wonderful Adventures of Nils* leaves Sweden and is read outside this imagined community, then the map of Sweden, the Swedish geography, still works as the main theme and forms the structure of the plot, while *The Adventures of Pinocchio* could just as well have taken place anywhere else across the globe. According to Emer O'Sullivan, when Pinocchio crosses cultural borders, he usually loses both his passport and his identity, but this is due to the various universalising ways in which he is domesticated into the target languages and cultures, "being left to toss and turn on a sea of constant reinterpretation and instrumentalization", and not due to the original text, which is, one might perhaps say, lost in the internationalising ocean (O'Sullivan, 2005, p.152).

But, actually, when examining the original novels' respective Swedishness or Italianness, the opposite pattern can be discerned. The Swedishness of *Nils* can easily be transformed into any other "-ness", in the sense that "it provides a blueprint for the conception of any

---

15 "Com'ero buffo, quand'ero burattino!" (Collodi, 2002, p.234)

nation, a conception that is non-aggressive and self-contained" (Sundmark, 2008, p.183). In contrast—and this is the most crucial point when comparing the two stories, I think—the Italianness of *Pinocchio*, which lies not in the scenery and the descriptions of it, but in the plot and on a merely metaphorical and symbolical level, is perhaps not at all that easy to transform or transgress. I rely here on the interesting 2007 study by Suzanne Stewart-Steinberg, *The Pinocchio Effect. On Making Italians 1860-1920*. This will be further discussed later when I will also question this described Italianness.

Anyhow, both stories can be regarded as mere fairy tales about boys growing up and learning, in one way or another, how to cope with the world, a world that is more or less fantastically represented. They both thus lend themselves to radical adaptive changes and have also had great adaptation success, especially within the ambit of popular culture (as, for example, cartoon films). *Pinocchio* was 'Disneyfied' in 1940, and *Nils Holgersson* has twice been 'Mangafied' within the Japanese anime tradition, in the eighties and again in the first decade of the twenty-first century.

Comparing the figure of Nils with the figure of Pinocchio is like placing the characters of Dickens side by side with those of Kafka; and yet, on the surface, the two stories have much in common. But Nils, just like Oliver Twist, manages to grow up in one piece. In the end, Nils cries out: "Mother! Father! I'm big! I'm a human being again!" (Lagerlöf, 2014, p.644). Pinocchio, by contrast, according to Stewart-Steinberg (2007), embodies the fundamental split of the modern self, both as a puppet without strings, and, in the final scene, where the former puppet remains in the corner as a reminder to the real boy of the past he now has to reject ("How funny I was when I was a puppet!"—Collodi, 1996, p.170) if he is to stay where he is. Pinocchio's shame is an existential on; he can never escape the shame of existence.

Although he becomes a real a boy, one may, as Stewart-Steinberg does, argue that this transition is purely a negative one: from puppet without strings to boy with (metaphorical) strings. As she puts it, leaning on Žižek, Pinocchio is "the allegorical brother of [...] Gregor Samsa and other Kafkan characters who confront the ideological state apparatus in the form of a blind, nonsensical bureaucracy but who are not integrated into that apparatus" (Stewart-Steinberg, 2007, p.47).

According to Stewart-Steinberg (2007, pp.2-4), "the formulation of an Italian [post-liberal] national self was predicated on a language that posited marginalization and powerlessness as fundamental aspects of what it meant to be modern Italians". Other aspects were "superficiality, rhetoricism, absence of essence and a childlike nature". So, the rhetoric of the project of 'making Italians' was "not about the emancipation of adults, but instead about the education of children. Even when the focus was on the literal education of children, as in the case of Maria Montessori's work, the metonymic referent was in fact a nation composed only of children". She continues by arguing that the "educational and gendered language by which Italians were to be made circled almost obsessively around three concerns [...]—the crisis of liberalism, the crisis of religious conscience, and the crisis of paternal, masculine performativity". This produces an anxious and fundamentally split ego, an uncontrolled puppet who lacks all kinds of autonomy.

I would now like to focus on the opening of *The Adventures of Pinocchio*. It all begins with corporal maltreatment: "Don't hit me too hard!" the piece of wood says "pleadingly" (Collodi, 1996, p.1).[16] Already, there are serious reasons to be suspicious, because it does not say 'please, don't hit me': it says: 'don't hit me too hard'. In this light, it is no paradox that Pinocchio is, indeed, a transitional figure, about to turn into a human being, but not in the sense of growth and grounding as is Nils. Pinocchio is, in Stewart-Steinberg's words, "more accurately subject to Kafkan metamorphosis, whereby his transgressions increasingly take on an aspect of perverse pleasure" (Stewart-Steinberg, 2007, p.52).

---

16   "Non mi picchiar tanto forte!" (Collodi, 2002, p.5)

Pinocchio and Nils as two different responses to modernity

However, I would like furthermore to suggest that what Pinocchio and Nils embody is perhaps not so much national selves as two versions, two alternative and equally possible roads to take in modernity or even in late modernity: suppressed shame or reconciled guilt. On a collective level, Pinocchio's is the non-processed, deeply traumatised history, while Nils represents the more utopian solution of empathy and solidarity facing the truth. On an individual level, Pinocchio is perhaps the emblematic neurotic, trying to escape or reject the too strong affects lodged in his body, or the psychotic projecting of them onto some kind of metaphorical screen as paranoid fantasies—an escape from or rejection of the actual situation, which becomes a prison under the force of these fruitless attempts to escape or reject. Nils, on the other hand, stands for a more grounded solution, where good and evil coexist and are possible to talk about.

If Nils and I had had the chance to take Pinocchio up into space to look down upon earth, instead of just the Tuscan or the southern Swedish landscape, I think we would have shown him the world as a whole and the immense variety of stars and planets which surround it in the universe. The power of empathy lies in the imagination. With the help of imagination, imaginative power, every limit is, in the end, transgressible. All strings can be cut; we can all become human beings.

The motivation for awarding the Nobel Prize to Oe may, at first glance, perhaps seem very similar to the motivation for awarding it to Selma Lagerlöf back in 1909, over a hundred years ago. Oe "... with poetic force creates an imagined world, where life and myth condense to form a disconcerting picture of the human predicament today", while Lagerlöf received the honour "...in appreciation of the lofty idealism, vivid imagination and spiritual perception that characterize her writings".[17] One could also easily argue that the difference between the two statements of motivation has more to do with the changing context than with the literary texts in themselves. But let us focus on the word "disconcerting". I think this is where Collodi and Oe coincide and unite.

So, finally, I would like to argue that, after all, perhaps Collodi, just like Kafka, actually offers a much more constructive solution than does Lagerlöf, since the Collodian one—by using the lie about happiness and wholeness as a cover-up for the paradox of shame—actually and truly paradoxically sticks to the truth instead of projecting a utopian image of the future. "Pinocchiology", as Stewart-Steinberg (2007) refers to it, could actually be seen as something, which not only mirrors or performs things as they are; in criticizing the state apparatus, the nonsensical bureaucracy, the norms of the society, the acute and problematic problems of the modern and split self – in the end, perhaps it also offers a solution for how to transcend and overcome them. But, of course, we do need the utopias. So, the best alternative seems to be a combination of the two. The utopia of Lagerlöf combined with the dystopia of Collodi could conceivably produce a heterotopia (according to Foucault), an 'other' place (Foucault, 1984).

In that other place, there would still be both guilt and shame, of course. There are shameless places, but shamelessness is not the disappearance of shame, since shame can never truly disappear. Shame can only be more or less mentalised; that is, made conscious. Shamelessness would therefore be the same as suppressed shame. There is no such place as a place without shame. But the *other* shame, in this *other* place, this heterotopia, would maybe and hopefully always be productive, always possible to regulate, formulate and therefore also

---

17   http://nobelprize.org/nobel_prizes/literature/laureates/1994/index.html. To be compared with: "in appreciation of the lofty idealism, vivid imagination and spiritual perception that characterize her writings": http://nobelprize.org/nobel_prizes/literature/laureates/1909/index.html

to transform into more manageable and conscious feelings, such as guilt, fear of being left out and fear of shame itself.

References

Anderson, B. (1991). *Imagined communities*. London: Verso.
Bohlin, A. (2018/19). Nils and the social mother as a migrating goose. Tijdsschrift voor Skandinavistiek 3(2).
Collodi, C. (2002). *Le avventure di Pinocchio*. Edizione illustrata. Milano: Garzanti.
Collodi, C. (1996). *The adventures of Pinocchio*. Translated with an introduction and notes by A. L. Lucas. Oxford: Oxford University Press.
Edström, V. (1984). *Selma Lagerlöf*. Boston: Twayne.
Foucault, M. (1984). Des espaces autres. *Architecture Mouvement Continuité, 5*. [(1986). Of other spaces. Transl. J. Miskowiec. *Diacritic*, 16(1)].
Lagerlöf, S. (1906). *Nils Holgerssons underbara resa genom Sverige I*. Stockholm: Bonniers. Retrieved from www.litteraturbanken.se
Lagerlöf, S. (1907). *Nils Holgerssons underbara resa genom Sverige II*. Stockholm: Bonniers. Retrieved from www.litteraturbanken.se
Lagerlöf, S. (1967). *Brev I: 1871-1902*. Y. Toijer-Nilsson (Ed.). Lund: Gleerups.
Lagerlöf, S. (1992). *Du lär mig att bli fri. Selma Lagerlöf skriver till Sophie Elkan*. Y. Toijer-Nilsson (Ed.). Stockholm: Bonniers.
Lagerlöf, S. (1999). *The wonderful adventures of Nils* [I] and *The further adventures of Nils* [II]. Transl. V. S. Howard. London, New York: Puffin (Penguin).
Lagerlöf, S. (2014). Nils Holgersson's wonderful journey through Sweden. Transl. P. Graves. London: Norvik Press.
Nathanson, D. (1992). Shame and pride. Affect, sex and the birth of the self. New York & London: Norton.
Oe, K. (1994). *Japan, the ambiguous, and myself*. Nobel lecture, December 7 1994. Retrieved from http://nobelprize.org/nobel_prizes/literature/laureates/1994/oe-lecture.html
Oksanen, S. (2003). *Stalinin lehmät*. Helsinki: WSOY.
O'Sullivan, E. (2005). Does Pinocchio have an Italian passport? What is specifically national and what is international about classics of children's literature? *Comparative children's literature*. New York: Routledge.

Scheff, T. J. (2011). Emotions and depression. Finding and facing intense emotions. *Psychology Today*. Retrieved from https://www.psychologytoday.com/blog/lets-connect/201107/emotions-and-depression-0

Skårderud, F. (2011). Sofi Oksanen—skammens politiske geografi. *Tidskrift for Norsk Psykologforening, 48*(5).

Smedberg Bondesson, A. (2018). Gösta Berling på La Scala. Selma Lagerlöf och Italien. Göteborg & Stockholm: Makadam förlag.

Stewart-Steinberg, S. (2007). *The Pinocchio effect. On making Italians 1860-1920*. Chicago & London: University of Chicago Press.

Sundmark, B. (2008). Of Nils and nation. Selma Lagerlöf's The Wonderful Adventures of Nils. In *International Research in Children's Literature, 2*.

Thomsen, B. T. (2007). *Lagerlöfs litterære landvinding. Nation, mobilitet og modernitet i* Nils Holgersson *og angrænsende tekster*. Amsterdam: Scandinavisch Institut.

Tomkins, S. (1995). Exploring Affect. The Selected Writings of Silvan S. Tomkins. V. E. Demos (Ed.). Cambridge: Cambridge University Press.

Vinge, L. (1999). Nils Holgerssons uppgift: att bli människa igen. *Artes. Tidskrift för litteratur konst och musik, 1*.

5.
When we dead awaken: To die of shame

Kjell R. Soleim

When We Dead Awaken,[1] written in 1899, was to be Henrik Ibsen's last play; the author gave it the subtitle "A Dramatic Epilogue". We find the signifiers of the title in a dialogue between the two protagonists towards the end of Act 2:

> IRENE. We see the irretrievable only when... (Breaks off)
> PROFESSOR RUBEK. (Looks inquiringly at her) When...?
> IRENE. When we dead awaken. (Ibsen, 1936 (HI), p.238)

To this, I have added: – to die of shame. As a matter of fact, the world-famous sculptor and his model, who are the main characters, die by the end of Act 3. They perish in an avalanche up in the mountains, like the fanatic priest Brand does in Ibsen's play from 1864. But, as the title of the play from 1899 tells us, its two protagonists were *already* dead. They were ghosts who had risen from the dead – and, after that, they died. This intermediate stage – between the awakening and the second

---

[1] The translations from Ibsen's play *Når vi døde vågner* are taken from the eBook of *When We Dead Awaken*, Project Gutenberg, 2013, translated by William Archer. As the online version has no page numbers, reference is made to page numbers in the Norwegian version fra 1936, *Hundreårsutgave. Henrik Ibsens samlede verker.*

death – will be the theme of my contribution. My assumption is that this intermediate stage has to do with shame: the dead awaken so that shame can finally put an end to their lives. In other words: what awakens them is shame.

We understand from the plot that the awakening was provoked by a chance encounter at a bathing establishment on the west coast of Norway. Professor Rubek and his wife Maia are both Norwegians, but live somewhere in Central Europe, by a lake called Taunitzer See; and now, at the height of summer, they are travelling through their native country. Here, Irene suddenly appears; she is a patient accompanied by a nurse (a "sister of mercy") who carries a straitjacket in her suitcase. Some years earlier, Irene worked for Rubek as a nude model for his masterpiece "The Day of Resurrection", which made him rich and famous. We learn from the dialogue between the two of them, in Act 1, that very tense, erotic feelings developed between them during the work sessions and weekends spent in an old farmhouse by the Taunitzer See. But as a young man, the artist was under the delusion that he would jeopardize his natural gift if he got sexually involved with his model. Thus, Ibsen has him pronounce the following words towards the end of Act 1:

> PROFESSOR RUBEK. In those days I was still young, Irene. And the superstition took hold of me that if I touched you, if I desired you with my senses, my soul would be profaned, so that I should be unable to accomplish what I was striving for... And I still think that there was some truth in that. (HI, p.271)

Uttering these words, Rubek admits his desire. He admits his fear concerning the consequences of his desire. Later, towards the end of Act 2, Irene tries to make him remember how he *dealt with* his desire back then. She says that he took both her hands and held them warmly, and now she reminds him of what he said on that occasion:

> IRENE. And then you said: "So now, Irene, I thank you from my heart. This, you said, has been a priceless episode for me." (HI, p.265)

"At that word", she had left him and they were not to see each other again before meeting at the bathing establishment many years later. In the meantime, Irene has been performing as a nude:

> IRENE. I have posed on the turntable in variety-shows. Posed as a naked statue in living pictures. Raked in heaps of money. That was more than I could do with you. (HI, pp.233-234)

The sculptor soon started raking in heaps of money, too – thanks to the fame he gained through the masterpiece inspired by Irene: from then on, he was an uninspired artist, but then again, he did not need any more inspiration. He would simply produce portrait-busts of wealthy gentlemen and ladies. Irene married rich men, whom she partly drove mad, partly drove into suicide and perhaps killed. Finally, she went mad and was locked up for a while. Rubek married Maia, a shabby-genteel lady, who for a while enjoyed her status as Frau Professor and mistress of a lovely house, but who was soon enough bored to death.

After Irene left him, Rubek made some changes to "The Day of Resurrection", to the "most ideal woman," "awakening from the sleep of death." The figure that Irene had posed for eventually ended up "a little subdued, perhaps." It was now surrounded by other figures; in fact, the artist had placed himself in the foreground of the group:

> PROFESSOR RUBEK. In front, beside a fountain – as it were here – sits a man weighed down with guilt, who cannot quite free himself from the earth-crust. I call him remorse for a forfeited life. He sits there and dips his fingers in the purling stream – to wash them clean – and he is gnawed and tortured by the thought that never, never will he succeed. Never

> in all eternity will he attain to freedom and the new life. He will remain forever prisoned in his hell.
> IRENE. (Hardly and coldly.) Poet!
> PROFESSOR RUBEK. Why poet?
> IRENE. Because you are nerveless and sluggish and full of forgiveness for all the sins of your life, in thought and in act. You have killed my soul – so you model yourself in remorse, and self-accusation, and penance – (Smiling.) – and with that you think your account is cleared. (HI, p.263)

That was a clear message. Rubek calls himself an artist, but Irene bluntly rejects this idea and calls him a poet.

Ibsen, at this point, lets the dialogue take a typically feminist turn: a woman calls a man to order, telling him a few home truths. One of these truths is transmitted by the signifier "poet". Rubek is made aware of the mysterious power emanating from this title: it dulls his mind and provides forgiveness for his sins, thus allowing him to just sit still, feeling remorse like the statue that is continuously washing its hands as long as the water from the fountain trickles through its fingers. The statue portrays a pretty common pleasure, or perhaps rather a *jouissance*, an enjoyment mixed with pain, and which has to be repeated endlessly since there will always be a need for *more* forgiveness. The hand-washing statue could thus be seen as an emblematic case of the Lacanian *plus-de-jouir* (surplus enjoyment).

For a long while, Rubek has kept a safe distance to the cause of his present situation, i.e. from Irene, whom he calls "the fountainhead of my achievement." She was more than a model to him; she was the source of his work as an artist; but then she changed position in relation to him, becoming his source of remorse and self-pity, the deadening *jouissance* that is presently drowning his desire. There seems to be no reason why Rubek should not continue to be immersed in this affect. But one summer's day, Irene shows up at a seaside hotel on the west coast of Norway, scornfully calling him "poet". She sees him as somebody who profits from this label in order to enjoy life peacefully without creating anything, nor desiring anything. He is fully aware that she perceives him as playing this role. He realizes that he has been found out, and that he must do something about it. He simply cannot escape her sharp eye. He is put to shame. And he tries to find a way out through Irene. There is nobody else around who is able to save him. Rubek says to his wife Maia that Irene holds the key to the locked casket, which contains all his visions, and he says that Irene took the key with her when she went away. When he tells Irene that she could open all that is locked up inside of him, she replies that she no longer has the key.

We have to go back several years in order to make sense of the dialogues at the bathing establishment.

Irene and Rubek worked together on "The Day of Resurrection". Parallel to this work, they experienced a mutual erotic awakening, which came to nothing. But something was nonetheless *produced* during the process and they called this something "our child," a child made out of clay. Irene describes the artist and the work process as follows:

> IRENE. (...) the artist who had so lightly and carelessly taken a warm-blooded body, a young human life, and worn the soul out of it – because you needed it for a work of art. (HI, p.259)

Rubek tries to defend himself, pointing to the fact that Irene played along with him and claiming that she had invested her desire in the work:

> RUBEK. And you can say that – you who threw yourself into my work with such saint-like passion and such ardent joy? – that work for which we two met together every morning, as for an act of worship. (loc. cit.)

This conversation takes place in Act 2, far up in the mountains. But the day before, in Act 1, down by the seaside hotel, Rubek had emphasized ideals of purity rather than sensual desire:

> RUBEK. Thanks and praise to you, I achieved my great task. I wanted to embody the pure woman as I saw her awakening on the Resurrection Day. Not marvelling at anything new and unknown and undivined; but filled with a sacred joy at finding herself unchanged – she, the woman of earth – in the higher, freer, happier region – after the long, dreamless sleep of death. (More softly.) Thus did I fashion her. – I fashioned her in your image, Irene.
> IRENE. (Laying her hands flat upon the table and leaning against the back of her chair.) And then you were done with me... (HI, p.238)

Here, Ibsen presents the work process from two different perspectives. Seen from Rubek's point of view, the artist becomes a medium used by the woman to rediscover herself since he is instrumental in producing a harmonic relationship between the heavenly and the earthbound aspects of the woman. From Irene's standpoint, however, her work is seen as an alienating process of abstraction, a sort of theft.

The manner in which Ibsen lets Irene portray this process as the artist's usurpation of the work done by his model may recall Jacques Lacan's description of the function of philosophy in his 17th *Seminar, The Other Side of Psychoanalysis*: "What does philosophy designate over its entire evolution? It's this – theft, abduction, stealing slavery of its knowledge, through the manoeuvres of the master" (Lacan, 2007, p.22).

Here, Lacan introduces a distinction between two levels of knowledge, developed by Hegel in his dialectics of slave and master in The Phenomenology of the Spirit. At the first level we have a sort of elementary, practical knowhow used during the work process by the slave. On the next level, this knowhow is exploited by the slave's master, who develops it for his own use in a more sophisticated manner. Lacan shows this by reference to Plato's dialogues:

> The entire function of the *episteme* insofar as it is specified as transmissible knowledge – see Plato's dialogues – is always borrowed from the

technique of craftsmen, that is to say of serfs. It is a matter of extracting the essence of this knowledge in order for it to become the master's knowledge. (Lacan, 2007, p.22)

In both cases – the modern sculptor and the ancient Greek philosopher – it is a question of exploiting the work and the knowledge of the Other as material for the "extraction" of a sort of "essence." Lacan formalized this process through his schema for the Master's Discourse

$$\frac{S_1 \rightarrow S_2}{\$ \mathbin{/\mkern-6mu/} a}$$

Here, the Master is represented by S1, the master signifier, ("philosopher", "artist" or "poet"), who by means of his intervention reorganizes the knowledge (S2, the articulated chain of signifiers) that has already occupied the place of the Other, represented by the slave, the craftsman or the nude model. This arrangement works smoothly enough as long as the master signifier is treated with the respect belonging to a glorified ideal. But, at some point during the time span separating Plato from Ibsen, something must have come to pass, complicating the position of the Master and making it more difficult for him to use ideals as a screen against the gaze of the Other, even in cases where the place of the Other is occupied merely by a worker, a servant or a model. To his own disadvantage, Rubek did not realize this; his miscalculation is amply demonstrated the moment he thanked Irene heartily and said that this had been a priceless episode for him. The more precarious situation suffered by the modern Master could be illustrated by the variant of the Master's Discourse that Lacan presented in his Milano Lecture (Lacan, 1978) as "The Discourse of the Capitalist":

$$\frac{\$ \rightarrow S_2}{S_1 \mathbin{/\mkern-6mu/} a}$$

Here, the Master appears in the exposed position of a divided subject, who does not hide his lack or his divided state, but who, on the contrary, plays a sort of game of honesty, admitting that he is looking for pleasure and enjoyment. In his article "On Shame", Jacques-Alain Miller presents the following reflection on this issue: "(...) we are in a system that produces impudence and not shame, that is, in a system that annuls the function of shame." (Miller, 2007, p.26). However, the system to which Miller refers belongs to our own hypermodernity, an age of permissiveness, not to Henrik Ibsen's modern times. The sculptor of *When We Dead Awaken* certainly admits that his mind is split and that he is feeling remorse, but even so, he never stops trying to cover up his *jouissance,* the painful pleasure secretly aimed at through shame and remorse, and his very explicitly cherished ideals of purity keep him at a safe distance from hypermodern imperatives of happiness (the object *a* below the bar to the right in Lacan's schema, denoting the *jouissance* produced by the discourse of the capitalist). Yet, a subject ($) such as Rubek could be seen as situated in the place of *semblant* (the place of the agent, somebody who relies on a make-believe authority), directly exposed to and challenging the Other (S2 as constituted knowledge) inasmuch as he impersonates a *modern* Master who has to pay for his make-believe function of a Master with a parcel of shame when he has to face an Other who implies that his ideals are his instruments of *jouissance*.

On Lacan's schemata of the discourses of the Master and the Capitalist, the little *a* object, denoting *plus-de-jouir,* is situated at the place of "production" (beneath the bar to the right), the effect produced by a certain discourse. According to Irene's perspective on the work she had been involved in, Rubek exploited her "saint-like passion" to produce something they called "our child" – until he thanked her heartily for this "priceless episode." By doing so, he also revealed that this "child" was, in fact, the product of a process of extraction whereby the artist "so lightly and carelessly" took a warm-blooded body, a young human life, and "wore the soul out of it." As a matter of course, the child was a work of art, a statue made of clay, but perhaps this product contained something that the Master was neither able to see nor to mould into a shape befitting his professed artistic ideals: a *surplus product* brought about by shared labour. This would render it the product which constitutes the difference between 1) the work performed by the naked body of the Other (S2) while "the soul" (signifiers, elementary units of language) is being torn out of it, and 2) the pay, the heartfelt thanks by the Master (S1) for the service. This surplus product is neither more nor less than the Lacanian *plus-de-jouir*, the *surplus enjoyment* that is so difficult to deal with.

Where do we find this product? It may seem to have vanished the same way that Irene vanished. It may for a while have been locked up behind barred windows and padded walls – but then, one summer's day, it reappears in the shape of a loss, a loss of meaning, an *ab-sens,* for which Rubek tries to find a compensation through notions such as "resurrection" and "transfiguration". However, Irene refuses to give her pain a meaning. In this manner, by her very refusal to accept an imaginary substitution for the irreparable, Irene acts ethically. Yet, by the end of Act 3, she is finally carried away "up in the light" by Rubek's hands, and a by a seductive rhetoric, he denies the reality of the irreparable:

> PROFESSOR RUBEK. (Drawing her along with him.) We must first pass through the mists, Irene, and then... (HI, p.283)

Then, of course, they meet their doom.

Could it still be possible to claim that they die of shame? In my view, that is exactly what Ibsen demonstrates by letting Irene and Rubek die twice. Throughout his work together with Irene, Rubek was driven by his desire, but when he suddenly shied away from the consequences of his desire and thanked Irene heartily for her help, he paid for his betrayal in the form of shame. And through shame, he lost his inspiration and died as an artist.

For her part, Irene sought oblivion through her own version of prostitution, selling her body and her soul to rich viewers and rich husbands until she went mad. Insofar as shame can be seen as an affect that limits senseless *jouissance,* Irene is a character whose acts are not subdued by this affect – until one summer's day, when the two protagonists accidentally meet and "awaken." They see each other, each of them feeling captured by the gaze of the Other. Rubek admits as much in the middle of Act 2:

> PROFESSOR RUBEK. You have a shadow that tortures me. And I have the crushing weight of my conscience.
> IRENE. (With a glad cry of deliverance.) At last! (HI, p.258)

This liberating confession of shame clears the way for the rather candid conversation that carries on throughout the rest of Act 2. Neither of them could foresee the consequences of this deliverance. Shame was obviously related to their failure to deal with the product of their common work, their shared *plus-de-jouir;* now that they have admitted their respective flights into madness and bad conscience, where are they to go? After this moment of truth, where can they continue to hide? Where else than in the reality of an avalanche? When Rubek says that they will hold their marriage-feast up on the mountain top that Irene names the Peak of Promise, we are supposed to understand that this ultimate flight is impossible. And it is this impossibility that is consecrated by Maia's song, which is heard just before Irene and Rubek's bodies are buried in masses of snow:

> MAIA. I am free! I am free! I am free!
> No more life in the prison for me!
> I am free as a bird! I am free! (HI, p.283)

Ironically, these words also constitute Ibsen's epilogue as a dramatist.

References

Ibsen, H. (2013). *When We Dead Awaken*. Translation by W. Archer in *The Project Gutenberg EBook*. https://www.gutenberg.org/ebooks/4782

Ibsen, H. (1936). *Hundreårsutgave. Henrik Ibsens samlede verker.* Oslo: Gyldendal norsk forlag, bind XIII.

Lacan, J. (1978). Discourse of Jacques Lacan at the University of Milan, May 12, 1972. Translation by Jack W. Stone. In *Lacan in Italia 1953-1978*, La Salamandra.

Lacan, J. (1998). *On Feminine Sexuality. The Limits of Love and Knowledge*. New York: Norton.

Lacan, J. (2007). *The Other Side of Psychoanalysis, The Seminar of Jacques Lacan,* Book XVII. Translation by R. Grigg. New York: Norton.

Miller, J.-A. (2006). On Shame. Translation by R. Grigg. In J. Clemens and R. Grigg (eds.), *Jacques Lacan and the Other Side of Psychoanalysis*. Durham and London: Duke University Press.

6.
A short reflection on some scenes of shame

Carin Franzén

> *Then the eyes of both were opened, and they knew that they were naked; and they sewed fig leaves together and made themselves aprons.* (*Genesis*)

It is as hard to tell whether shame is an innate affect or a result of culture. Anyhow, it is easy to recognize shame when one feels it and the many instances of shame appearing in literature and philosophy from antiquity onwards say something about its importance in culture. The purpose of this essay is not to define shame, but to reflect upon some of its manifestations throughout history in order to better understand its role in a contemporary society proclaiming individual freedom. One obvious point at which to start is the widespread idea that shame is related to seeing and, more precisely, to being exposed to the gaze of the Other in a specific context. The nature of such a context can be described as a revelation of affairs that ought to be kept behind the scenes. Let us begin by a disappointed lover speaking in the aftermath of what could have been such a revelation.

Scene I

In one of the fragments of his discourse on love from 1977, Roland Barthes writes about the production, within the amorous field, of a counter-image of the beloved object in the following terms: "It is as if the alteration of the Image occurs when *I am ashamed* for the other" (1978, p.26).[1] This fragment offers a short analysis of why this alteration comes about. The image of the beloved changes, Barthes writes, when the lover sees that the beloved is subjected to the gaze of others – "caught up in the platitude of the social world."[2]

Barthes is, in a sense, inverting a traditional scene of shame, which is that of being seen, as Bernard Williams puts it in a classic study of ancient Greek morality (1993, p.78): "inappropriately, by the wrong people, in the wrong condition." From this traditional perspective, it is the beloved who ought, in the eyes if his lover, to be ashamed because he is lowering himself to the level of the social world instead of remaining in mutual idealisation with his lover. The disappointed lover continues his analysis: "The other alters if he sides with the banalities the world professes in order to depreciate love."[3] In this analysis, the lover feels ashamed when confronted with the opinion of the social world, which depreciates his intimate feelings, which are themselves mediated through and thus betrayed by the beloved when he sides with the world.

One can also say that the lover in this scene feels ashamed not only for the other, but also because he discovers that he has been fooled by his own ideals. Barthes indicates such an interpretation when he, in the same fragment, refers to Plato's dialogue *Phaedrus* and the connection between love and shame in ancient Greek culture.

---

1 Barthes (1977, p.34): "On dirait que l'altération de l'Image se produit lorsque *j'ai honte pour l'autre*".
2 Ibid: "pris dans la platitude du monde social".
3 Ibid: "l'autre s'altère s'il se range lui-même aux banalité dont le monde fait profession pour déprécier l'amour".

He notes parenthetically that the fear of being ashamed for the other kept Greek lovers on the straight and narrow path, "each obliged to care for his own image in the other's eyes."[4]

It is not coincidental that a reflection upon shame starts with a scene that deals with love problems. From a historical perspective, shame has often been connected with love as a passion that makes people unreasonable, a folly that produces shame when it passes and reveals the reality behind the glorified image of the beloved. This view can, for example, be sensed in François de La Rochefoucauld's maxims (five editions between 1664 and 1678) even though the homosexual code of love in Barthes and Socrates is altered here into a dominant heterosexual culture. In Maxim 71 in the last edition from 1678, La Rochefoucauld writes: "There are few people who would not be ashamed of being beloved when they love no longer."[5] This maxim evokes a scene in which the idealisation of love has disappeared, and this is the situation Barthes' disappointed lover finds himself in. Although the conception of love in the seventeenth century still bore affinities with ancient Greek culture, La Rochefoucauld's words are articulated in a situation where shame has become a piece of exchange in heterosexual power relations. I will come to this change, but let us first take a closer look at Barthes' parenthetical reference.

Scene II

If shame concerns a sudden exposure of the reality behind an idealized image, it also implies – from the revealed person's perspective – the necessity of covering up. In *Phaedrus* (c. 350 BC), just before Socrates

---

4   Ibid: "chacun devant surveiller sa propre image sous le regard de l'autre".
5   La Rochefoucauld (1976, p.55): "Il n'y a guère de gens qui ne soient honteux de s'être aimés quand ils ne s'aiment plus". English trans. J.W. Willis Bund 1871, retrieved from http://www.gutenberg.org/files/9105/9105-h/9105-h.htm

gives one of his discourses on love, he says that he will keep his eyes covered and get through his discourse as fast as he can, for if he looks at Phaedrus he will feel ashamed (1925, p.237a).

Why is Socrates covering his face and galloping through his discourse on love? One rather explicit answer is that Socrates is actually unprepared. In the dialogue (1925, p.236d), he says that, unlike the famous sophist Lysias, a master of his art, he is an amateur "without preparation to speak on the same subject." In other words, compared to Lysias' rhetorical skills, Socrates stands naked before the god of love – *Eros* – who is the final addressee of his discourse, and his first reaction is to cover himself. However, it may also be that concealing his face and emphasizing that he is improvising is an ironic gesture or false modesty, considering that Socrates is the only one among his contemporaries who really knows what love is. As Lacan points out (2001, p.16), Socrates claims to know nothing, except for the ability to recognize what love is.

At any rate, the actual discussion of love in *Phaedrus* deals at first with the sort of shame a lover feels once he returns to reason, and this apparently results in the rather paradoxical consequence that one ought not to love a person who is in love because it is unreasonable. However, such a conclusion is an offense against Eros. Socrates (1925, p.243b) retracts his first discourse in favour of another, stated thus "head bare this time, not, as before, covered through shame." Socrates' initial shame is here explained in terms of defaming love or, more precisely, as being shameless regarding *true* love: Though still a madness, love is described as the greatest of heaven's blessings. At this point in the dialogue, Socrates formulates the idea of love as an ascending force towards a higher good, an idealisation, and this way of viewing love remains paradigmatic for a very long time.

From antiquity onward, shame in Western culture is a recurrent theme in literary and philosophical debates on love and sexuality, reflecting a social order in which virtue and honour are key concepts. It is also easy to note that, in its idealized form, love seems to protect against shame, but when love is debased, shame emerges. Then again, why is debasement – or depreciation – of love related to shame, not only in a culture based on honour, but even in a modern text such as Barthes' discourse on love? One answer upon which we have already touched could be that debasement of an ideal signifies a revelation of the real. Yet, regarding our lovers mentioned above, shame also seems to emerge when this revelation results in the loss of an image that is part of one's self-image.

This suggestion can be developed more clearly if one regards love as grounded in primary narcissism, as Freud claims (1957 [1914], p.88). According to Freud, the overvaluation of the other is "derived from the child's original narcissism and thus corresponds to a transference of that narcissism to the sexual object." From this perspective, one can argue that, in the cases of both Barthes and Socrates, shame arises when the discrepancy between the ideal image and the real is disclosed, and the narcissistic transference is impeded.

However, both Barthes and Socrates demonstrate that the devaluation of the ideal is above all a question of discourse. Socrates feels ashamed and covers his face because he knows that he will offend true love (as this is developed in the palinode) with his first ironic discourse, as if loving and telling the truth about love (the platonic *eidos*) were one and the same thing. In Barthes' fragment, the alteration of the image of the beloved emerges when he hears him utter a banal phrase, "flattening the specialty of the rapport by a conformist formula" (1978, p.26).[6] In both cases, one can say that shame occurs when the overvaluation of love is exposed for what it is, namely a flaw, and therefore causes the lover to feel shame. One can also say, however, that this process occurs within a discursive order that defines the subject and its limits.

---

6 Barthes (1977, p.34): "aplatissant la spécialité du rapport sous une formule conformiste".

Scene III

Shame's relationship to one's self-image is also a perspective that can be observed in René Descartes' *Les Passions de l'âme* (Passions of the Soul, 1649), in which Article 205 defines shame as "a species of Sadness, also founded on Love of ourselves, arising from our opinion that we are being blamed or our apprehension that we will be" (1989, p.130).[7]

In Article 66, Descartes defines shame as a passion, a kind of self-interest that refers to the opinion others may have of it. If this narcissistic passion is conceived of as evil, it produces shame; if it is considered good, it results in glory. However, as long as the good or the evil remains within us, this passion leads to neither shame nor glory. Shame can thus only be ignited by the opinion of others and by being blamed. Furthermore, because shame is related to the opinion of others, according to Descartes it incites the subject to virtue. In fact, this view draws heavily upon the classical tradition, which relates shame to a specific moral system.

In *Rhetoric* (c. 329-323 BC), Aristotle makes a long and detailed list of all the "bad things" that ought to arouse shame if committed (1924, p.1384a). It is also clear that shame is defined in relation to honour or virtue: As Aristotle states in the *Nicomachean Ethics* (c. 367-247 BC), shame is "a kind of fear of dishonour" (1925, p.1128b). This connection between honour and shame can be generally felt in pre-modern literature and philosophy, as for example in La Rochefoucauld's aforementioned maxim. Thus, both ancient Greek culture and the courtly or aristocratic culture that still constituted a hegemony in seventeenth century Europe, especially in France, can be designated as cultures of honour and – in consequence – as cultures of shame. It is significant that the French word for shame – *honte* – derives from the Old Saxon *hōnitha*, "déshonneur".

---

7   Descartes (1996, p.225 art 205): "une espèce de tristesse, fondée [...] sur l'amour de soi-même et qui vient de l'opinion ou de la crainte qu'on a d'être blâmé".

It is furthermore clear that shame and honour, as they appear in early modern literature and philosophy, both seem to regulate and be regulated by the period's power relations and gender roles. It is significant that the most paradigmatic scenes of shame in this period concern the loss of honour, which in turn reveals the power relations between the sexes. On the one hand, women's honour is bound to a regulation of their sexuality, as stated for instance in Marguerite de Navarre's *Heptaméron* (1559), "the forbidden goal of a lady's honour" (2004, p.140).[8] On the other hand, women are subjected to men in this societal order and, in this context, honour stems from the masculine power over the other. The consequence, simply put, is that honour is based on chastity for women, whereas for men it is tied to their reputation (or that of their wives). This kind of dialectic can be demonstrated by Madame de Lafayette's novel *La Princess de Clèves*, which she published anonymously in 1678. In one key scene in the novel, Madame de Lafayette describes the torments of Monsieur de Clèves, when he discovers that his wife loves another man, the Duke de Nemours, with the word *honte*: "the mortification [*honte*] of being deceived by a woman" (1994, p.94).[9]

The woman in question, the Princess de Clèves, was married to Monsieur de Clèves at the age of 16, as an object of trade in the aristocratic system of alliances. Yet her husband never possessed her heart, as it were. The princess, for her part, refuses to overtly admit her love for another and is ashamed of not telling the truth: "She was also ashamed […] to hide the truth from a man who had so good an opinion of her" (1994, p.40).[10] This shame of not living up to Monsieur de Clèves' ideal image pushes her to finally confess the secret of her heart, at which point her shame at being unable to master her pas-

---

8 Marguerite de Navarre (2000, p.144) "ce que l'honneur des dames defend".
9 Madame de Lafayette (2003, p.160): "la honte d'être trompé par une femme".
10 Ibid (2003, p.72): "Elle sentit aussi de la honte […] de déguiser la vérité à un homme qui avait si bonne opinion d'elle".

sion passes to her husband in the sense that it deals his reputation a heavy blow.

The scene reveals how shame is determined by a specific social order – the culture of honour among the aristocracy – and its fixed gender roles.[11] From a more modern perspective, it could be argued that the princess' dilemma is based on the social restrictions imposed upon her in her choice of object, to paraphrase Freud (1957, p.89). To be sure, in the princess' case, the element of choice is nearly non-existent, and the novel is famous for the princess' refusal to allow her love for the duke to be fulfilled.[12] As the princess says at the end of the story, after their last meeting when she tells the duke that she loves him but must nevertheless leave him, "this conversation fills me with shame" (1994, p.105).[13]

As a married woman at a court at which, as the author writes, "love was always mingled with politics, and politics with love" (1994, p.10),[14] the princess chooses retreat as compensation for a social restriction that will undoubtedly lead to her degradation if she accepts becoming the duke's mistress or wife. The final dialogue between the two indicates the kind of power relationship that surrounds love in a courtly context.

Social restrictions also provoke a fear of degradation on the part of the husband, for his reputation is based on that of his wife or, more precisely, on his power or loss of power over her. The author underlines that the nature of his loss (and hence shame) is tied to his

---

11 The classical care for one's image in the other's eyes, or the importance of one's appearance, is reinforced by a courtly and late feudal system in which dissimulation becomes a royal talent, as Jean Rohou points out (2002, p.386).
12 Slavoj Žižek (2001, p.75) has suggested that it is the predominance of the pleasure principle, or a will to keep an inner peace against passion or *jouissance*, which guides the princess' renunciation. I think, in line with Freud, that this kind of self-contentment must be put in relation to the social context.
13 Madame de Lafayette (200, p.178): "voici une conversation qui me fait honte".
14 Ibid (2003, p.20): "l'amour était toujours mêlé aux affaires et les affaires à l'amour".

"pride and honour" (1994. p.78),[15] which are sorely wounded. Thus, behind the story's social interplay of power relations, we can detect the torments of inflated self-images. We also sense that, in early modern scenes of shame, social opinion comes to the fore.

Against this backdrop, one can understand why *impudence* involves being insensitive to the opinion of others – displaying "a scorn of shame", as Descartes puts it in Article 207 in his treatise on the passions (1989, p.131), thus indicating a certain freedom with regard to social restrictions.[16] Considering that modernity is based on a strong belief in the freedom of the individual, we can moreover say that we are living in a society in which the ideal is exactly the scorning of shame in contrast to a pre-modern subjugation to the rules of a culture of honour. However, even though shame is nowadays regarded as something we ought not feel, because we are free and independent individuals, it is nevertheless the case that we do feel shame. Why is this so? One tentative answer could be that freedom from shame does not produce freedom but a state of shamelessness, which does not preclude the return of shame.

Scene IV

The return of shame in a shameless society can be generally felt if we turn our attention from the scenes of love above to the late capitalist and neoliberal discourse. In a modern society based on crude self-interest rather than on a moral authority that identifies 'bad things', the return of shame takes on new guises. One current example is the European debate concerning people begging in the streets. The interesting aspect of this debate is that shame, in relation to this social and political problem, is not concerned with the act of begging or of

---

15 Ibid (2013, p.134): "sa gloire et son honneur".
16 Descartes (1996, p.225): "un mépris de honte".

being poor as such. The issue instead is that members of the welfare society feel ashamed when they see poor people on the street, and that this feeling is unpleasant. In a sense, this kind of shame felt by the wealthy can also be explained as a revelation of the real behind an idealized image. Being reminded of social injustice when one goes shopping points to a failure in the good image of the welfare state, and a common response to this phenomenon is to make begging illegal in order to keep the image intact.

In a more subtle analysis of the shame of the wealthy, Agamben (1999, p.106) suggests that it can be conceived as a fear of being recognized as akin to the poor or, more precisely, the fear of recognising oneself in an alterity that cannot be assumed. In this sense, shame still concerns a loss, yet it is not only the loss of an idealized image but, more radically, the loss of one's own subjectivity. In Agamben's word's, "In shame, the subject thus has no other content than its own desubjectification."

Shame thus seems inevitable, even in a time based on the emancipation from shame, not only because it is what moves the process of subjectification in Agamben's description, but also because shamelessness is shameful. For if the shameless scorns shame as a kind of social barrier obstructing the expansion of self-interest, this expansion simultaneously reveals the exposedness of the self. Without the other's gaze and the social bounds it implies, the shameless is exposed to the never-ending imperative to maximize self-interest and the concomitant anxiety of failure. Thus, in today's society, the scorning of shame opens the door to anguish, which could be taken to indicate that the neoliberal late capitalist discourse has more power over the subject than do the classical and early modern shame cultures.

In other words, contemporary shamelessness bears witness to an internalisation of shame. The shame-provoking gaze has been transformed into an inner voice commanding a maximisation of self-interest in the name of individual freedom and self-sufficiency. This shift from an external to an internal authority under the guise of liberation or emancipation has been noted by both psychoanalysis and critical theory, as indicated for example by Herbert Marcuse's notion of "repressive desublimation" (1966, p.72).

Going back to the scene of people begging on the street, modern shame seems on the one hand to derive from the fact that we continue to live in world based on social and economic injustice, which we – unlike pre-modern society – cannot justify by referring to, for instance, God's order or the king's divine right. On the contrary, the beggar is part of the same system that produces the wealthy consumer. Thus, in late capitalist society, the other's shame-provoking gaze is no longer based on authority, but comes directly from social reality – or, as Lacan puts it (1991, p.220), from a system that produces shame in the form of impudence.

Yet, in comparison to the above discussion of shame and love, we can note that the same mechanism of revelation is involved in this more directly political scene of shame. What we see here is a revelation of the reality of the other (the beggar in the example above) and the loss of an idealized image, which in this case is the welfare state. In this case, the welfare state comes across as an empty signal word that conceals the lack of desire for political change.

It is interesting to note that it is shame and not guilt that seems to possess this direct relationship to politics, at least at the level of reaction if not as a reflection. Perhaps this is because guilt is the voice of the super ego critiquing transgressions of prohibitions, while shame is connected to the subject's relationship to a self-image, which is seen and confirmed by the other. In other words, guilt stems from breaking internal or external rules with the fear of punishment, while shame is anchored in self-interest and the fear of losing one's *raison d'être*. When guilty, I feel that I owe something to someone and that I can (attempt to) repair the wrong that has been done. When I feel ashamed, it is my identity that is at stake; the feeling concerns my subjectivity rather than my actions. The desire to cover up oneself or even to disappear points to this desubjectification.

In a shameless neoliberal society, however, it is as if shame also produces another wish, that of making the very gaze that evokes shame disappear. Not only the extreme right, but also more moderate politicians defend regulations aiming to cleanse the streets of beggars, immigrants, refugees, etc. This analysis could be elaborated upon further by the notion of disgust or abjection as something that must be separated from the subject in order to maintain its identity.[17] I wish, however, to return to the dialectics of shamelessness and shame that has become so apparent in the liberal and neoliberal tradition, this time using another example taken from modern literature, which can perhaps point to an upheaval of this very dialectic.

Scene V

There are probably as many forms of shame as there are forms of shamelessness, and these seem, in turn, to be shaped by the social hegemony current at any given moment. I will thus wrap up this short reflection with a modern literary configuration of shame taken from Marguerite Duras, who called her first novel *Les impudents* (*The Impudent Ones*). The book was published in 1943 and Duras later refuted it, with reference to its aesthetic value, as something of which she seemed to be ashamed. It is, however, interesting to note that the novel was conceived during a rather traumatic time: It was not only published in the middle of the Second World War, her father died in 1941, her first son died at birth in 1942, and her younger brother died this same year. Against this backdrop, writing a novel could, as Levinas says in an article published in the journal *Les temps modernes*

---

17 Julia Kristeva (1980, p.12) speaks of abjection as something that disturbs an order and draws attention to the fragility of the law. In this sense and for the formation of the subject, one can say that shame is more primordial than guilt, which is bound to the law in the sense that it arises from the transgression of the law.

(*Modern Times*) in 1948, be seen as shameless escapism, "as feasting in times of plague."[18] According to the philosopher, such an act ought to be corrected by an act of responsibility through a relationship to the other.

For her part, Duras later says that writing is "the thing that makes life bearable,"[19] and she emphasizes that writing must be freed from moral constraints. Furthermore, this idea of 'impudence' in the sense of freedom of expression can be said to characterize modern literature in general.

Les impudents is the story of a bourgeois family, and it can easily be regarded as a 'Familienroman' in Freud's sense. The novel – which centres on the young girl Maud, her two brothers, a mother who is overbearing with respect to the oldest brother, and a passive, rather absent, father – could be analysed from a biographical perspective. A salient feature, indicated by the title, is the insolence or *impudence* that the family members express toward social and economic transactions. In this more or less cynical and at the same time severely moralistic rural bourgeois milieu, the reader follows Maud's emancipation. Her efforts are articulated as a scorning of the morals surrounding her: She refuses to accept an arranged marriage to a wealthy farmer and starts a sexual relationship with another man. To be sure, her act is described as scandalous, and Maud's reaction to the reprobation she receives from her family demonstrates a process of desubjectification: "Maud would have liked to disappear into the shadow, diminishing until becoming as the shadow itself, nothing."[20] Nevertheless, she escapes her family and marries the other man, although the novel ends with

---

18   Levinas (1994, p.146): "comme de festoyer en pleine peste". English translation is mine.
19   Duras (quoted in 2011, p.1407): "la chose qui rend le plus supportable la vie". English translation is mine.
20   Duras (2011, p.90): "Maud aurait voulu disparaître dans la flaque d'ombre, s'amenuiser jusqu'à devenir, comme l'ombre elle-même, rien". English translation is mine.

certain disillusion on her own part and with her finally pleasing her family by the very act of marriage, which is never questioned.

Duras' realistic and, it seems, somewhat involuntarily conventional narration is in a way congenial to the novel's oppressive moralistic ambience. Moreover, Maud foreshadows the female figures in novels such as *Le Vice-Consul* (1966) and *Le Ravissement de Lol V. Stein* (1964) in offending social expectations. They are all shameless, as it were.

Through Duras' work, one can follow the vicissitudes of shame and shamelessness from the traditional bourgeois family to its bankruptcy in the 1960s and 1970s, framed by the major catastrophes and crises of the twentieth century. During this period, Duras' writing changes from a traditional realistic narration to her famous elliptical poetic style. However, the awareness of impudence and the need to elaborate upon her 'Familienroman' seems to follow her all through her writing, which also becomes more openly political and critical of contemporary society and its capitalist order.

Duras was 70 years old when she wrote her great public success, *L'Amant* (The Lover, 1984). She comments on the novel's autobiographical nature by closing the loop, stating that she started writing in an environment that directed her towards an experience of pudeur, implying a strong notion of shame, the negation of which is impudence (1985, p.8).[21] She goes on to explain that, for the people in that milieu, writing was still a moral activity. In the following lines, Duras is not exactly judging this background, but she does compare it to what seems to be her experience of the presence (1985, p.8):

> Nowadays it often seems writing is nothing at all. Sometimes I realize that if writing isn't all things, all contraries confounded, a quest for vanity and void, it's nothing. That if it's not each time all things confounded into one through some inexpressible essence, then writing is nothing but

---

21 Duras (1984, p.14): "J'ai commencé à écrire dans un milieu qui me portait très fort à la pudeur".

advertisement. But usually I have no opinion, I can see that all options are open now, that there seem to be no more barriers, that writing seems at a loss for somewhere to hide, to be written, to be read. That its basic unseemliness is no longer accepted.[22]

Duras' description of contemporary literary writing as "nothing at all" could be read as an indication of a literary institution conditioned by the liberty to say everything and to say it in the way one wants. Nevertheless, Duras insists that this "nothing at all" or absence of literary moral constraint must be directed by something that is impossible to express in public. If this quality is lacking, "writing is nothing but advertisement." Thus, even though writing is no longer a moral occupation, Duras points to the necessity of some sort of protection or shelter, "somewhere to hide, to be written, to be read." In other words, if writing is to be something besides a more-or-less automatic response to the demands of the market, it must obey something essentially ineffable, which seems to be equivalent to literature's "basic unseemliness." What is this "unseemliness," when it is no longer connected to moral constraints?

A final scene

In one respect, literary unseemliness is what protects writing from being reduced to "nothing at all" or to mere publicity. Duras uses the

---

22 Ibid (1984, p.14-15): "Écrire, maintenant, il semblerait que ce ne soit plus rien bien souvent. Quelquefois je sais cela: que du moment que ce n'est pas, toute choses confondues, aller à la vanité et au vent, écrire ce n'est rien. Que du moment que ce n'est pas, chaque fois, toutes choses confondues en une seule par essence inqualifiable, écrire ce n'est rien que publicité. Mais le plus souvent je n'ai d'avis, je vois que tous les champs sont ouverts, qu'il n'y aurait plus de murs, que l'écrit ne saurait plus où se mettre pour se cacher, se faire, se lire, que son inconvenance fondamentale ne serait plus respectée".

French word inconvenance, which also indicates a negation of conventions or of the ruling order. In Duras, this aspect has a political side that becomes clear when, in her discourse on writing, *Écrire* (Writing, 1993), she speaks of "the horror of the capitalist regime" and the place of the writer in such a social order: "The other work, that of the writers that sometimes makes them feel ashamed, the kind that usually provokes the most violent political regrets."[23] In other words, Duras and her modernist credo of the necessary unseemliness of art and literature is here articulated as a sense of shame that rediscovers the fundamental relationship between shame and the reality of the other.

To conclude this brief and schematic reflection on some of the historical configurations of shame in European literature and philosophy, one can at least say that, even though shame can be seen as an innate and basic affect, its forms and effects seem to be intimately related to a given social and cultural order.[24] However, what is the source of shame when shame is no longer dependent on an Other who holds authority or an ideal (as it was in the ancient and early modern cultures of honour) or is no longer tied to a bourgeois hegemony that in some respects is constructed on an appropriation of preceding aristocratic values, especially with respect to gender roles? A simple answer may be that the gaze of the Other (God, king, public opinion, father, etc.) has been internalized in the name of the firm belief in individual freedom that dominates our current, neoliberal social order. Yet, as Foucault (1976, p.211) has noted in another context, we believe that it is a matter of our liberation when we are just following a *dispositif* of power, which in the case of shame is the late capitalist

---

23 Duras (1993, p.50): "l'horreur du régime capitaliste", ibid (1993, p.49): "L'autre travail pour les écrivains est celui qui quelquefois fait honte, celui qui provoque la plupart du temps le regret d'ordre politique le plus violent de tous". English translation is mine.

24 See for example Sedgwick's (1995, p.5) account of the American psychologist Silvan Tomkins, who in 1960s developed a theory of shame as one of eight innate affects.

dictate of maximizing one's self-interest and realizing oneself.[25] It could therefore be a good idea to disobey this dictate in order to meet the gaze of the real other – not to avoid shame but to better understand what is at stake in every subjectification. And in this way, perhaps, a "most violent political regret" could be transformed into resistance.

References

Agamben, G. (1999). Shame, or on the Subject. In *Remnants of Auschwitz. The Witness and the Archive.* Trans. D. Heller-Roazen. New York: Zone Books

Aristotle (1924). *Rhetoric*. Trans. W. Rhys Roberts. Retrieved from http://rhetoric.eserver.org/aristotle/rhet2-6.html September 18, 2014.

Aristotle (1925). *Nicomachean Ethics*. Trans, W. D. Ross. Retrieved from http://classics.mit.edu/Aristotle/nicomachaen.4.iv.html September 12, 2014.

Barthes, R. (1977). *Fragments d'un discours amoureux*. Paris: Seuil.

Barthes, R. (1978). *A Lover's Discourse. Fragments*. Trans. R. Howard. New York: Hill and Wang

Descartes, R. (1996). *Les Passions de l'âme*. Ed. Pascale d'Arcy. Paris: Flammarion.

Descartes, R. (1989). *The Passions of the Soul*. Trans. S. Voss. Indianapolis: Hackett Publishing Company.

Duras, M. (1984). *L'Amant*. Paris: Minuit.

Duras, M. (1985). *The Lover*. Trans. B. Bray. New York: Pantheon Books.

Duras, M. (1993). *Écrire*. Paris: Gallimard (folio).

Duras, M. (2011). *Œuvres complètes I*. Ed. G. Philippe. Paris: Gallimard.

La Rochefoucauld, F. de (1976). *Maximes et Réflexions diverses*. Ed. J. Lafond. Paris: Galimmard (folio).

La Rochefoucauld, F. de (1871). *Reflections; Sentences and Moral Maxims*. Trans. by J.W. Willis Bund, and others. Retrieved from http://www.gutenberg.org/files/9105/9105-h/9105-h.htm September 12, 2014.

---

25 To be sure, Foucault (1976, p.211) is here discussing the history of sexuality and its relationship to power, but I think that his idea of a *dispostif* of power that uses a discourse of 'liberation' also elucidates the political and psychological implications of shame in late capitalist society.

Foucault, M. (1976). *La volonté de savoir. Histoire de la sexualité 1*. Paris: Gallimard.

Kristeva, J. (1980). *Pouvoirs de l'horreur: essai sur l'abjection*. Paris: Seuil.

Kosofsky Sedgwick, E. and Frank, A. (1995). *Shame and its Sisters. A Silvan Tomkins Reader*. Durham: Duke University Press.

Lacan, J. (1991). *Séminaire XVII, L'envers de la psychanalyse*, ed. Jacques-Alain Miller. Paris: Seuil.

Lacan, J. (2001). *Séminaire VIII, Le transfert*, ed. Jacques-Alain Miller. Paris: Seuil.

Lafayette, M. de (1994). *The Princess of Clèves*, trans. John D. Lyons. New York: Norton.

Lafayette, M. de (2003). *La Princesse de Clèves*. Paris: Hatier.

Levinas, E. (1994). La réalité et son ombre. Reprinted in *Les imprévus de l'histoire*, ed. P. Hayat. Paris: Fata Morgana.

Marcuse, H. (1966). *One-Dimensional Man. Studies in the Ideology of Advanced Industrial Society*, Boston: Beacon Press.

Navarre, M. de (2000). *L'Heptaméron*. Ed. Nicole Cazauran. Paris: Gallimard.

Navarre, M. de (2004). *The Heptameron*. Trans. P. A Chilton. London: Penguin.

Williams, B.A.O. (1993). *Shame and Necessity*. Berkeley: University of California.

Plato (1925). *Phaedrus*, trans. Harold N. Fowler. Cambridge, MA: Harvard University Press. Retrieved from http://www.perseus.tufts.edu/hopper/text?doc=Perseus%3Atext%3A1999.01.0174%3Atext%3DPhaedrus September 15 2014.

Rohou, J. (2002). *Le XVIIe siècle, une révolution de la condition humaine*. Paris: Seuil.

Žižek, S. (2001). *On Belief*. London: Routledge.

7.
Friendship as the friend of thought: Franz Kafka and the gesture of shame

Alexander Carnera

Man is the creature that cannot escape himself. Samuel Beckett
'Like a dog,' he said, it were as if shame [die Scham] should survive him.
Franz Kafka, The Trial

In his book *Nudità*, the Italian philosopher Giorgio Agamben writes about how nudism, exposure of the body, prostitution and pornography confront us with the question of the grace of nudity and glory of the Garden of Eden and thereby with the question of shame and its intimate relationship with this nakedness (Agamben, 2011, p.66). In becoming aware of each other's nakedness, Adam and Eve were not submitted to the sensation of shame (Genesis 1:2:25). According to Agamben, the "metaphysical transformation that results from sin is "...the loss of the clothing of grace that hid the naked corporeality of the first couple" (Agamben, 2011, p.60). In a paradoxical formulation, Adam and Eve were dressed naked. In contrast, we talk about animals as naked even though they are covered by fur, feathers or the like. Clothes do not parallel the fur of animals: it is only man who wears clothes. One is reminded of Hans Christian Andersen's fairy tale *The Emperor's New Clothes* in which the naked emperor walks around the city as if he were not naked. So how is the naked body dressed in the sublime grace of clothing? Agamben claims that the idea of sublime grace is attached to the metaphysical transformation of recognition. The crucial moment is when Adam and Eve leave the Garden of Eden. It is at this moment that it is no longer possible to be dressed in the clothes of grace, they must now submit to a material covering. We might, for instance, speculate whether 'the other's gaze' already had a role to play in terms of the experience of nakedness. Were the eyes of Adam and Eve opened without a conscious public opinion? Initially, the celestial city did not have a need for human clothes—or rather, not until Adam and Eve were covered with clothes could they be said to be human. Hence, the exposure of the emperor by the little boy is nothing but the discovery of the emperor's humanness. However, it is not only the power of sovereign monarchy and its political and legal iconography that are intimately connected with this theological longing and perfection attached to the grace of clothing: so, too, are modern fashion, performance and work-life.

In what follows, this paper argues that shame is attached to what we wish to hide but cannot cover up. This 'cover-up' has eventually become part of the performance society that characterizes modern working life and the individual fashioning of the modern self in late capitalism. The first part of this paper argues that shame can be located as a gesture on the border between language and non-language. The second part of the paper follows Gilles Deleuze and Samuel Beckett, arguing how the awareness of shame is an important instrument for authorship and artistic thinking. Furthermore, this potential of shame is illustrated as a central theme in the writings of Franz Kafka.

The impossibility of escaping our self

The characteristic thing about shame is that we are submitted to our selves and cannot escape our own basic nakedness. Initially, we experience shame as a response to our fellow humans: we feel this way in our everyday relationships with spouse or children in the aftermath of situations devoured by anger rather than understanding and love. Hence, the first and basic premise of shame seems to be rooted in our capacity for reflection. The word 'shame' is used as a noun, "a shame", and as a verb, "to be ashamed". Shame is the name given to an impulse or affect that we inflict upon ourselves—a kind of auto-affection. Yet, when we feel shame, we are not only submitted to ourselves, but also lost to our selves. This fracture or strangeness is captured within the mode of shame. The self is split between two—between the living and speaking creature, between something human and non-human. As a divided self, man is the creature who can survive himself. Even though K. in *The Trial* dies an unworthy death, in the end shame is able to speak for him in his place. Hence, man can survive himself because he never possesses himself. Therefore, because he can be split off from himself, he can be ashamed of himself or on behalf of humanity. We are here reminded of Primo Levi's writings on Auschwitz. Regardless of how much the Nazis tried to rob the Jews of any kind of subjectivity, they never entirely succeeded. Levi's comments on the Russian soldiers' arrival at the camp is important here:

> They did not greet us, nor did they smile; they seemed oppressed not only by compassion but by a confused restraint, which sealed their lips and bound their eyes to the funereal scene. It was that shame we knew so well, the shame that drowned us after the selections, and every time we had to watch, or submit to, some outrage. (Levi, 1995, p.16)

The revelation of the camp is not necessarily the revelation of man as essentially a beast. Rather, the camp exposes the armature of habits that ties the body to a social pattern, which only the most extreme conditions can penetrate. Taking away all dignity will not necessarily eliminate social ties and social behaviour; yet, what Primo Levi describes is our encounter with the power of shame as a necessary force outside of social performance and self-reflexivity. Agamben characterizes this as "the radical impossibility of escaping from itself" (Agamben, 1999b, p.205). We can hardly bear it. We tend to turn our face away. In a bizarre way, we feel exposed. It is similar to the type of embarrassment we might feel when confronting people placed in a mental institution whose behaviour puts us in an awkward situation. Here is someone without dissimulation, someone who is not playing a social role. Of course, there are exceptions; but the point here is that we are confronted with a person who cannot be anything other than what he or she is. To some extent, this is what Lars von Trier exposes in his film *The Idiots*. Does this film (notwithstanding the group-sex scenes), in fact, bring us closer to our own lives? If this is so, it might be because our confrontation with this necessary element forces us to be human. In other words, the confrontation seems to constitute a point at which we cannot escape our own self no matter how much we try. Confronting a world without dissimulation makes it difficult to continue our own life in the same way. No matter what we do, we are confronted with our own fracture; this is the affect by which shame forces us to think, to reflect on who we are, on what our relations to other human beings may be. However, in meeting the idiot, most of us will do the same as the Russian soldiers when they reached the concentration camp. The discomfort bites us from behind.

Shame as gesture

Nowadays the borders of shame and disgrace have been pushed into previously unknown territories. The popularity of our leadership is apparently untouched by any level of disgrace: Clinton's sexual episode with Monica Lewinsky while he was president, the US warfare in Iraq or Berlusconi's shameless behaviour. It is said that we have the kind of leaders we deserve. To put it differently: the shameless behaviour of our leaders is accepted because vulgar behaviour, vulgar language and a shameless banality have seeped into our very way of behaving. Historically, shame is tied to guilt and degradation, as exemplified in the treatment of Jews in the concentration camps. Within modern working life and the performance society with its demand for self-optimisation and individualisation, and its constant demands for visibility and exposure, the absence of shame seems to dominate our era when we consider the superficiality of competitive behaviour within consumerism and the self-optimisation of human capital. And yet, looking at the case of capitalism more closely, we not only experience shame in extreme situations, such as the one described by Primo Levy, but also as part of our everyday struggle in social life to cope with dissimulation, insecurity and self-development. As Deleuze and Guattari emphasize,

> We also experience shame [...] before the meanness and vulgarity of existence that haunts democracies, before the propagation of these modes of existence and of thought-for-the-market, and before the values, ideals, and opinions of our time. The ignominy of the possibilities of life that we are offered appears from within. We do not feel ourselves outside of our time but continue to undergo shameful compromises with it. (Deleuze & Guattari, 1994, pp.107-8).

With an increasing focus on the individualisation of human capital and modern work-life based on recognition, the social network and modes of exposure, shame often occurs as a hidden factor behind the more visible moral and legal authorities. Hence, shame reveals itself in our everyday encounter, confronting the other's gaze, the gesture of the boss or the colleague, the degrading look, the lack of trust. It is this world of gestures, no matter how insignificant they may appear, that expresses an important part of the foundation of the social being.

The prose of Franz Kafka displays a world of such gestures: within the apparently most insignificant human relationships, Kafka puts everything at stake all the time. In particular, Walter Benjamin placed great emphasis on the gesture. In his famous study on Kafka, he writes: "Each gesture is an event—one might even say, a drama—in itself" (Benjamin, 1968, p.121). A teacher or an employer raising his eyebrow might be decisive for your future destiny. Kafka exposes our powerlessness in the social jungle, how the sensation of shame is intimately related to the constant pressure of the environment in our social relations, as well as in our particular work situation. Gesture captures what Walter Benjamin calls "a world of theatre". Human behaviour as a gesture "is the name of the intersection between life and art, act and power, general and particular, text and execution" (Agamben, 2000, p.100). Gesture is the name used by Agamben to address the event of the praxis, the *principium individuationis*:

> If production is a means in view of an end, and praxis is an end without means, the gesture then breaks with the false alternative between ends and means that paralyses morality and presents instead means that, as such, evade the orbit of modality without becoming, for this reason, ends. (Agamben, 2000, p.101).

The assertion is that, in Kafka's universe, each gesture is a world in itself, bringing out the social machines of recognition and judgement.

Discreditation and degradation are not only governed by laws and the authority of law (for instance, a verdict on slander, violence or a cry of negligence), but also through a multitude of signals that accompany the reaction from the surrounding world. You are kept outside of the circle. The others are whispering when you pass them in the hallway. You are not sitting at the right table during lunch hour. You are not a member of the running club. You have an awkward reaction when meeting the leader outside the office. It is all being absorbed by the impersonal affect of not taking proper part in the overall performance of success. The shame of being a failure is most visible through the daily dramatization of the human field and its gestures. This is the staging of the world theatre, as Benjamin would phrase it. According to Agamben (2005), gesture operates as an enunciation of a non-transparent law—law-enforcement without any concrete, written law and composed of invisible levels of operation. Kafka exposes power and the machines of recognition not through the direct order coming from the boss or the transparent codes of institutions, but through the power of desire, gestures, the other's gaze, daily patterns of reactions and performance known today as the highly ambiguous concept of self-management. Modern organisations, corporations and institutions not only want our power of labour—they want our soul. They appeal to our sense of freedom, independence, enjoyment and our own initiative through images and stories of competences, courses of self-realisation and work-life-balance programmes. However, what looks like freedom is, instead, a social machine in which we learn to desire our own enslavement. The Italian sociologist Maurizio Lazzarato is not far from the truth when he considers the machine of execution from Kafka's short story *In the Penal Colony* as an image of how power today operates within modern work life:

> The paradigmatic body of our societies is no longer a mute body shaped by disciplines, but the body and soul are marked by signs, words, images (companies' logos) registered in us in the same way that Kafka's machine or 'prison colony' grafts its commands on the skin of the condemned. (Lazzarato, 2004, p.191)

The machine of judgment penetrates the human body. The overweight and the anorectic are the two poles in this corrosion of the body. On the one hand, starvation of the body takes place when pressure from the surroundings leads to resignation and distancing (isolation). On the other hand, the dilated, constantly gorging body will reach its breaking point. Shame is now part of the demands imposed by the doctrine of self-realisation and individualisation, living in the precarious balance between production and failure, between success and degradation. The constant search for applause, combining self-exposure with confession, is the need for attention and recognition. Within modern working life, it is not enough to perform; you have to show 'who you are'. The capitalisation of the self is now an intense part of the confessional industry in which we mirror ourselves in famous people's lives. Talking about our problems and enjoying our sins now seems to be a part of the confessional self-seduction. Enjoyment and guilt change positions. "I might be a bit crazy, manic, depressed, but I am still productive. Let me express myself" (Taylor, 2009, p.4). Now, it is all about mobilising a suppression and pathology, so you have a reason to confess, to visit a therapist, a doctor, your boss, girlfriend, the media. Indirectly, we use shame to justify our existence. We confess not because we are suppressed; we confess and hide something so that we can perform confession (Deleuze, 1992, p.105). Hence, shame will now play a problematic part in the performance theatre of our increasing love of pleasure, narcissism and inferiority.

The language of impotence, or: shame and thought

> "The shame of being a man—is there any better reason to write?" Gilles Deleuze

"Why do you write?" This is the first question asked by the interviewer. The author is already tired. After a while he says, "Because something insists on breaking into my world." "But what is it?" she asks. "Hard to say. Could be my father's death, my powerlessness in life, my impotence in handling things, dissimulation in my social relations, but it could also be something else." The interviewer wonders, "But could you not be more specific?" He answers, "The truth is, certain images keep haunting me. They insist. Like necessity. Hence, I write to give this unclear image (chaos) some kind of shape."

This fictive interview brings out a common sensation when addressing the problem of shame: the creation of distance and the impossibility of escaping the moment of exposed existence. But in confronting shame, the thought has to overcome its own self-defence.

In the following, I will use the work of Kafka to analyse the animal as a literary tool to capture the language of powerlessness attached to shame. Rather than a neo-romantic view of animals, the animal affect is a potential exit from the powerlessness of shame. Perhaps in writing about shame, one has to penetrate into the human through confronting the non-human? As a writer, this exercise requires paying much attention to the language itself. This has to do with our responsibility towards language, not only for Kafka, but for any serious writer. Confronted with this responsibility, the French author Leslie Kaplan writes:

> I do believe that the writer has a responsibility. But it seems to me that the writer first of all has a responsibility towards language. This means a responsibility towards every aspect of language as such and primarily towards the potential of language; its possibility, its fiction. Which means, even if someone writes about what takes place nearby, the author should be concerned with and feel himself responsible for how things could be different. It is something that is included within language. Everything we say contains the possibility of something else. Something that could be a different world, another regime or another word. (Kaplan, 2013, p.117)

In this particularly attentive use of language, literature has a responsibility to break through to another reality. Lack of imagination belong to a culture of acceleration that also affects language. We only have to scratch the surface to realize how powerless we are when it comes to being taken seriously and to be heard. In this sense, we all experience this powerlessness on a daily basis—and, not least, an increasing experience of vulgarisation and stupidity, including one's own.

And yet the impulse of this shame may be converted into an active force, a political force. A transvestite in my son's high school class was silent and awkward to begin with, but one day his agony and pain burst out and enlightened the classroom dialogue about identity, gender, boys and girls, etc. My son described this as a powerful moment where he suddenly felt a political force that took the shape of a transformative power emanating from this isolated and distressed young classmate. The impulse of shame makes us write, fabulate and think. Perhaps this is the true power of shame. A writer's most important task is to confront those forces that he is not prepared to confront in the first place. Confronting this cul de sac, and yet, moving on, he might overcome something he does not like about himself or the other: shame, perversion and madness. Important literature does this. This is not an ethical obligation or a moral command as such, but ethics, in its capacity to rethink our relationship to degradation, vulgarisation and stupidity. When these affects and impulses of shame become visible as an extension of man, they become intense, because they lose their ideological and transcendent dimensions. And as Deleuze and Guattari suggest we sometimes imitate the gesture of the animal, because "thought itself is sometimes closer to an animal that dies than a living, even democratic, human being" (Deleuze & Guattari, 1994 p.108). "We become animal so that the animal also becomes something else" (Deleuze & Guattari, 1994, p.109).

Shame and the language of animals

In his later writings, Franz Kafka seems to have turned this idea into something we might call a strategy. In his writing, it is among the animals and those closest to them that we will encounter an outside force that cannot be countered with a reflexive reaction. This encounter leaves us devoid of any recognisable psychological emotion of refuge. We find ourselves in the midst of something that we cannot possess and cannot quite comprehend. In a rather subtle manner, the animal is part of a process of metamorphosis that distances it from what is perceived as human, and yet the distance from this so-called human world produces a number of other-governed impulses that pushes the human gaze and perception to the extent of the possible. The animal offers a language for powerlessness that is difficult for man to reach all by himself (Agamben, 2011, p.44). Walter Benjamin has called the animal creatures of Kafka's universe "mysteriousness with the utmost simplicity", and, as he adds, "It is possible to read Kafka's animal stories for quite a while without realizing that they are not about human beings at all" (Benjamin, 1968, p.122). Kafka has seen how man has become a stranger to his own gestures. "Kafka, he divests the human gesture of its traditional supports..." (Benjamin, 1968, p.122).

However, we should be careful not to see this 'animalistic' extension of the human as a political way out of the deadlock. There are other writers—for instance, Brian Massumi—who talk about a continuum between animal and man. Kafka's "becoming animal" [...] "shows us a way out" (Massumi, 2014, p.112). Massumi no longer reads Kafka's writing on animals as a force of fiction, but as a force of affective biology with political implications; a new kind of reversed biopolitics based on the transformation of bodily affects springing from the world of animals. Combining Kafka and biosemiotics, Massumi argues for new ecological possibilities re-analysing the continuum of the man-animal axis. That line of thought will not be pursued any further here; rather, we will focus on the literary figure of the animal and its potential as the friend of thought, which might be the beginning of a critical ethos.

In Kafka's short story *The Metamorphosis*, non-human forces play an active role in teasing and extending human perception. When young Gregor Samsa wakes up transformed into a huge insect, human attributes are gradually lost. The further away from his humanness he grows, the stronger his ability to think becomes. Towards the end, almost lost and a complete stranger towards his human element, he is deeply moved by the violin playing of his sister. He himself wonders why he is now moved so vehemently by her violin playing that he intends to keep her in the room and "he will never let her leave [...] feeling the way to the unknown nourishment he longed for was being revealed" (Kafka, 2009, p.32).

In Kafka's writings, it is rare for human beings to be affected in the way that Gregor is, despite the fact that the emotional capacity for being moved and for being affected are essentially human features and characteristics. Animals, the creatures termed "the defected" by Benjamin, are affected by a gesture, a small scene, a piece of music. On the other hand, the feeling of being repelled seems to be the most common sentiment attached to humans in Kafka's writings—a main characteristic of the protagonists in *The Trial, The Castle* and *America*. The fact that the protagonists look at music, dance, bodily performance and gestural expression with mistrust is due to the fact that they are already chosen, and therefore captured, between two worlds: the otherworldly (transcendent) from where the selection takes place, and the earthly (immanent), the empty world of law, the world of shame, degradation and rigid gestures. The animal and the defected are still capable of being affected since they live within the world of immanence, the world in which gestures, singing, sounds have not yet lost the element of naïve innocence and its peculiar uniqueness. In the short story *Investigation of a Dog*, Kafka stresses how the event that occurred to the dog as a "child" is an event that tore the dog's world to pieces, a gesture so strong that the dog was convinced that it would be its death. The event is caused by seven dogs playing music, all of them suddenly stepping out while "... from the empty air they conjured music" and created a noise both thrilling and captivating (Kafka, 1971, p.281). The power of Kafka's literature is to capture this ambiguity of gesture. This irresistible and devastating music fills the air from nothing:

> ...but from the empty air they conjured music. Everything was music, the lifting and sitting down of their feet, certain turns of the head, their running and their standing still, the positions they took up in relation to one another, the symmetrical patterns which they produced by one dog setting his front paws of the back of another... (Kafka, 1971, p.281)

In this ambiguous music lies the pledge of hope. Through music, the dog is connected to its own shame where it is prey to the immanent play of inhuman and human forces:

> ...but while I was still involved in these reflections the music gradually got the upper hand, literally knocked the breath out of me and swept me far away from those actual little dogs, and quite against my will, while I howled as if pain were being inflicted on me, my mind could attend to nothing but this blast of music which seemed to come from all sides, from the heights, from the deeps, from everywhere, surrounding the listener, overwhelming him, crushing him, and over his swooning body still blowing fanfares so near that they seemed far away and almost inaudible. (Kafka, 1971, p.282)

The gesture of shame resonates out of pure nothingness and deviates from the given norms and rules. The dog admires the musical – performing dogs and the deviation of the moral interiorisation of shame. "Those dogs were violating the law. [...] They were uncovering their nakedness, blatantly making a show of their nakedness" (Kafka, 1971, p.283-4) and they were overwhelmed by the scathing musical performance. The investigating dog has no desire to instruct the musical dogs on the conventions of common sense, but insists on pointing out the error as the type of defect that shakes their understanding and brings it to a different path: "...but even if it was an error it had nonetheless a sort of grandeur, and is the sole, even if delusive, reality that I have carried over into this world..." (Kafka, 1971, p.314). The immanence of the animal brings out the powerlessness and impotence of language. Agamben characterizes the language of impotence and impotentiality as the heart of potentiality. In contrast to animals, negativity is part of the capacity of being human. Human beings have "a potentiality that is not simply the potential to do this or that thing but potential to not-do, potential not to pass into actuality" (Agamben, 1999a, p.179-180). This isolation of impotence is something that belongs specifically to humans. Something that is only potential can both be and not be. "To be potential means: to be one's own lack, to be in relation to one's own incapacity. Beings that exist in the mode of potentiality are capable of their own impotentiality; and only in this way do they become a permanent chance of life as power, *potential*" (Agamben, 1999a, p.182). We could say that Kafka uses the figures of animals to pay attention to the impotentiality of language. The true power of gesture is "therefore not that something is being produced or acted, but rather something is being endured and supported. The gesture, in other words, opens the sphere of ethos as the more proper sphere of that which is human" (Agamben, 2000, p.57). A world that reduces gestures to spasms (in playback and political spins) and pornographic nakedness leaves out the ethical and political potential of gestures. Hence, the ethics of shame in the literature of Kafka give form to the transformative aspect of our shameful encounters without relying on interiorization of the emotion of shame itself.

Rather than referring to a thing that takes on a clear shape, shame refers to an event through which an indefinite life passes. This raises ethics above the singular and presents it as a shared element, because rather than referring to particular beings, it points to the singular act in which the subject becomes a carrier of shame.

References

Agamben, G. (1999a). *Potentialites*. Stanford, California: Stanford University Press.

Agamben, G. (1999b). *Remnants of Auschwitz. Witness and the archive*. New York: Zone Books.

Agamben, G. (2000). *Means without end. Notes on politics*. Minneapolis. London: Minnesota University Press.

Agamben, G. (2005). *State of exception*. Chicago: University of Chicago Press.

Agamben, G. (2011). *Nudities*. Stanford, California: Stanford University Press.

Benjamin, W. (1968). "Franz Kafka. On the tenth anniversary of his death". In *Illuminations. Essays and reflections*. H. Arendt (Ed.). New York: Schocken Books.

Deleuze, G. (1992). *Difference and repetition*. New York: Athlone Press.

Deleuze, G. & Guattari, F. (1994). *What is philosophy?* New York: Verso.

Kafka, F. (1971). *The complete stories and parables*. N. M. Glatzer. (Ed.). New York: Quality Paperback Book Club.

Kafka, F. (1995). *Franz Kafka: the complete stories*. New York: Schocken Books.

Kafka, F. (2009). *The metamorphosis*. Classix Press.

Kaplan, L. (2013). *Overskridelsen—Fabrikken*. (Danish version of fr. *L'exces – l'usine* (1982)). København: Basilisk.

Lazzarato, M. (2004). From capital-labour to capital-life. *Ephemeraweb.org, 4*(3). London.

Levi, P. (1995). *The reawakening*. New York: Touchstone.

Massumi, B. (2014). *What animals teach us about politics*. Durham: Duke University Press.

Taylor, C. (2009). *The culture of confession from Augustine to Foucault*. London: Routledge.

8.
Poetics of shame and guilt
Freud and Woolf on shame and guilt in creative writing and the pleasures and pains of reading

Anna-Klara Bojö

In the transcribed and translated seminar "Creative writers and daydreaming" (1959 [1908]), Freud attempts to outline the source of creativity and its affects. In the space of a few pages, Freud sets out to lay bare not only "from what sources that strange being, the creative writer, draws his material", but also "how he manages to make such an impression on us with it and to arouse in us emotions of which, perhaps, we had not even thought ourselves capable" (1959, p.143). For the purposes of analyzing the source of creativity, Freud asks his readers to consider the layman's activity of daydreaming, for daydreaming, or imagining, is the grown man's substitution for the childhood activity of play, and a child's play is, actually, the same thing as creativity.

Most adults, however, do not become writers. Indeed, most adults, according to Freud at least, will not admit to the fact that they fantasize at all. Rather, Freud explains, the adult "is ashamed of his phantasies", and "as a rule he would rather confess his misdeeds"—that is, he would rather admit his guilt than confess to the pleasures of daydreaming (1959, p.145). The creative writer, however, has somehow managed to overcome his shame and becomes, in Freud's own words, a "dreamer in broad daylight" (1959, p.149). In sharing his fantasies, the writer also manages to touch his readers and evoke in them emotions of which they did not know themselves capable.

In a different context, Virginia Woolf has, in her transcribed "Speech of January 21 1931" (1978), later published under the heading 'Professions for women' (1966), analyzed the specific situation for women writers.[1] Similar to Freud, Woolf ascribes the source of creativity to the activity of daydreaming; or, more precisely, she describes writerly creativity as dependent on the workings of an undisturbed unconscious that can "sweep unchecked round every rock and cranny of the world that lies submerged in our unconscious being" (1966, p.xxxviii). This feature of creativity as the free exploration of unconscious desires is, according to Woolf, gender neutral: men and women writers alike depend on it. There are, however, other aspects of the question of creativity that appear to be connected to gender. One such substantial difference is women writers' apparent sensation of guilt as their imagination attempts to transcend the moral codex of sex-appropriate behaviour.

According to Woolf, male writers "who can let their imaginations go much further than women can" (1966, p.xxxix) are in a much more favourable position than are women. For a woman writer to tell the truth such as she sees it is simply not possible; the restrictions that gender conventions put on her freedom makes the task of expressing her subjective truths an impossible endeavour: "I should need the courage of a hero" (1966, p.xxxix), Woolf explains, in order to tell the truth about, for example, women's passions or bodies. But, she continues: "I doubt that a writer can be a hero. I doubt that a hero can be a writer" (1966, p.xxxix). For Woolf, the heroic leap puts the art

---

1 "Speech of January 21 1931" is a transcribed and originally untitled manuscript from the Berg Collection archives at Sussex University. The manuscript is published with its corrections in *The Pargiters* (1978). Also, Woolf rewrote and published a much shorter version of her speech titled "Professions for women", to be read in the *Collected Essays by Virginia Woolf* (1966). Unless otherwise indicated, I take my citations from the transcribed original.

of literature at risk, for it jeopardises the style and tone of literature proper and effectively turns literature into preaching or criticism. Furthermore, the sensation of guilt and heroic preaching, which we know from Woolf's reading of Charlotte Brontë's *Jane Eyre* and other women novelists in *A Room of One's Own* (2000 [1928]), has a way of seeping into the text, affecting its rhythm and ultimately ruining the book's integrity and the act of reading, too.

Freud and Woolf offer two in many ways similar, yet substantially different, poetics. Whereas the focus of the Freudian poetics is on the writer's overcoming of shame and the subsequent pleasure this brings to the reader, Woolf is preoccupied with the woman writer's need to overcome her sensation of guilt, while also giving a more detailed and elaborate theory of the pleasures and pains of reading. In the following pages, I will outline more carefully the logics of Freud's and Woolf's poetics, respectively. Discussing the difference between shame and guilt in the process of creative writing, I suggest that the two different approaches, though sensitive to the question of sexual difference, should be analyzed primarily in relation to the different aesthetics proclaimed by each thinker. I suggest that Freud's aesthetics of escapism—which ultimately consider fantasizing as a strategy employed by the individual subject to cover up sensations of displeasure by way of daydreaming—should be viewed as opposed to Woolf's aesthetics that carry a strong revelatory truth claim. The different aesthetics pertain to two different views on the function of daydreaming, as well as of writing, and I will pay special attention to, on the one hand, daydreaming and literature as a means to uphold a certain existing order, and on the other hand, daydreaming as a potential challenge to that order—what we might call daydreaming out of place. The different aesthetics and the different ways of understanding the function of daydreaming have some bearing on how the two thinkers understand the creative process in relation to shame and guilt and how they theorize the feelings associated with reading.

Freud. On shameless writers and joyous readers

At the beginning of his seminar on the creative writer and the affects of reading, Freud poses the following question: "Might we not say that every child at play behaves like a creative writer, in that he creates a world of his own, or rather, re-arranges the things of his world in a new way that pleases him?" (1959 [1908], pp.143-144). In this single passage, Freud gives us three foundational aspects concerning his theory of creativity: 1) the source of creativity can be traced to activities in childhood, something Freud later supports with the claim that man can never give anything up, but "only exchange one thing for another" (1959, p.145) by way of substitution; 2) the creative act is understood as an act of rearranging things in an already existing world—that is, it is not really a creation of something previously unthought of or unheard of, but a rearrangement of already known material; and 3) the act of rearrangement-creativity is pleasurable in that it corrects an unsatisfying reality and grants the subject fulfilment of an unsatisfied wish.

There is a fourth significant aspect to Freud's understanding of daydreams and poetics, and that is their nature of unreality, or perhaps rather their testification to an imaginative register, an unconscious sphere in man's being. Referring to *The Interpretation of Dreams*, published eight years previously, Freud suggests that "night-dreams are wish-fulfilments in just the same way as day-dreams—the phantasies that we all know so well" (1959, p.149). Literature, like dreams, testifies to those repressed wishes of which man is ashamed, but which must be taken into account if science is to comprehend the nature of man and his desires. Thus, Freud explains, "[t]he opposite of play is not what is serious but what is real", and he continues: "He [the creative writer] creates a world of phantasy which he takes very seriously—that is, which he invests with large amounts of emotion—while separating it sharply from reality" (1959, p.144).

Literature then, like dreams, opens up for an acknowledgement of and an investigation into a sensational register, a mode of pleasure that stands out:

The unreality of the writer's imaginative world", Freud explains, "has very important consequences for the technique of his art; for many things which, if they were real, could give no enjoyment, can do so in the play of phantasy, and many excitements which, in themselves, are actually distressing, can become a source of pleasure for the hearers and spectators at the performance of a writer's work. (1959, p.144).

What Freud thus highlights is the subject's split existence between an external and an internal reality to which different pleasures correspond.

In relation to literature, genres such as murder mysteries and romances come readily to mind. To actually live through even the blandest murder mystery would be absolutely awful, and, while romantic adventures in real life seldom live up to their fictive counterparts, they can turn the world upside-down and shake the foundations of one's subjective being nonetheless. Yet, the immense popularity of both genres arguably testifies to the presence of a certain pleasure involved in reading, and it is this pleasure that Freud takes as his steppingstone to discuss the affects of reading. However, before turning to the question of the affects of reading in Freud's aesthetic theory, I wish to dwell a while longer on the question of shame and on the connection between, not creativity and daydreaming, but shame and daydreaming.

Let it first be noted that Freud, despite his attempt to differentiate between writers who work by means of taking over "material readymade" and writers who "originate their own material" (1959, p.149), is really only concerned with those writers who reorganize already familiar ideas. As I understand it, Freud's first type of writer rewrites and reorganizes already known pieces of literature, while the other type of writer is engaged in reorganizing ideological goods in accordance with the bourgeois daydream of getting both the job and the girl and then living happily ever after. According to Freud, almost all daydreams pertain to those two definable groups—ambitious wishes and erotic ones—and we often find both types enmeshed in the same daydream or work of literature, the one supporting the other.[2] While we may deplore the limited nature of man's imaginative register, we have no reason to doubt Freud on this account. But, one may ask, why must we hide our fantasies and unfulfilled wishes? That is, wherein lies the shame of daydreaming?

Returning briefly to the passage where Freud discusses daydreaming and shame, it is noteworthy that, whereas children display an uncomplicated attitude towards the activity of play, adults usually develop an awkward attitude towards fantasizing. Freud says:

> People's phantasies are less easy to observe than the play of children. The child, it is true, plays by himself or forms a closed psychical system with other children for the purposes of a game; but even though he may not play his game in front of the grown-ups, he does not, on the other hand, conceal it from them. *The adult, on the contrary, is ashamed of his phantasies and hides them from other people. He cherishes his phantasies as his most intimate possessions, and as a rule he would rather confess to his misdeeds than tell anyone his phantasies.* It may come about that for that reason he believes he is the only person who invents such phantasies and has no idea that creations of this kind are widespread among other people. (1959 [1908], p.145; my italics)

---

[2] Here, Freud makes a distinction between women's and men's fantasies, suggesting that: "In young women the erotic wishes predominate almost exclusively, for their ambition is as a rule absorbed by erotic trends. In young men egoistic and ambitious wishes come to the fore clearly enough alongside erotic ones" (1959 [1908], p.147). However, Freud concludes that: "we will not lay stress on the opposition between the two trends; we would rather emphasize the fact that they are often united. Just as, in many altar-pieces, the portrait of the donor is to be seen in a corner of the picture, so, in the majority of ambitious phantasies, we can discover in some corner or other the lady for whom the creator of the phantasy performs all his heroic deeds and at whose feet all his triumphs are laid" (1959, p.147).

If we differentiate between guilt as a reaction to a transgression of internalized moral norms and shame as a sensation of unease linked to a failure to live up to one's ego-ideal shaped according to moral norms (Tangney & Dearing, 2002, pp.12-13, 113-115), we can understand daydreaming in this passage as shameful because it is a symptom of a failure in the subject to live up to his ideal image.[3] "We may lay it down that a happy person never phantasises" (1959, p.146), Freud proclaims. Consequently, if the subject were to reveal his daydreams, it would be the same thing as not only acknowledging but flaunting his failure to live up to an ideal image. In other words, the prime motive for concealing our fantasies is that they bear witness to our wish for a different life.

This analysis of the function of daydreams and its connection to shame brings about consequences that Freud does not explicitly elaborate on, but which I would argue are important for understanding his theory of literature and the affects of reading, because man in general detests failure: instead, in wanting to be his ideal, man works hard and fabricates fanciful illusions to convince himself that he is at least close to it, and here the function of secret daydreaming is crucial. For while man lies in language, he nurtures his self-deception in silence. With this in mind, daydreaming takes on the function of covering up or modifying the subject's sense of himself and his position without actually having to take responsibility for the disagreeable situation that he finds himself in. Daydreaming, or psychical reality, as Marcos Aguinis has explained, allows man to take "liberties in the reorganization and evocation of factual events, sometimes even changing them out of all recognition" (1995, p.24). As long as the subject fantasizes in private, where he si-

---

3   The theoretical literature on the subject of shame and guilt shows that a clear definition of either concept is hard to establish. However, there appears to be some agreement on a differentiation between an understanding of shame as an emotion linked to sensations of failure and shortcomings in relation to a self-image, whereas guilt is linked to the transgression of limits and wrongdoing connected to external conventions (Deigh, 1996; Tangney & Dearing, 2002).

lently reorganizes the misfortunes of his real life, he can tranquilly go on living his misfortune supported by that other psychical reality, which gives him enough pleasure to get by. To speak, however, or to write, is to put that inner reality to the test. Writing is setting oneself up for potential failure, not just in the sense that one might get bad reviews or fail to attract any readers, but, in relation to Freud's aesthetics, the writer also takes a risk in the very utterance of the wish for the girl, the job and the happy life—he becomes, again, "a dreamer in broad daylight", with his lacks and desires displayed to any and all.

However—and now we turn to the question of affects and reading—Freud explains that if a layman were to convey his fantasies to us it would give us no pleasure, but rather "[s]uch phantasies, when we learn them, repel us or at least leave us cold" (1959, p.153). Tales of "His Majesty the Ego, the hero alike of every day-dream and of every story" (1959, p.150) far from grant us enjoyment. The central question is what it is in the creative writer's way of conveying his admittedly banal daydreams that makes us, the readers, experience great pleasure. Roland Barthes's humble question—"Does writing in pleasure guarantee—guarantee me, the writer—my reader's pleasure?" (1975 [1973], p.4)—is useful in this context. Barthes himself replied no; and while Freud acknowledges that the answer to the question of the pleasures of reading must be complex and the sources many (aesthetic method being one such source), he ventures a clear answer: "our actual enjoyment of an imaginative work", Freud suggests, "proceeds from a liberation of tensions in our minds. It may even be that not a little of this effect is due to the writer's enabling us thenceforward to enjoy our own day-dreams without self-reproach or shame" (1959, p.153). Thus, Freud concludes, the writer's overcoming of his shame in creative writing may in turn help the reader to shamelessly indulge in his own fantasies. Therein lies the reader's pleasure.

At first glance, this appears to be a horrific fate for literature and its potential. Instead of understanding reading as a way of relieving us from shame in the face of our own daydreams, one might suggest that literature offers us escape from the monotony of our own imagination and preconceived ideas. But, at a second glance, there may be something of value in Freud's theory of literature and its affective pleasures. While his theory cannot say anything of the pleasures of a flight of mind that transcends new horizons, Freud does say something about how a certain type of literature might work to fortify our sense of security and order. If we consider again murder mysteries and romances, it is not far-fetched to interpret the immense popularity of both genres as a symptom of widespread fears of death as inevitable and suspicions that we are fundamentally alone, or existentially separated. They also tell of acute wishes to control those fears and eliminate those suspicions by means of fictive heroic intervention that affirms that law and romantic order are still in place.[4] In other words, our unwillingness to face the harsh reality that romantic love is impossible and that we are all mortal is supported by heroic fiction and daydreams that allow us to think otherwise. Freud's theory of reading thus points to a consolidating type of pleasure that is associated with being allowed to fantasize about an invariable, secure and solid order.

But what about all those readers who, instead of seeking to be affirmed in what they already know or dream of, read in order to think new thoughts and experience new emotions? What about those readers who are not content with the moderate pleasure of eradicating displeasure, but who yearn to expand their cognitive and emotional register? What about the curious reader who wants to know all possible facets of life, who wishes to constantly transcend his limits and broaden his horizons, and who celebrates the unknown and is open

---

4 Even though Freud admits that not all imaginative writings follow the model of a "naïve daydream" (1959 [1908], p.150), he still claims that the psychological novel, as well as the modern and the realistic novel, share traits of the logic pertaining to daydreams. The modernist novel, for example, wherein the narrator "sees the actions and sufferings of other people pass before him like a spectator", can be compared to non-normative individuals whose daydreams testify to the fact that "the ego contents itself with the role of spectator" (1959, p.151).

to meeting the yet unheard of, from a distance and in the comfort of his own reading chair?

Woolf. On guilt-ridden poetesses and the pleasures and pains of reading

It is tempting to read Virginia Woolf's "Speech of January 21 1931" as a direct response to Freud's "Creative writers and daydreaming" Herein, Woolf, similar to Freud, develops a theory of creativity based on a notion of the subject's exploration of unconscious desires. Woolf also picks up on the notion of the heroic gesture in literature, which she, contrary to Freud, rejects, and she relates her poetics to questions of truth and reality. However, instead of drawing on the Freudian notion of fantasy as a rearrangement of a dissatisfying reality into a more agreeable one, Woolf claims that creative writing may be a way to explore and express subjective experience or desire that transcends or transgresses moral convention. For Woolf, then, literature is the ideal place to convey a certain subjective sense of reality, and the central question is whether there are any limits to what can be conveyed through literature.

While the creative writer desires "to be as unconscious as possible" in order to reassure that "nothing may break the illusion; that nothing may disturb the flow, that nothing may interrupt the mysterious nosings about, feelings round, darts and dashes, and sudden discoveries of that very shy and illusive fish the imagination" (1966 [1931], p.xxxvii), the Woolfian exploration of the unconscious is by no means a conjuration of a fantasy world or a psychic reality that functions to cover up discontent in life. On the contrary, the imaginative work of Woolf's creative writer is an exploration of the truths that lie hidden in "the depth of her subconsciousness" (1966, p.xxxvii). There, in the unconscious, the creative writer can access all kinds of queer knowledge about "womens [sic] bodies for instance—their passions—and so on" (1966, p.xxxix).

It is no simple task to give an account of Woolf's poetics. Those familiar with *A Room of One's Own* (2000 [1928]) know her complex and somewhat contradictory aesthetic theories. In *A Room of One's Own*, literature is conveyed as dependent on both the author's subjective experience of truth and as the outcome of many years of thinking in common; literature is said to depend on the author's material conditions, yet complete freedom of mind is regarded as essential for any author who wishes to create a convincing piece of literature. And, perhaps the most complex topic of them all, regarding the question of sexual difference, the great writer is arguably required to be unconscious of her sex, yet men and women are declared not to be able to create in the same fashion, nor is an eradication of sexual difference deemed desirable. I have no pretention to say anything exhaustive on Woolf's poetics here. Instead, I will settle for a much more modest inquiry into the relation of women's creativity and the experience of guilt that Woolf observes in her "Speech of January 21 1931".

In the speech, then, Woolf takes it upon herself to describe the creative process of the woman writer, a task she describes as very difficult[5]—so difficult, in fact, that she turns from the language of theory to the employment of fiction in order to convey to her listeners/readers the implications involved. "The image that comes to my mind when I think of this girl", Woolf starts out:

> is the image of a fisherman lying sunk in dreams on the verge of a deep lake with a rod held out over the water. She was letting her imagination sweep unchecked round every rock and cranny of the world that lies submerged in the depth of our unconscious being. *Now came the*

---

5 This passage in the "Speech of January 21 1931" is so filled with corrections that a citation would not only be unnecessarily long, but it would also risk creating confusion. Thus, I have cited the corresponding passage in the shorter, revised text 'Professions for women'. The point of argument in reference to the question of guilt is the same, but it is more succinctly expressed in "Professions for women". For comparison, see "Speech of January 21 19312, pp. xxxvii–xxxviii.

experience that I believe to be far commoner with women writers than with men. The line raced through the girl's fingers. Her imagination had rushed away. It had sought the pools, the depths, the dark places where the largest fish slumber. And then there was a smash. There was an explosion. There was foam and confusion. The imagination had dashed itself against something hard. The girl was roused from her dream. *She was indeed in a state of the most acute and difficult distress. To speak without figure, she had thought of something, something about the body, about the passions which it was unfitting for her as a woman to say. Men, her reason told her, would be shocked. The consciousness of what men will say of a woman who speaks the truth about her passions had roused her from her artist's state of unconsciousness.* She could write no more. The trance was over. Her imagination could work no longer. (Woolf 1966 [1931], pp.287-288; my italics)

The story of the woman writer as a fisherman and the interfering and inhibiting function that reason—or we could say morality—lays upon the creative process offers a clear picture of the woman writer's specific situation that Woolf is trying to convey. Woolf does not use the word guilt in the cited passage, but working from the definition of guilt as discussed above, that is an experience associated with the subject's sense of transgressing boundaries or her sense of wrongdoing towards an acknowledged authority we can recognize the logic at work. As the woman writer in the story encounters reason—that is, as she becomes self-conscious of "what men will say of a woman who speaks the truth about her passions"—her creativity withers and she is pulled away from that necessary "artist's state of unconsciousness." The internal struggle between the creative impulse to explore and express subjective experience and the internalized prohibitions of a superego that does not allow women to write their pleasures or desires is clearly a cause of conflict, and this conflict will make itself known in language—or, in Woolf's case, in the lack of language.

According to Woolf, her own experience is that the conflict arising from attempting to transgress moral boundaries leads to silence. Too conscious of society's unwillingness to hear of women's bodies and passions, and arguably too conscious of her own internalization of those moral boundaries, she is prevented from exploring the subject any further. The writer may hint or allude (as Woolf herself does in the cited passage above), but there is no vocabulary, syntax or grammar suitable to convey a woman's pleasure. One might say that Woolf dwells silently on the emotion of guilt so as not to risk being shamed by the gaze of the other. Thus, Woolf writes: "I will wait until men have become so civilized that they are not shocked when a woman speaks the truth about her body." (1966, pp.xxxix–xli). Indeed "the future of fiction", Woolf concludes her speech, "depends very much upon what extent men can be educated to stand the free speech in women" (1966, p.xl).

The silencing effect that Woolf connects to the topic of women's passions recurs in her writing on poetics. Writing of the fictitious Mary Carmichael in *A Room of One's Own*, a figure of the woman writer to come who touches upon women's desire for other women, Woolf returns to the same idea of waiting. "It will be a curious sight, when it comes, to see those women as they are", Woolf writes, "but we must wait a little, for Mary Carmichael will still be encumbered with that self-consciousness in the presence of 'sin' which is the legacy of our sexual barbarity. She will still wear the shoddy old fetters of class on her feet" (2000, p.88).

The suggestion that literature await passively society's change is somewhat puzzling, and it is hardly congruous with Woolf's admiration for those professional women who came before her and to whom she pays homage in several of her key writings. However, the primary question here may not be that of sexual difference and desire—or at least not that alone—but rather a question of aesthetics. As Woolf scholar Anna Snaith has argued, Woolf was apprehensive about the politically motivated 'new woman' literature that emerged on the literary scene in the 1890s. "[N]ovels by women for women", as Snaith describes the 'new woman' literature, portrayed "[t]he single, financially independent, sexually and physically liberated woman who often questioned marriage, motherhood, and legal and educational inequalities" (2000, p.46). For Woolf, however, literature should not be reduced to a political tool; nor should it be a place for displaying personal grievance. Literature might be experimental in both choice of subject and style, but it must "absorb the new into the old without disturbing that infinitely intricate and elaborate balance of the whole" (2000, p.84), as she expresses it in *A Room of One's Own*. For aesthetic reasons, then, which here get tangled up with questions of sexual morality, Woolf draws a line that renders literature unable to portray female desire. In order to avoid aesthetic shame, Woolf accepts the sin and guilt connected to woman's desire. On that topic, Woolf writes: "The only way for you to do it […] would be to talk of something else", and in "words that are hardly syllabled yet" (2000, p.84).

Woolf's preference for silence over representation might be understood as an aesthetic contribution attempting to rescue literature from a guilt-laden tone of voice that makes itself heard in political contestation. For while literature proper demands that the writer tell the 'truth', the voice of a guilty conscience is a shrill and awkward one which, according to Woolf's aesthetic principles, has ultimately ruined the work of many of her female colleagues and predecessors. For this last query, then, on the subject of the pleasures and pains of reading, I will turn to Woolf's discussion on reading as outlined in the essay *A Room of One's Own*. Here, Woolf discusses in a rather detailed manner the specificity of women's literature together with both the pleasures and pains of reading. Contrary to Freud, who connected the pleasure of reading to an escapist flight from reality and its displeasures, Woolf perceives the pleasures of reading to be gained through encountering new emotions and thinking new thoughts. The Woolfian reader, contrary to finding confirmation of her thoughts and world views, seeks in literature to experience another subject's singular and peculiar perspective. Or, in other words, the reader enjoys what

Woolf terms "integrity" (2000, p.72) – that is, "the conviction that he [the novelist] gives one that this is the truth. Yes, one feels, I should never have thought that this could be so; I have never known people behaving like that. But you have convinced me that so it is, so it happens" (2000, p.72). In the light of a strange but convincing truth, the reader is filled with excitement and pleasure as her imaginative and experiential horizons broaden.

Those strange truths that come to the reader from a great piece of work must, however, be conveyed with integrity. They cannot be written in anger or in an argumentative mode; if they are, the necessary tone of integrity will be ruined. The famous passage where Woolf in *A Room of One's Own* reads Charlotte Brontë's *Jane Eyre* offers insight into the guilt-laden affects that ruin the pleasures of reading and the art of writing, too. The feminist indignation, if we may call it that, the indignation that makes woman protest that she is "as good as a man" or that makes her admit that she is "only a woman"—in other words, that self-conscious notion that drags "anger" and "personal grievance" into the work of art—ruins literature at its core (2000, p.74). "One has only to skim those old forgotten novels", Woolf writes, and:

> listen to the tone of voice in which they are written to divine that the writer was meeting criticism; she was saying this by way of aggression, or that by way of conciliation. She was admitting that she was 'only a woman', or protesting that she was 'as good as a man'. She met that criticism as her temperament dictated, with docility and indifference, or with anger and emphasis. It does not matter which it was; she was thinking of something other than the thing itself. Down comes her book upon our heads. There was a flaw in the centre of it. (Woolf 2000 [1928], pp.74-75)

Aggression and contestation then, affect the art of literature and make for a painful reading experience. The tone of voice, its hint of anger or servitude, of transgression and protest, clouds the essence of any truth and hinders it from taking on a clear shape. Woolfian poetics have a strong and revelatory truth claim, but one that is far removed from that of journalism or criticism. Fictive truth is not only a matter of depicting existing reality as truthfully as possible, nor is it a scene for political argumentation. Rather, is it a place for making truths come into being, for giving subjective truths shape and form; and, when it works, literature offers a possibility for the reader to encounter something hitherto never felt or imagined.

Literature, human creations of other worlds, of new worlds and new sensations, can potentially be radical. At best, literature opens new imaginative horizons, both in the writing and the reading subject. But the imaginative flight of mind does not necessarily entail a movement towards an open-ended future or a constant becoming other. In the case of Freud's poetics, the imaginative workings can just as well be employed to let the split subject enjoy a little bit of fantasmatic pleasure in an otherwise apparently petrified world. If literature, as Freud suggests, remains within the ideological boundaries of its time, it arguably misspends its potential to make a difference. Instead of seeping into the world and modifying its boundaries, literature risks fortifying an already existing order as it simply produces a little bit of by-pleasure, while the misfortunes of real life calmly continue. Furthermore, not only literature, but daydreams, too, are inflicted and regulated by convention and, as both Freud and Woolf observe, it is hard work, not only for women, to daydream outside of one's designated place.

References

Aguinis, M. (1995). A masterpiece of illumination. In E. S. Person, P. Fonagy, & S. A. Figueira (Eds.), transl. P. Slotkined, *On Freud's creative writers and daydreaming*. New Haven and London: Yale University Press.

Barthes, R. (1975 [1973]). *The pleasure of the text*. New York: Hill and Wang.

Deigh, J. (1996). *The sources of moral agency. Essays in moral psychology and Freudian theory*. Cambridge: Cambridge University Press.

Freud, S. (1959 [1908]). Creative writers and day-dreaming. In J. Strachey (Ed. and transl.), *The standard edition of the complete psychological works of Sigmund Freud. Vol. 9 1906-1908*. London: The Hogarth Press.

Snaith, A. (2000). *Virginia Woolf: public and private negotiations*. Hampshire and New York: Palgrave.

Tangney, J. P., & Dearing, R. L. (2002). *Shame and guilt*. London and New York: The Guilford Press.

Woolf, V. (1966 [1936]). Professions for women. In *Collected essays by Virginia Woolf. Volume 2*. London: The Hogarth Press.

Woolf, V. (1978 [1931]). Speech before the London/National Society for Women's Service, January 21 1931. In M. A. Leaska (Ed.), *The Pargiters* (xxvii–xliv). London: The Hogarth Press.

Woolf, V. (2000 [1928]). *A room of one's own*. London: Penguin Books.

9.
Where being and thinking is the s(h)ame: Nightwood, sub specie ruboris

Magnus Bøe Michelsen

If not *sub specie aeternitatis*, that is to say, from the perspective of eternity, as in Spinoza's philosophical interrogations, then at least *sub specie vanitatis*, from the perspective of that which passes – or, to put it more colloquially, from the perspective of our times – we can assert that Djuna Barnes' *Nightwood* (1936) has risen to its rightful position as a modernist classic. Its position is warranted not only on account of its bold, formal experiments, such as its bewildering poetic qualities and the dreamlike ramblings of Doctor Matthew-mighty-grain-of-salt-Dante-O'Connor but also on account of its content. We find in *Nightwood* many of the recurring motifs and constituent themes of modernism, such as the disintegration of values; the crisis of culture implied by industrialization and urbanization and the consequent questioning of identity, subjectivity and sexuality; the impending feeling of being everywhere and nowhere at home, of belonging to all and to none, having the possibility of everything and nothing.[1] *Nightwood* revolves around the rootless and enthralling itinerant Robin Vote and the miseries and misfortunes that wreak havoc upon the people sur-

---

1   See *e.g.* Bradbury and McFarlane (1976:19-55).

rounding her: Baron Felix Volkbein, her husband, obsessed with the dead and gone nobility of 'Old Europe'; their son, Guido Volkbein, of meagre mental and corporeal means; the first lover Nora Flood, an incurable home-builder, as unable to let Robin go as to hold onto her; the second lover Jenny Petherbridge, a squatter by nature and nurture, who loves only things and only in the ways that others have loved before her; and lastly the unlicensed gynaecologist/cosmogonist Doctor Matthew O'Connor, be-it-all and know-it-all, suffering from a seemingly incurable logorrhea. If Robin is to be conceived as the cause of their miseries, then it is Doctor O'Connor who is at the centre of the plot and relating its course. In want of the always-missing Robin, characters as well as readers of the novel are consigned to the endless monologues of the Doctor.

There are numerous comparisons of Barnes' book to James Joyce's *Ulysses* (1922), for instance the seminal essay by Jane Marcus, "'Laughing at Leviticus'; *Nightwood* as Woman's Circus Epic", which describes the former, in all its learned and linguistic extravagance, as "the logos-loving match" of the latter (Marcus, 1989, p.163). Marcus is, however, eager to underline that the differences are as evident as any similarity, claiming that if "Joyce in *Ulysses* writes ancient and modern patriarchy, mythologizes woman and Others the mother, Djuna Barnes in *Nightwood* laughs at Leviticus, brings all the wandering Jews, blacks, lesbians, outsiders and transvestites together in a narrative which mothers the Other" (Marcus, 1989, p.157). It is due to this difference that Marcus proffers the ludicrous proposition that, to a much greater extent than Joyce, Barnes exposes "Freudian psychoanalysis's collaboration with fascism in its desire to 'civilize' and make 'normal' what it considers to be the sexually aberrant misfit" (Marcus, 1989, p.164). In this mercilessly deconstructive parody, the Doctor plays the role of the analyst, thus privileging the limp penis and the lost womb to the detriment of the phallus and its *nomos* (Marcus, 1989, p.157). But not all readings are as depreciative of psychoanalysis as that of Marcus. Taking Merrill Cole's "Backwards Ventriloquy: The Historical Uncanny in Barnes's *Nightwood*" as an example, we encounter a reading that focuses on loss and abjection and "celebrates that alterity's escape" (Cole, 2006, p.392) on the grounds of an "unsupportable joy" (Cole, 2006, p.401) portrayed in the persona of Robin, perceived as a representation of the unrepresentable. To Cole, Robin thus represents that which "psychoanalysis designates [as] desire's correlatives – in full recognition of naming's inadequacy – as the uncanny, the extimate, the real and jouissance" (Cole, 2006, p.393). The Doctor, who is seen as possessing "a dark knowledge that the other characters seek" (Cole, 2006, p.394), a knowledge, that is, of the *jouissance* that is Robin, is depicted as a *sujet supposé savoir*, as Cole observes in a footnote (Cole, 2006, n. 7). With some mutations of terminology these are also the main tenets of Teresa de Lauretis' reading in '*Nightwood* and the "Terror of Uncertain Signs"', in which Robin is perceived as a manifestation of pure sexuality, pure drive, while the Doctor performs the function of presenting, at least in part, a theoretical framework for this representation of sexuality (Lauretis, 2008, p.120-1). According to Cole, who acknowledges *Nightwood*'s modernist credentials, it is the bending beyond recognition or comfort of traditional narrative architecture allowing Barnes to represent the unrepresentable, in contrast to the discarding of articulated architecture that takes place in, for example, *Ulysses*. In Barnes' novel, the representation of the unrepresentable is performed primarily on the narrative level, in the frustrations and excursions caused by the Doctor's incessant interruptions of the narrative movement – as a sort of mimic of desire's eternal postponement (Cole, 2006, p.405).

Though it might benot the first thing that would associate with bold experiments of modernism, I would argue that an examination of modernism *sub specie ruboris*, from the perspective of shame, could prove fruitful.[2] Does shame not ravage the mind of Leopold Bloom, the publicly cuckolded and emasculated man, from morning till midnight, in Ulysses, the novel by 'Shame's Voice'? As for *Nightwood*, as Mary Wilson comments, "many critics have noted [that it] is a text marked by failure, shame, loss and despair" (Wilson, 2011, p.429). But noting the mark of shame still leaves wanting the proper examination of this mark's significations, its cause-and-effect structure, its *modus operandi*, etc. Jacques Lacan demonstrates how the road from being to shame, or from shame to being, is never long, as *ontologie* becomes *hontologie* with a slight slip of the pen, thereby turning the study of being into a study of shame, or into a shameful study of being. Despite the term *hontology* occurring (to my knowledge) but once – on 17th June 1970, during the last lecture of his Seminar XVII, *L'Envers de la psychanalyse* – one might still dare argue that Lacan's teachings have hardly been anything but a systematic elaboration of the concept as such, of the relationship between shame and being, seeing how this relationship entwines with the subject, in the subject's division between meaning and being, through the registers of the imaginary, the symbolic and the real. Redefining the saying by Bishop Berkeley, for whom *esse est percipi*, we could say, after Lacan, that *esse est rubere*, to be is to be ashamed. Or redefining the saying by Parmenides, for whom being and thinking were the same, we could say, in Lacanian terms again, that being and thinking are the shame. The connection thus indicated between thought and being, between language and being, being seen and being ashamed, is more than merely incidental. It is fundamental, as the examination of *Nightwood sub specie ruboris* will illuminate. In so doing, some light may fall upon the topic of modernism as well, as it addresses the disintegration and questioning of values, identity and subjectivity in the early half of the 20th century.

---

2   Besides the reference to Spinoza, I owe an inspirational debt to Gisle Selnes and his interrogation of Western literature *sub specie naufragii*, conducted at a public event in Bergen some years ago. See also his *Det Fjerde Kontinentet* (2010).

The Cause of Shame

There is ample textual evidence to corroborate the thesis that Robin figures as the cause of shame, just as it falls upon the Doctor to cure this very shame, as it ravages the lives of the Baron and Nora. Chapter 1, 'Bow Down', provides important information concerning the functions and interrelations of this quartet of main characters. Simultaneous with the first appearance of the Doctor, the Baron and Nora are introduced with the epigraph of 'the embarrassed': "He [the Baron] had become the accumulated and the single – the embarrassed" (Barnes, 2006, p.11), while Nora, approaching the Doctor, "seemed embarrassed" (p.21). The Doctor, in contrast, is posited confidently at the centre of attention, encircled by someone else's guests and faking the role of host, with "a heavy way of standing that was also apologetic" (p.17). Hence the scene is set. Whenever the Baron or Nora encounter the awkwardness of their existence – when the Baron's illusion concerning the noble families, which is causing him to be both the accumulated and the single, proves thin and bereft of any future, and when Nora, stuck on the outskirts of civilized conversation, must acknowledge that she cannot give the world or anybody in it a home and anchorage – it is the Doctor they seek out, or at least with him they end up, for him to excuse their incompatibility with life, for him to cover up the voids in their existence with his endless tales and incomprehensible chatter. Robin, significantly, is conspicuously absent.

Lacan began his seminar *Les quatre concepts fondamentaux de la psychanalyse* "in the hole, in the split, in the gap characteristic of cause," observing that "in short, there is cause but in that which doesn't work" (Lacan 1973, p.30-1).[3] The examination of *Nightwood sub specie ruboris* also revolves around the hole, the split, the gap that characterizes Robin, as she is absent from the scene during most of the novel, represented there only in the third person and *per voci*,

---

3   All translations are mine, unless otherwise noted.

as the subject of others' conversation. But it is precisely *in absentia* that Robin, in her function as cause, affects her former companions the most.

The most direct linkage between Robin and the affect of shame is presented in Chapter 6, 'Where the Tree Falls'. The perspective, however, is thrice removed, as we are told how the Baron tells the Doctor what Mrs. Petherbridge told him. During her stay at the Petherbridge residence, the young Sylvia was unfortunate enough to develop some delicate affection for Robin, who relished in this newfound attention. However, having been away on holiday, Sylvia later returns to find that Robin "had so obviously forgotten all about her that the child was 'ashamed'," that "shame went all over her" (p.124). The decisive factor for the child's overflowing with shame is the concrete *tête-à-tête* with Robin in her presence, which may be described as an absent presence. It is not simply a matter of Robin not being there in the same way as she was missing during the short holiday. Shame occurs in full force as Robin shows herself to be beyond reach even though she is right there. In other words, Robin is the cause of shame because she, as fickle as she is in matters of love, renders herself unattainable, thereby revealing the hole she formerly filled in the life of the person who desires her, in this instance the young Sylvia. What we observe here is the occurrence of shame at the moment when Sylvia is reduced to nothing. Due to the absent presence of Robin, Sylvia comes "looking for someone who is not there" (p.120), and she comes to realise that she herself is not desired in return, that she can satisfy neither her beloved Robin, nor, as a consequence, her love *for* Robin; instead, she is quite literally reduced to nothing in this relation.

David Bernard, defending his doctoral dissertation on psychopathology, *L'Hontologie*, in 2005, which was later reworked into the book *Lacan et la honte; de la honte à l'hontologie* (2011), conceives of hontology as a valuable tool for the psychoanalytic cure, as it designates a fundamental condition of our speaking being, a specifically human ontology. In his presentation 'La Honte et la névrose' at the conference *Qu'est-ce qu'une névrose?* in Liège (2005), he elaborates on the colloquial parlance of *se taper l'affiche* as an expression for shame. In English, we might speak of *losing face* if we perceive someone who is being publicly exposed as a fraud. This expression indicates how shame is tied to the failure and the falling apart of the ego, of the specular image of the subject, in its status as an imposture, created and constructed to conceal the fact that the subject is nothing but an empty place, a simple effect of the signifier. "In short, the speaking being would prefer to show itself as that which it is not and as that which it has not, $(-\phi)$" (Bernard, 2005, p.7), that is, as being the imaginary phallus. It is a matter of the speaking being identifying itself with the "small fetish of the Other," of "veiling the castration of the mother as much as its own" (Bernard, 2005, p.6) and thereby presenting itself as something rather than nothing, as being rather than void, and significant rather than nonsensical. Shame, on the other hand:

> reveals the structural and egoist imposture of the subject, reveals its lie of being, and shatters the imaginary identifications by which these subjects want to reinforce itself, and thanks to which it wants parade. In sum, shame, and this could be its merit, is always the denunciation of the imposture of this phallicised and 'strong ego'. (Bernard, 2005, p.10)

As the imaginary identification with the phallus is destroyed, Bernard claims, shame is ontological by structure, because it affects the subject in its very existence, shattering its very *raison d'être*. What is the subject supposed to be if not the object of the Other's desire? And more disturbing still, not being this imagined object, why is the subject there at all; what possible justification does its existence hold? Being reduced to nothing, the speaking being, by still being all the same, suffers the shame "of being too much, which again is being less than nothing" (Bernard, 2005, p.11) – a waste, an excess.

> To put it otherwise, behind the image of the subject, there is not only its want-to-be, $, of which the phallus is the signifier, as Lacan would say, but also its being as *jouissance*, a, which – φ tempers or glosses. To put it otherwise again, there is masked behind the image of the subject its ontology, that is to say, what it is as subject of the signifier, $, but also what it is as subject of *jouissance*, that is, as body affected in its *jouissance*, a. In short, there is masked behind the image of the subject its being-there [*être-l(a)*], this excess body [...]. There is masked behind the image of the subject, which always lies a little, the ontological secret of the subject, that it is nothing, $, if not it [ç(a)]. (Bernard, 2005, p.15)

For Bernard, the concept of hontology designates that specifically human ontology accounting for Lacan's three orders of the speaking being in its relation to shame – the shame of its wanting-to-be or lack-in-being on the one hand and its being-too-much or excess-being on the other – as well as those faltering images that fail to keep it all together and covered up.

Returning to the Sylvia case from *Nightwood*, does it not present precisely the denunciation of a potent specular image? Does Sylvia not fancy the image of herself as the object of Robin's desire, and does shame not occur at the very instant this image is shattered for all to see when Robin does not even remember the young girl? And, being in this manner reduced to nothing, in her own eyes and certainly in those of Robin, does her very presence there not become questionable, if not outright excessive?[4] Furthermore, it is not only the actuality of the potent image that is shattered in this case, but also the potentiality of ever fulfilling the promise the image pretends

---

4   Although Sylvia is not there to satisfy the desire of Robin, she nonetheless satisfies a desire of Mrs. Petherbridge. The readers will know, as Mrs. Petherbridge has told the Baron and the Baron has, in turn, told the Doctor that the only reason for Sylvia to return after the holiday was due to Mrs. Petherbridge's desire to check, *per experimenta*, whether or not Robin had a heart. *QED*. Having performed her function in this regard, Sylvia is once again reduced to nothing.

to bear. It is not only that she is not, but also that she will never be the one to satisfy Robin that is revealed to Sylvia at this moment. In other words, although Sylvia may be the only one to lose face as it is revealed that she neither is nor has what she wants-to-be and wants-to-have, her own castration is not the only castration she comes to face. There is also the castration of Robin, who, despite many attempts to disregard the fact, is a mother herself. Marcus insists that the 'yes' of Joyce's Molly Bloom "is answered by Robin Vote's 'no' to marriage, 'no' to motherhood, 'no' to monogamous lesbianism" (Marcus, 1989, p.160). But in saying 'no' to these things, does Robin not present herself as a paradigmatic example of the desire of the mother in its errant character, always directed elsewhere, the unsatisfiable desire *par excellence*? Robin will never be satisfied, no matter how Sylvia portrays herself to her, but will forever go on seeking her satisfaction elsewhere.[5]

(H)ontology spelled properly

Unfortunately for Sylvia, she does not partake in the privilege of the Doctor's company and therefore cannot ask for his recommendations, as do both the Baron and Nora, when she is confronted with the empty truth behind her self-images. When Robin finds herself dissatisfied with fostering the future bloodlines of the Volkbein baronage or with shaping and partaking in the doll's house of Nora, her absence leaves the Baron and Nora at a loss and they turn to the Doctor and his oral remedies. Certainly, his endless monologues are of the essence in *Nightwood*. Already in his 1937 'Introduction' to the novel, T.S. Eliot

---

[5] As if to underline the insatiable desire of Robin, the Doctor himself makes reference to William Shakespeare's poem 'Who is Silvia' (in which Silvia is portrayed as the supreme object of desire and adored by all), but symptomatically misstates the title as 'Who is Sylvia' (Nightwood, p.164).

observed how "most of the time [the Doctor] is talking to drown the still small wailing and whining of humanity, to make more supportable its shame and less ignoble its misery" (Eliot, 1937, p.*xx*). The Doctor himself admits to being:

> the greatest liar this side of the moon, telling [his] story to people like you, to take the mortal agony out of their guts, and to stop them from rolling about, and drawing up their feet, and screaming, with their eyes staring over their knuckles with misery which they are trying to keep off, saying, 'Say something, Doctor, for the love of God!' (Barnes, 2006, p.144)

However, with every truth having the structure of fiction, there is no such thing as a simple lie. There is an ambiguity in the Doctor's recommendations, in his responses to his patient listeners and their experiences of loss and shame, in much the same way as there is an ambiguity in the possible understandings of the term 'hontology'.

There is another conception of hontology in addition to that of Bernard, in which the term is taken at its most depreciative and derogatory meaning, designating more or less the opposite of any proper or true human ontology. Instead of referring to the lack and excess of being behind a faltering specular image, hontology will now denote the exact opposite movement, namely the covering up of that lack and excess of being with a false image. Perhaps the difference is best grasped by pointing out that the pun in this last instance is not so much directed at joining shame with being, *la honte* with *tò ón*, but at linking it with *lógos*. It is no longer being as such that is shameful in and of itself, but the study or theory of it, the discourse on being, that ancient philosophical exercise known as ontology. Such is the reading indicated by Badiou in his seminar on the anti-philosophy of Lacan (Badiou, 2013, p.61). For Badiou, hontology is not so much a conceptual tool for the cure, but an insult directed at the philosophical endeavour of thinking being-*qua*-being, which is then considered as a shameful exercise, at least as performed in its Aristotelian tradition.[6] In short, ontology is a shame because it is a sham; it misconceives both its object and its own operation in purporting to grasp the meaning of being and the being of meaning. The Saussurean lesson as elaborated by Lacan, according to Badiou, argues that there is no "content of meaning in the order of being" (Badiou, 2013, p.61). Rather, "it is but by excluding being from the consideration of meaning as thinkable that it is ascertained that meaning is, effectively, scientifically thinkable" (Badiou, 2013, p.60). That is to say, meaning never simply is what it is or becomes what it should be, as an essence or inherent nature, but can only be thought as an effect of signifying matter, which is furthermore dependent upon the evacuation of being from its field for the said effect to occur. It is only in the hole, the split, the gap between signifiers, always two or more, that meaning is effectuated. Ontology fails to appreciate this fact, and, in pursuing the thesis of *the One is,* covers up the hole, the lack-in-being, at the heart of its own signifying operations with an imaginary representation or unary trait, presented as the real deal, instead of interrogating these very operations and their effects, in line with the thesis of *the One happens* [*yad'lun*] – where the One is not, unless it is the mark of an empty place, a void (Badiou, 2013, p.69-71).[7] Ontology is but chasing the ghosts of its own making without being able to acknowledge that this is what is going on, presenting them instead as being.

In his Seminar XX, *Encore*, Lacan addresses the correspondence between ontology and the master's discourse, seeing the latter as the one in the wake of which every dimension of being is produced, by means of a proffering of the signifier (Lacan, 1975, p.42-3). Cor-

---

6   See *e.g.* (Cassin, 2010, p.23): "From the perspective of [Aristotelian] philosophy, the meaning of a word, given in its definition, utters the essence of the thing, and that is why there can only be univocity: a 'man' is a man."
7   See (Lacan, 1999, p.5), translator's footnote 19, where Bruce Fink offers this as another possible translation of Lacan's statement *y a d'l'Un*, together with "there's such a thing as One" and "there's something like One."

related to his earlier statements on the relation of shame and being, this observation is enlightening with regard to "(h)ontology spelled properly at last" (Lacan, 2007, p.180), as he comments in his Seminar XVII, *L'Envers*. It concerns, Lacan explains, the subject's "being towards death, that is, the visiting card by which a signifier represents a subject for another signifier", but which "never arrives at the right destination, the reason being that for it to bear the address of death, the card has to be torn up" (Lacan, 2007, p.180).[8] In other words, it concerns precisely that which the formalization of the master's discourse spells out, namely the representation of the split subject ($) for another signifier (S2), through the master signifier (S1) in the position of a semblance, a make-believe of a potent and unified entity. In the master's discourse, there is a master signifier presumed to represent the subject as One, as whole, as undivided, as this ego being itself, this 'me being myself' [*m'être*] or what Badiou designates as the subjugation of an abject real by a sublimated semblance, under the mark of the One (Badiou, 2013, p.67). Such a representation remains dissatisfying, however, as the subject is not One, not whole, not undivided, not that specular image of the strong and potent ego, but is instead always too little and too much. Lacan tells us rather bluntly, in Seminar XIX, ...*ou pire*, that "ontology – that is to say the consideration of the subject as being – is a shame" (Lacan, 2011, p.116), in the sense that, if one aspires to get to the heart of the matter, one cannot speak *of* the Thing, which is what the master would venture to do. The key is instead to let the Thing itself do the talking [*moi, la vérité, je parle*]. Ontology is a shame, because one simply does not get to grips with being by way of talking about it. Instead, talking about it only leads to covering it up and concealing it under "a jungle of shadows and reflections," to borrow an expression by Jacques-Alain Miller (Miller, 2011, p.16).

---

8   See (Lacan, 1991, p.209).

Being and thinking are not the same, as Parmenides claims, but are instead the shame.[9]

There are two contradictory conceptions of hontology, as seen from within the field of philosophy proper, as with Badiou, or from a psychoanalytic perspective *stricto sensu*, as with Bernard, with the latter revealing what the former conceals. "Philosophy makes of being an essence, an absolute reality. Hontology evokes being, the Lacanian being, that of language," as Jean-Paul Clément puts it (2004, p.159). The psychoanalytic perspective demotes the specular image and reveals the lack and excess of speaking being, while philosophy proper promotes the specular image to maintain enshrouded the empty place it conceals. Bearing this ambiguity in mind, one might venture the thesis that Doctor O'Connor *hontologizes* over his patients and their loss. The Doctor is neither a common liar nor a simple soothsayer, for there is both a revealing and a concealing taking place. On the one hand, the Doctor's talks become a defence, as Eliot notes, against the shame in having to confront desire and its cause, a sort of veil against the void. On the other hand, the topic of his rants is often nothing but the destitution, the fundamental non-being of human being as such. But still the question remains for whose benefit these operations of concealment and revelation take place. Whose shame and being are hontologized by the Doctor's monologues? Eliot and the Doctor himself would answer 'humanity' or 'people like you', that is, Nora and the Baron, but as we shall see, there is more to the doctor-patient relationship than first meets the eye. There is shame in the Doctor's own sauce as well.

---

9 See the many references to and rephrasings of the Cartesian cogito by Lacan, notably in his *L'Instance de la lettre dans l'inconscient ou la raison depuis Freud*: "I am thinking where I am not, thus I am where I am not thinking" (1966, p.517).

The Doctor's solution...

In Chapter 5, 'Watchman, What of the Night?', during the scene that Marcus reads as a deconstructive parody of the analytic session, while intruding upon the Doctor in his attic abode, Nora entreats him with a very specific request, namely to tell her everything he knows of the night (p.86), that time and place in which Robin wanders out of reach of Nora, who knows nothing of the driving forces of her beloved. She soon rephrases her request into the question "What am I to do?" (p.91) – in order to regain her lost love's favour. The Baron also approaches the Doctor with an honest question: "What I particularly wanted to ask you was, why did she marry me? It has placed me in the dark for the rest of my life" (p.121). What are these questions but variants, addressed to a third party and therefore in the third person, of that famous *che vuoi?* of phantasy: What does she want of me? What am I to her?[10] In failing to answer of their own accord and thereby failing to maintain their specular image, as the Baron's choices of words often accentuate, they approach the Doctor, that theoretician of nightly sexuality and *sujet supposé savoir* of whom Lauretis and Cole have spoken, for him to provide them with the answers they seek and thereby reconstruct and re-buttress their broken ideals. In a more-or-less perfect imitation of the hysteric's discourse, Nora and the Baron address the Doctor as if he were a master, for him to bestow upon them the knowledge they lack, the truth as to what Robin wants and, consequently, what they themselves would be.[11] The

---

10 For the graph of desire and the *che vuoi?*, see Lacan's "Subversion du sujet et dialectique du désir dans l'inconscient freudien" (1966, p.815).

11 For the hysteric's discourse, see (Lacan, 1991, p.35 ff.). If Robin figures as the paradigm for the desire of the mother, she might well be said to function as the cause of desire (a) underpinning the divided, desiring subject ($), which is acting in the hysteric's discourse by addressing the figure of the master (S1), for him to produce the knowledge the subject lacks (S2). One might even elaborate upon how *Nightwood* distinguishes between the hysteric and the obsessive in differentiating the formulations of their questions. Nora might be said to be more concerned with her-

Doctor, for his part, does not refrain from parading in the guise of a master, however odd his impersonation, boasting that "the reason the doctor knows everything is because he's been everywhere at the wrong time" (p.89). He will respond to his patients' complaints as best he can, through a sort of *free association* filled to the brim with strange formulations and imagery intertwining the motives of death and desire, sexuality and sin, all mined from the labyrinthine depths of the many experiments and experiences of his own dysfunctional self.

With regard to the Baron's concern regarding his nuptial agreements with Robin, the Doctor explains the underlying motivations of the latter's marriage by way of a parable:

> Take the case of the horse who knew too much, [...] looking between the branches in the morning, cypress or hemlock. She was in mourning for something taken away from her in a bombardment in the war – by the way she stood, that something lay between her hooves – she stirred no branch, though her hide was a river of sorrow; she was damned to her hocks, where the grass came waving up softly. Her eyelashes were gray-black, like the eyelashes of a nigger, and at her buttocks' soft centre a pulse throbbing like a fiddle. (Barnes, 2006, p.121)

With regard to Nora, he informs her of "the peculiar polarity of times and times" of "Sleep the slain white bull," of "how the day and the night are related by their division" and how "twilight is a fabulous reconstruction of fear, fear bottom-out and wrong side up" (p.87), as a way of introduction to the metonymic movements of Robin, as she slips through the night from one pair of arms to another, ending in the knowledge of "what the world is about, knowing it's about nothing" (p.132). He has no qualms about preaching the fundamental

---

self not being like Robin or *vice versa*, that is, with the hysteric's question of *what a woman is* – while the Baron, left in the dark as to Robin's motivation – portrays the masculine position of the obsessive in his quest for *what a woman wants*.

division of human being between night and day, lust and law, with the added imperative to "think of the night the day long, and of the day the night through, or at some reprieve of the brain it will come upon you heavily" (p.90). In other words, he induces his patients to be "as the Frenchman, who puts a *sou* in the poorbox at night that he may have a penny to spend in the morning" (p.91), that is, to be attentive and appreciative of their fundamental division rather than ignoring it, in order to avoid the ailments of shame implied by everyday humanity.

To recapitulate, the Doctor, at the request of Nora and the Baron, expounds on their shame, its cause and consequences, on the lack and excess of being behind their faltering specular images. One can easily read the parody on analysis, as Marcus does, with the Doctor doing the talking, drawing upon his own experience and his own ego, to prop up those of his patients. The Doctor being an impotent transvestite, "the Old Woman who lives in the closet" (p.146), "the other woman that God forgot" (p.151), if not that unsexed doll, "the uninhabited angel" (p.157), one might also agree with Marcus that *Nightwood* favours the limp penis over the phallus, with the proviso, however, that the phallus in question would be the imaginary one, that image of potency, and not the one of symbolic castration. From the perspective of shame, the Doctor's disfavouring of the phallus cannot merely serve as the recuperation or restoration of a historical abject, the sexually aberrant misfit, as Marcus reads it, or as the outline of a "loss of access to history, to language, and to representation in general for those consigned to the margins of culture," as Victoria L. Smith argues (1999, p.194-5). Instead, the disintegration of the phallic image must serve as a token of the impotence and impossibility implied in human being *tout court*. If the Doctor privileges the limp penis, the Doctor himself is not privileged. On the contrary, the Doctor is as obliged by the imperative of Chapter 8, entitled 'Go Down, Matthew', and as inclined to shameful being as anyone else. As Badiou reminds us, there is but one humanity (1992, p.258).

... *dissolves the Doctor*

As Cole observes, despite the Doctor "taking pains to show how her narcissism is unhealthy," Nora nonetheless "proves recalcitrant to his advice" (Cole, 2006, p.400) and remains reluctant to accept her predicament, nor does the Baron seem to heed the moral paraded in the Doctor's parables. If they listen to him, they do not listen to his words, let alone act upon them. This should probably come as no surprise: To someone seeking consolation because of a broken ego, the affirmation of the omnipresence of division and the omnipotence of a pulse throbbing like a fiddle would hardly seem comforting, that someone would be hard put to re-buttress his or her self-esteem. Besides, hysterics are known to questioning their masters' knowledge. But their circumvention of the Doctor's advice raises the question anew as to what their motivation might be and what the function of the lie might be. Nora's very first words form the seemingly naive question of whether the Doctor is saying what he really means or "just talking" (p.21). Later she gives a clue as to which alternative she prefers, when she joins in the chorus urging him to "say something, oh, God, say something" (p.155). There is as much consolation and comfort in the mere soothing voice of the wine-soaked servant of medicine itself as there would be in any assisted conclusion as to the whys and wherefores of Robin, it seems. Without it being a matter of what the Doctor is talking about as long as he keeps talking, his words will keep the void at bay, concealing the empty hearts and fending off the worst of the impending shame, enamelling his listener's existence in that jungle of shadows and reflections gathered from his own selective herbarium. The Baron finds the Doctor "a great liar, but a valuable liar," reminiscent of Old Europe in the way of "a servant of defunct noble family, whose movements recall, though in a degraded form, those of a late master" (p.33), seeing in the Doctor simply what he wants to see, making the Doctor the perfect tool to keep propping up his noble illusions.

Cole argues further, against both Marcus and Smith and their recuperative readings, that the novel as such does side with the Doctor in his diagnosis – we are all fucked in wanting to be fucked – even if Nora and the Baron do not heed his advice (Cole, 2006, p.400). The fact that the novel tears the Doctor asunder towards the end of the penultimate chapter can be read as an all the more authoritative indication of how the Doctor is actually in the right, as it provides the hard empirical evidence of our all-impending doom. If his analysis is correct, it is all the more difficult to read his destruction as a recuperation of the historically abjected and marginal. But I find it just as hard to come upon any trace of actual celebration of loss or alterity's escape, as Cole does. Regardless, the Doctor's breakdown does have some bearing from the perspective of shame.

The breakdown comes creeping but culminates as Nora, by extolling her own conclusions of the mysteries and miseries of being, experienced at the "moment [she] stood in the centre of eroticism and death" (p.167), makes it clear that the Doctor has outplayed his doctoral or masterly function. At this point, the Baron has already left for Austria, content to live in his grandiose illusions but already shocked to have observed, even just for a split second, the Doctor's "unobserved self," "older than his fifty odd years would account for," moving "slowly as if he were dragging water," "as if in a melancholy that had no beginning or end" (p.117). That is to say, the image of the Doctor, as the immaculate and untouchable be-it-all and know-it-all, had already begun to falter. And then, as it becomes clear that Nora is able to conduct her own reasoning on "love and life" (p.167), the last layers fall from the Doctor's façade, and the formerly unstoppable well of words well-chosen finally goes silent, gets his hat and coat, and stumblingly leaves. In the safety of the *Café de la Mairie du VIe*, he exclaims, in a peerless peroration, both to the point and off the mark as to his own predicament:

> May they all be damned! The people in my life who have made my life miserable, coming to me to learn of degradation and the night. [...] God, take my hand and get me out of this great argument – the more you go against your nature, the more you will know of it – hear me, Heaven! I've done and been everything that I didn't want to be or do – Lord, put the light out – so I stand here, beaten up and mauled and weeping, knowing I am not what I thought I was, a good man doing wrong, but the wrong man doing nothing much, and I wouldn't be telling you about it if I weren't talking to myself. I talk too much because I have been made so miserable by what you are keeping hushed. (Barnes, 2006, p.171-2)

Certainly, his talking too much has been caused by the silence of others, and as he comes to realize that his soliloquies have, in the end, amounted to nothing, the image of himself as the good man, able to salvage his co-cosmopolites from the pain of their existences, disintegrates. They do not listen to him anyway.[12] But the question remains as to what their silence has been suppressing. It is more than possible that he has been mistaken in his auto-diagnosis. As an anonymous bystander observes, the Doctor is "a funny little man [...] Never stops talking – getting everybody into trouble by excusing them because he can't excuse himself – the Squatting Beast, coming out at night–" (p.172). In other words, the apologetic stance, which has served as his *leitmotif*, has not been primarily to the benefit of his embarrassed interlocutors, whether the Baron, Nora or another forlorn person, as it was intended, unless that listener were, in fact, the Doctor himself.

---

12   Whether Nora and the Baron actually do listen to the Doctor, whether they actually disregard his advice or come to some conclusion of their own or not, is debatable as there are some indications that the Baron at least has taken the Doctor's words into account, seeing that he is reported as feeling a certain embarrassment when bowing to the assumed "Grand Duke Alexander of Russia, cousin and brother-in-law of the late Czar Nicolas" (p.131) once he arrived in Austria. But the debate is less relevant from the perspective of shame with regard to the Doctor, all the while his function as doctor, as master, will have outplayed itself regardless.

Instead of saving his ill-befitted neighbours, as he thought he did, touching upon what they dared not touch and thereby illumining the dark truths of their dreams and desires, the Doctor's mad soliloquies have served but for his own salvation, in concealing his own desolate being and keeping his own shame at a distance.

At this point, one could of course argue that there is no shame at all in the Doctor, seeing how he unflinchingly reports his own unfortunate position, as that sexless doll or woman forgotten by God, uninhibitedly unveiling his limp if not lacking "Tiny O'Toole" to God and Earwicker alike on numerous occasions. But such an objection would fall prey to the essential or 'contential' mistake of traditional ontology and its endeavour to grasp the One in its being instead of its operations and effects. The issue here is not so much the Doctor's actual condition, his being sexless or not, as it is how this condition comes to be applied or appropriated by the one in question, the Doctor himself. It is perhaps paradoxical, as is the nature of the *pharmakon*, but it is nonetheless the Doctor's unfortunate predicament that has made him able to pose and posit himself in the image of Doctor-mighty-grain-of-salt-Dante-O'Connor, the master and know-it-all of the calamity called human being and, as such, has given meaning and consistency to his existence. It has been the idea of him being the unashamed, the flagrant and scandalous renegade Doctor, the one to dare venture where no man or woman ever went before, to the easement of all suffering masses, which has propped up his image and kept his real shame at bay. His torrential talk, even if mainly of his own wants, has covered up his own wants, his void and, by sustaining the image of himself as the universal scapegoat, he has believed himself to have escaped his own downfall. But when these illusions disintegrate, as they do, and he proves to be as impotent in his professional as in his purely physical matter, his real desolation becomes overwhelming, disastrous. Talking, which in the end is all he ever knew, will no longer suffice, meaning that there is nothing left for him, no reason and no justification for his being there. It is, as he observes, the end, which is wordless, "now *nothing, but wrath and weeping*" (p.175).

In conclusion

Having argued for the perspective of shame in reading *Nightwood*, I would like to end on a further prescription for a widening of this view by pointing out some occasions where the perspective of shame could cast light on the modern era in general. By drawing some lines to the already mentioned *Ulysses* of Joyce, I would like to present the hypothesis that shame, in the dual aspect of hontology, might be seen as foundational to the modernist project as such, even if the shame in question here might be a voluntary or even lauded shame. I have mentioned the disintegration of values, the crisis in culture and civilization brought about by the industrial revolution and its consequences for the question of subjectivity. In psychoanalytic terms, one could speak of the fall of the Father, that is to say *le nom-du-père, the primordial signifier* that structures and ensures a certain stability as far as one's meaning and being are concerned. The Baron's incessant quest for a noble ancestor is perhaps the most direct expression of the Father's retreat in the case of *Nightwood*, but the Doctor's sexual indeterminacy, Nora's disintegrating homes and Robin's errancy can be understood as no lesser implications thereof. In much the same way, *Ulysses* can be said to portray the fall of the Family, precipitated by the fall of the Father, Leopold Bloom himself. Neither Molly nor Stephen will play their roles of Mother and Son respectively in any more convincing a manner, the first equipped with a barren bosom and the latter denying the very concept of affiliation as such. One can debate to which degree shame is a defining issue for these two characters, but seeing how the fall of the Father, due to the structuring function of his name, will affect the stability of one's specular image and its significance, one could argue that the concept of hontology offers an interesting point of entry into the question of the disintegration of values, with regards to both its cause and how it is handled. The many and varying literary exceptions of the time could then be read, perhaps, as just so many attempts to come to terms with the lack and excess in being revealed behind the traditional images of men and women: The great interchanges with canonical works, of which *Ulysses* is but the paradigm, could be read as attempts to reach some remainder of truth, positive or negative, behind the veils of tradition's formerly potent images, while the bold experiments in form and content of the many -isms of modernist art could be seen as efforts to either have done with the traditional images and remove their last remnants or to construct new ones to cover up what the former concealed or, as perhaps the case would be with Dada, to tear down the old while violently overriding the void thereby revealed with noise. The point, at least in part, would be that the pioneers of the literary frontier at the time possessed a greater appreciation of the changes unfolding in the tumultuous world at the turn of the last century, exceeding the confines of the strictly Oedipal framework and, by their continuous questioning and challenging of the authoritative past and its presence, somehow prefigured the observation of Lacan half a century later – the observation that Doctor O'Connor cannot but personify in full – namely the observation that *the non-dupes err*.

References

Badiou, A. (1992). Qu'est-ce que l'amour? *Conditions*, Paris: Éditions du Seuil.

Badiou, A. (2013). *Le Séminaire, L'Antiphilosophie, Lacan*, Paris: Éditions du Seuil.

Barnes, D. (2006 [1936]). *Nightwood*. New York: New Directions Publishing.

Bernard, D. (2005). La Honte et la névrose. Presentation at *Le Forum du champ lacanien de Liège*, vol. 20, 2005. Retrieved from www.lacanw.be September 05, 2014,

Bradbury, M. & McFarlane, J. (1976). The Name and Nature of Modernism. In *Modernism. A Guide to European Literature 1890-1930*, London: Penguin Books.

Cassin, B. (2010). L'Ab-sens, ou Lacan de A à D. In *Il n'y a pas de rapport sexuel; deux leçons sur 'L'Étourdit' de Lacan* (avec Alain Badiou). Paris: Éditions du Seuil.

Clément, J.-P. (2004). Faire onte au sujet. *L'En-je lacanien*, vol. 1, no. 2, 2004. Retrieved from www.cairn.info/revue-l-en-je-lacanien-2004-1-page-149.htm September 05, 2014.

Cole, M. (2006). Backwards Ventriloquy: The Historical Uncanny in Barnes' *Nightwood*. *Twentieth Century Literature*, vol. 52, no. 4, 2006, Hofstra University.

Eliot, T. S. (2006). Introduction. In *Nightwood*. New York: New Directions Publishing.

Lacan, J. (1966). L'Instance de la lettre dans l'inconscient ou la raison depuis Freud. In *Écrits*. Paris: Éditions du Seuil.

Lacan, J. (1966). Subversion du sujet et dialectique du désir dans l'inconscient freudien. In *Écrits*. Paris: Éditions du Seuil.

Lacan, J. (1973). *Le Séminaire de Jacques Lacan, livre XI; Les quatre concepts fondamentaux de la psychanalyse* (1964). Ed. J.-A. Miller. Paris: Éditions du Seuil.

Lacan, J. (1975). *Le Séminaire de Jacques Lacan, livre XX: Encore* (1972-73). Ed. J.-A. Miller, Paris: Éditions du Seuil.

Lacan, J. (1991). *Le Séminaire de Jacques Lacan, livre XVII; L'Envers de la psychanalyse* (1969-70). Ed. J.-A. Miller. Paris: Éditions du Seuil.

Lacan, J. (1999). *The Seminar of Jacques Lacan, book XX; Encore, On Feminine Sexuality, The Limits of Love and Knowledge* (1972-73). Ed. J.-A. Miller, trans. Bruce Fink. New York: W. W. Norton & Co.

Lacan, J. (2007). *The Seminar of Jacques Lacan, book XVII; The Other Side of Psychoanalysis* (1969-70). Ed. J.-A. Miller, trans. Russell Grigg. New York: W. W. Norton & Co.

Lacan, J. (2011). *Le Séminaire de Jacques Lacan, livre XIX;...ou pire* (1971-72). Ed. J.-A. Miller. Paris: Éditions du Seuil.

Lauretis, T. de (2008). *Nightwood* and the 'Terror of Uncertain Signs'. *Critical Inquiry*, vol 34, no. 2, 2008, University of Chicago Press.

Marcus, J. (1989). Laughing at Leviticus: *Nightwood* as Woman's Epic Circus. *Cultural Critique*, no. 13, 1989, University of Minnesota Press.

Miller, J.-A. (2011). *L'Année 2011*, Cours no. 6, 09/03/2011. In *L'Orientation Lacanienne III*, 13. Retrieved from http://psicoanalisisdigital.wordpress.com/2012/05/23/lun-tout-seul-2010-2011-2/ September 05, 2014.

Selnes, G. (2010). *Det Fjerde Kontinentet; Essays om America og andre fremmede fenomener*. Bergen: Vigmostad & Bjørke.

Smith, V. L. (1999). A Story Beside(s) Itself; The Language of Loss in Djuna Barnes' *Nightwood*. PMLA, vol. 114, no. 2, 1999, Modern Language Association.

Wilson, M. (2011). No Place Like Home: *Nightwood*'s Unhoused Fictions. *Studies in the Novel*, vol. 43, no. 4, 2011, John Hopkins University Press.

10.
Sweet November: Desire and shame in the age of serial monogamy

Lars Nylander

In this paper, I will address some narrative strategies for avoiding shame that we find in modern literature and film. For this purpose, I have found it necessary to use the notion of shame in its most general sense, as an emotion (affect, state, condition) that is directly tied to socialisation and thus closely related to notions such as embarrassment, dishonour and humiliation. In contrast to guilt, which is situated in the relationship between the ego and the super ego, these emotions are situated in our relationship to the social other. Shame is thus directly tied to the normative moral codes of the culture into which we are socialised. To be ashamed is to respond to the demand: "Shame on You!" A refusal to respond to this, coming from a person belonging to the same culture, will be taken as a display of social dissent.

This social dimension of shame, the fact that shame only exists to the extent that it is communicated, makes it a somewhat tricky concept to employ in literary analyses. If it is easy to find literary characters who are ashamed, literature itself has no shame. Even when an author expresses shame about writing or publishing a literary work (such as August Strindberg's two forewords to his novel *En dåres bekännelser* [*Confessions of a Madman*]), the fact that the work is nonetheless published makes such admissions highly ambiguous, if not outright ironic.

In more indirect ways, however, shame has always played an important role in literature and film, for example in the way in which it offers the reader strategies to avoid shame. In romantic comedies, lewd topics have always been counteracted by being presented in a farcical manner and a language filled with *double entendres*, in which laughter is mobilised against shame. Moreover, literature and film have always reflected and thematised conflicts relating to ongoing changes of ethical norms. In this paper, I address some aspects of such strategies of shame in relation to the changes that have occurred over the past 50 years with respect to the ethical norms surrounding marriage and sexual relationships.

Sexuality and marriage

At the centre of all of the emancipatory ideals and projects that characterized Western cultures in the late 1960s was the critique of the so-called 'bourgeois family', the traditional nuclear family with its roots in nineteenth century culture. The effort to break up this institution marked the true awakening of changes that had begun stirring in the 1950s with the shift from industrial production to production for domestic markets and the increase of married women joining the labour force. Combined with other more gradual changes (such as women's increasing political and legal power), this spurred a redefinition of the status and function of marriage, the most direct effect of which was an increase in divorces, which continued well into the 1990s.

With the introduction of the contraceptive pill, this underlying change gave rise to the 1960s countercultures that carried out social experiments with new, communal family units, in which the collective rearing of children became a central theme. In the most radical versions of these communes, critiques of the nuclear family turned into critiques of monogamy as such, resulting in experimentation with promiscuous community living. If these experiments remained rare, they nonetheless became emblematic of a more general practice of collective family units, which lasted into the 1980s and in which sexually monogamous relations were placed within larger family units.

As these social experiments gradually lost their emancipatory energy, the traditional, nuclear family was not replaced with some new, normative form. Rather, marriage was reduced to one 'relationship' among others. These love and life relationships, with or without marriage certificates and children, then took their place within the larger social practice ice, which subsequently became known as serial monogamy.

Serial monogamy was, then, never proclaimed as an explicit ideal and cannot be understood as a normative form. It is, instead, a practice that has emerged in the absence of normative forms, the internal norms of which must be established by negotiation between the individual agents: a pragmatic process of trial and error, conflict and renegotiation.

One effect of this absence of any officially proclaimed and socially policed moral norms is that today the super ego injunction to *obey* seems to have been exhausted and replaced by an opposing injunction to *enjoy*. Shame has thus become a highly ambiguous phenomenon, more immediately decoded as an indication of individual eccentricity and personal history than adherence to some social law.

As the notion of serial monogamy implies, this practice could be understood as a pragmatic compromise between the ideal of marriage-for-love and the demand for individual self-realization in a consumer society in which we primarily define ourselves as consumers of lifestyles, pleasures and experiences and, on the other hand, the need for emotional and familial stability, especially for children, which is closely associated with the traditional norm of lifelong marriage. In a somewhat ironic fashion, the combination of 'serial' and 'monogamy' demonstrates the paradoxical nature of this practice, which could also be described as a form of 'poly-monogamy'. As such, one might argue that the most paradigmatic expression of this practice is the growing popularity, over the past 30 years, of the practice of 'swinging': couples who regularly visit clubs or private homes at which they can enjoy sex with multiple partners, a practice that is often defended as a means of reinforcing a relationship or marriage and making it more sustainable.

Literature in the age of serial monogamy

How, then, are the problems related to the practice of serial monogamy reflected by and thematized in contemporary literature? The best answer is to say that this is done indirectly. Contemporary romantic novels constantly thematize conflicts and problems of present-day romantic relationships, but the fundamental logic of serial monogamy is now so well established and naturalized that it is seldom reflected upon as a social practice. One reason for this may be that it is difficult to problematize this practice without implying some false, sentimental longing for the 'good old days' when people (especially women) were presumed to marry for life. Problems and conflicts that emerge within the logic of serial monogamy are thus generally understood in other terms, such as gender differences or problems associated with fidelity.

There is, however, a non-fiction genre of writing in which the problems surrounding the practice of serial monogamy are discussed more directly, and this is the growing field of psychological and 'self-help' books. If the most central topic in this multifaceted literature has been the need for practical and personal techniques to make a marriage last longer than its initial romantic infatuation, another central topic has been how to manage the transition from one partner to another, from a predecessor to a successor in the individual's lineage of relationships and partners.

In this transition, the ego is easily exposed to all of the ambivalent ethical issues surrounding modern romantic relationships, in which feelings of failure to live up to the contemporary ideal of independence and self-governance may intermingle with shameful feelings of promiscuity that belong to an older layer of ethical norms. Unsurprisingly, the transitions between love and life partners have often been exploited in contemporary versions of the sentimental romance. In contrast to traditional feminine novels and romances, which explored the heroine's problem of finding a (good, stable, lovable, wealthy) husband in a society in which her options were severely limited, the contemporary heroine's quest is very different. This is more concerned with how to evade or displace feelings of shame arising from too fast or too slow a transition between partners. Too rapid a shift between partners may appear promiscuous, needy or as a devalorization of the new partner's personality, all of which could be difficult to combine with the need to sanctify the relationship in the name of love. Too slow a shift between partners, however, may appear as if the person is clinging to the role of the victim.

One example of a recent break-up-and-start-again novel that is largely structured by this moral syndrome is Elizabeth Gilbert's highly successful *Eat, Pray, Love* from 2006. This is a first-person story of 31-year-old Elizabeth, a successful career woman and writer who for six years has lived in a marriage consisting of a husband and a big house. As the marriage approaches the stage at which it would seem 'proper' to have a child, Elizabeth panics; leaves her work, house and husband, has a brief affair with a younger man and then understands that she does not need a new man. What she needs is to venture out in search of a new Self (or, as it is formulated on the cover of the book, a "search for everything").

Before giving us this background story, the novel opens *in medias res*, with a chapter in which our heroine faces the first moral challenge of her newly begun quest for everything, for "worldly enjoyment and divine transcendence" (2006, p.30). Her dilemma concerns an attractive young Italian by the name of Giovanni, whom she meets in Rome and from whom she is taking private language classes. Her moral crossroads is formulated as follows: Should she or should she not invite the charming Giovanni up to her room? She solves this dilemma with the following asserting of independence:

> "I have finally arrived at that age where a woman starts to question whether the wisest way to get over the loss of one beautiful brown-eyed young man is indeed to promptly invite another one into her bed?" Reaffirming her decision to spend one whole year in celibacy, she abstains from inviting Giovanni up to her room but returns alone to indulge in her "care of Self," her "newfound adventure of spiritual discipline." (Gilbert, 2006, p.25)

She then travels farther, first to India and then to Bali, where on a previous journalistic assignment she had met a man who now becomes her spiritual guide. Eventually, as she is rejuvenated and finds (or is found by) a suitable successor in her lineage of relationships, she has blocked her own erotic desires so successfully that her spiritual master must convince her that love is not an enemy of spirituality.

Fundamentally, then, Gilbert's novel is a story about a transition between partners, in which the initial breakup throws the protagonist into a life crisis, and she must transform herself before she is properly prepared to accept and enjoy a new partner in life and in love. But this is not the way in which the narrator herself describes her quest. She would find it insulting to suggest that her year of spiritual rebirth may be motivated by a need to cleanse herself of her earlier partner in preparation for finding a new one. In other words, this would turn her quest into something shameful. The desire that fuels her diary-like conversations with the reader is a desire to make her quest solely a search for a new self. This is a quest that, for reasons that remain unclear, precludes any romantic relationship.

Elizabeth could perhaps have achieved this transition of self as well as of romantic partner with much less spiritual discipline and self-enforced celibacy if she had come across a small article that recently appeared in a Norwegian tabloid paper. It announced the happy news that "People who find a new partner swiftly after a breakup are happier and more self-confident than those who take their time to mourn" (Svennes Bergland and Johansen 2014; my translation).[1] This 'discovery' is the result of an American study, which was then confirmed by a Norwegian relationship therapist, who states that "A month is a good guideline for how long you ought to mourn. After that, the body is normally ready for new impulses. [...] And when the body is ready to move on, so is the brain." (Svennes Bergland and Johansen 2014).[2] But such happy physiological and cognitive news would, of course, be difficult to turn into a bestselling novel.

If the topic of switching marriage partners has been commonplace in sentimental novels and films. over the past 20 years, including novels labelled 'chic-lit', which may include Gilbert's novel, it is somewhat more difficult to find genuine comedies on the topic. By genuine comedy, I mean a comedy in the classic sense of the term, in which all sentimental, psychological melodrama is countered by a plot and simplified character types that present an underlying fable concerning conflicts between Eros and social law. One successful example of this could be Mike Newell's *Four Weddings and a Funeral*. Another, more interesting, and today seemingly forgotten, example from the period in which serial monogamy was just starting to emerge as a standard practice is the American film *Sweet November* from 1968, directed by Robert Ellis Miller and written (originally as a stage comedy) by Herman Raucher. With its clever mixture of farce, melodramatic romance and a plot in which marriage is turned into a pragmatic form of self-managing therapy, the film stands out as a unique and entertaining commentary on the practice of serial monogamy. It thus deserves a closer reading.

---

1 "Personer som får seg ny partner raskt etter et brudd er lykkligere og mer selvsikre enn de som tar seg god tid til å sørge."
2 "En måned er en god tommelfingerregel på hvor lenge du bør sørge. Etter det er kroppen som regel klar for nye impulser. [... Og] når kroppen er klar til å gå videre, er også hjernen det."

Sweet November: serial monogamy in full speed

Where Gilbert's novel uses the protagonist's spiritual journey to de-centre the underlying theme and practice of serial monogamy, Miller's film *Sweet November* places it at the forefront, both by making it the central theme of the film and by structuring the plot between *two* transitions of partners. It is thus not a story about a protagonist's journey from one relationship to another but about one love story between two others. Here, the rejuvenation of the self does not occur between relationships but within them. The film starts with the meeting between Charles (Anthony Newly) and Sara (Sandy Dennis), as Sara is just about to end her relationship with a man she calls 'her October'. The day after this man has left her life and apartment, Charles moves in to become Sara's November man. The film ends with Charles' departure as Sara welcomes his successor, Mr. December. The fact that the film adopts Charles' perspective means that it offers an external view of Sara and the curious way in which she has formalised her need for serial monogamy.

The transition from Mr. October to Mr. November

When we first meet Charles, he is a slightly whimsical bachelor in his mid-thirties, who devotes his time to running a company that was left to him by his father, and which produces cardboard boxes. One day, he accidentally runs into the eccentric Sara, who at first mainly annoys him, but who then starts to question him about his life. As she hears that he devotes his life to the production of ordinary, six-sided cardboard boxes, she senses that Charles is a man who needs to be emancipated from himself. "Suppose someone came along and started to produce seven-sided boxes for the same price as six. What would happen then?" Her interest in him, together with her eccentric charm (and perhaps her matter-of-fact attitude, completely lacking self-irony and shame, which thwarts all of his efforts to hide behind irony) stirs his interest in her.

Sara invites him to see a flat that she's trying to sublet and, during this meeting, he learns that she is renting eight apartments, of which she sublets seven for a slightly higher rate. She also makes money as a "handy-man," taking on all of the repairs that need to be done in these apartments. Charles quickly becomes fascinated by her, and when he asks her out on a date, she accepts on the condition that "it can't be anything romantic."

After dinner, Sara brings Charles back to her apartment for a cup of tea. He is then introduced to an elderly, fatherly friend of Sara, Alonzo, who lives close by, as well as a whimsical man named Richard, who comes rushing into her apartment, demanding that she let him stay for longer than the month they have lived together. However, Sara firmly hands Richard his trunk with clothes and a clay figurine that he has apparently been working on during their time together, and she makes him leave.

Sara then explains to Charles that she has developed a special therapy for men "with special problems," after which she turns to him and states: "You have problems." When he asks what these are, she says that she is not quite certain, but it has something to do with his obsession with time, "your busy-busy-ding-dong," a phrase she coined earlier as a comment on his constant occupation with his wristwatch alarm, which keeps him updated with all of his business meetings. She asks what he dreamt of doing when he was younger and, after failing to avoid the question by means of silly, ironic remarks, he confesses that he liked writing poetry. But then, he declares, he left behind all such childish dreams and "became a man" – something Sara immediately corrects as: "You became a box."

She then presents her proposal: "I think you're worth saving. Would you like to be my November? To move in with me, write me poems, and leave when December comes?" He immediately accepts, in spite of the fact that the proposal implies that he must take a month's leave from his work and become her assistant caretaker. So, come midnight 31st October, Charles arrives with a trunk of clothes, which Sara immediately finds unsuitable for him, and he agrees to let her help him put together a new wardrobe. After this, they get into bed and start their one month of therapeutic, marriage-like relationship.

Charles' sweet November

On the second day, Charles discovers that Sara has left open a filing cabinet that she has previously shown him and in which she keeps records of all her one-month 'husbands'. He takes out the most recent file, which is on him, and read her first entry: "First night was, as expected, nothing unusual." When he complaints about this later in the day, she immediately takes the role of therapist and explains that the rules of their arrangement include that all complaints and discussions that might lead to a quarrel are forbidden. Instead, both should write down their thoughts and eventual criticisms of each other on a daily basis, after which they can read one another's comments and think about them. But they should not start any debates. Their November should be sweet, not quarrelsome.

They shop for more comfortable and less businesslike clothing for Charles, a change of style that he accepts and seems to enjoy. In this, as in many other respects, he gladly lets Sara take the role of a maternal wife.

After a couple of weeks, Charles has fallen deeply in love with Sara and follows all of her suggestions as to how he should renew his life and his self. But he has also started to worry about having to leave her. He tries to argue against this, at one point he even tries to manipulate the wall calendar in order to prolong his time with her, but Sara sticks to their agreement.

We also encounter another of Sara's former men, Clem, whom Sara warmly welcomes as an old friend. He tells Charlie that, during his month with her, his creative therapy was painting. He also announces to them that he is to be married. Sara is very happy for him and invites him and his bride-to-be to their Thanksgiving dinner. We and Charles thus come to see the kind of happy result that Sara seeks to achieve with her therapeutic love months.

Later, in bed, as Charles formally declares his love for her, she happily comments: "I really think you mean it! We're making great strides." She then shifts into a more melancholic mood and tries to explain how her love therapy is also intended for herself: "People must be remembered. Otherwise, it's as if they were not here at all. All we are is the ones who remember us."

As the meaning of Sara's words becomes clearer in a later scene, the film starts to shift to a more melodramatic mood. Charles has sought out Alonzo and urges him to tell him more about Sara. He has discovered that she keeps a large cabinet of medicine and suspects that she is seriously ill and that this is the reason for her strange monthly romantic relationships. Alonzo confirms his suspicions: "Sara... she's *temporary*, hasn't got much time [...] Now you understand why every month is like a year to her, and no man is allowed to stay longer. Not out of desire, but out of fear." When Charles asks what disease she suffers from, he reluctantly answers: "I have it written down somewhere. It's very rare, very incurable. It doesn't much matter what it's called." And when he complains that he cannot bear to lose her, Alonzo clarifies: "You can't lose what you really don't have; you can only borrow Sara. She has her own road to go. You just happened to cross it in November." If he really loves her, the best thing, according to Alonzo, is to do precisely what she wants.

In a subsequent scene, this psychological rationalisation of Sara's personality and conduct is confirmed in a dialogue between Alonzo and Sara. They discuss Charlie as a special "patient" to whom she has become strongly attached, and Alonzo suggests that this could be an opportunity for her to break her love therapy and venture into a lifelong relationship with him. But she stands firm: "I love him, Alonzo.

And because I do, I don't want him around when it comes. I don't want him to be part of *that*."

In this way, the light and at times farcical mode that dominates the first part of the film and the first weeks of their month gradually takes on a more melancholic tone, a change that accompanies and clouds Charles' personal change into a more emancipated, mature, self-confident and poetic man. His desire to make November last forever becomes an obsession and, as the time comes for their Thanksgiving dinner with Clem, his fiancée and Alonzo, Charles disappears, leaving only a present in the form of a seven-sided cardboard box. After the guests have gone, however, Charles returns to perform a kind of Broadway show for Sara, reciting his poem 'Sweet November' and giving her presents, including a bundle of 'thousand' pages of torn-out November almanac months, seeking to convince her to concede to his dream of making November last forever.

The transition from Mr. November to Mr. December

In terms of plot, the ending of the film becomes a direct repetition of the beginning. But the mood has now changed, so as Charles drags out his departure, he is still present when Mr. December nervously arrives with a trunk and a slightly clownish appearance. This brilliantly condenses the film's emotional register as the farcical mood of Mr. December clashes with the melodramatic mood of Charles' departure. When Charles eventually turns to walk away from Sara, he tries to live up to his emancipated status as a poet by whispering, as he holds her turned away from him and the door: "Don't turn around; I'd turn into salt," conflating the roles of Orpheus and Eurydice.

After Charles has left, Sara takes some time to subdue her grief, following which she turns to his successor with the words: "You know, I think December will be a very lovely month."

Playmate of the month

As the title indicates, the film is an ironic twist on the convention of 'calendar girls' and *Playboy*'s 'playmate of the month'. By changing this male fantasy of promiscuity into Sara's therapeutic romantic relationships and performing the story in a combination of farce, sweet romance and psychological melodrama, the film becomes a sympathetic commentary on the emerging convention of serial monogamy.

The sexual dimension of Sara's relationships is downplayed. On two occasions, on Charlie's arrival and in the scene in which he declares his love for her, we see them slip into bed together, but in line with the established convention of American film at the time, the scene fades out as soon as they embrace. But Sara's comment on and to Charlie about their first night together as "nothing unusual" and his reaction to this make us suspect that sexual enjoyment may, in fact, be of high priority in Sara's therapeutic program. Now and then, some of the comments from their conversation appear as voiceovers, but none of them concern sexual matters. Still, the fact that Sara's first entry concerned this topic indicates that it continues to play an important role, although always, of course, combined with sweet love. Her relationships are absolutely monogamous.

Her usage of the terms "clinical" and "therapeutic" should then be taken in the widest possible sense as including everything that enhances her and her partners' happiness and wellbeing. When Sarah tells Alonzo that she has found a man who will be her December, and he objects to this since he wants her to hold onto Charles, she hushes him with the words: "He is just someone to keep me company, purely clinically." Her program for fast-forwarded serial monogamy is as much motivated by her need to mourn one man in the arms of another as it is to leave life with a large number of happy, self-confident men, who will always remember her as the women whose love healed their "special problems."

Lastly, some ambiguities regarding Sara's illness remain. The manner in which Alonzo speaks of it make us suspect that it mainly served as a way for him to replace the shame of her monogamous promiscuity with a more sombre motivation. As if searching for the right words, he says: "She's ... *temporary*, hasn't got much time" and then clarifies that she does not want any man to stay long, "not out or desire, but out of fear." But what illness is this? "I have it written down somewhere. It's very rare, very incurable. It doesn't much matter what it's called." This opens our ears to an ironic understanding: Could the name of the terminal condition from which Sara suffers simply be life, the state of being alive, which is indeed 'terminal'? Similarly, when Alonzo says that Sara's imminent death makes every month seem like a year for her, he is of course using a figure of speech. But as always in figurative language, we can also hear the literal meaning, which in this case indicates that Sara's relationships, if she were completely healthy, would last about one year instead of one month. Even by today's standards, this pushes the notion of serial monogamy a bit too far. (Alonzo's words are also 'corrected' on the DVD cover, which presents the film thus: "For 30 days they lived the love of a lifetime").

There are other ironies in the dialogue, which similarly highlight the contradictions between plot and discourse and between the two moods of farce and melodrama. These are used to reveal and conceal the importance of Sara's sexual desire in her philanthropic program of fast-forwarded serial monogamy. The film thus illustrates how a character's fundamentally shameful conduct can be counteracted by opposing techniques and moods, offering the spectator a phantasy of promiscuous enjoyment while softening its shamefulness through the use of charmingly 'innocent' characters and a soothing melodramatic story.

Care of self

I have here used Gilbert's novel and Raucher's film as two opposing strategies for dealing with the social practice of serial monogamy. Whereas Raucher's film uses the generic techniques of comedy to create a comically enhanced version that highlights the underlying logics and problems of this practice, Gilbert's novel uses a thoroughly 'politically correct' first-person narrative of personal growth in order to decenter the underlying logic of modern romantic relationships and to give the story a happy ending, as is the convention for romances. (The thought that, six years down the line, Elizabeth's new marriage might suffer the same fate as her first does not seem to exist on her horizon.) By describing this as politically correct, I do not imply some laissez-faire attitude but instead something like a presupposed middle-class norm, an intimate agreement between narrator and reader that is inscribed in the style and modality of the discourse.

One example of this is the quote I gave above, in which Elizabeth ponders what to do with Giovanni. Another example could be the opening of Chapter 19: "Here's what's strange, though. I haven't been able to do any Yoga since getting to Rome" (Gilbert, 2006, p.58). This slightly chatty, conversational tone presupposes an intimate agreement that effaces the more problematic questions concerning the relationship between love and personal fulfillment in contemporary culture.

In spite of the many differences between this novel and Raucher's film, there remains one aspect in which they are in complete agreement. It is that – in contrast to the older ethical principles that guarded the institution of lifelong marriage by insisting (especially on the part of the wife) that care of self should be motivated by and put into the service of care of relationship – it is now care of relationship that is motivated by and put into the service of care of self. And therein lies the rub in our contemporary practice of serial monogamy.

References

Gilbert, E. (2006). *Eat, Pray, Love*. London: Bloomsbury.

Miller, R.E. (director) and Raucher, H. (author) (1968). *Sweet November*. DVD. Warner Brothers Archive Collection.

Svennes Bergland, C., and Johansen, L. (2014). Ny forskning om kjærlighetssorg: Slik kommer du raskest over bruddet. *Verdens Gang*, 26th marts, 2014.

11.
To write with the arsehole: Abject voices in contemporary literature

Lone Elmstedt Bild

"Write with the asshole, this is a piece of advice to a friend"
(Rasmussen, 2019, p. 8)

This strange invitation is presented in the Danish novel The Skin Is the Elastic Covering That Encases the Entire Body (transl. 2019, orig. *Huden er det elastiske hylster der omgiver hele kroppen*, 2011) by Bjørn Rasmussen.[1] The same idea can be found, albeit only implicitly, in the German novel *Wetlands* from 2009 (orig. *Feuchtgebiete*, 2008) by Charlotte Roche.[2]

This article examines two different ways in which the abject emerges in these two contemporary novels. It argues that the difference between them can be understood as a consequence of two different subject positions.

---

1   Bjørn Rasmussen, born 1983, was educated at The Danish National School of Playwrights and at The Danish Writers' School. *The Skin is the Elastic Cover Encasing the Whole Body* was his debut novel.
2   Charlotte Roche, born 1978, was born in England but has lived in Germany since the age of eight. In addition to being an author, she is a television presenter. *Wetlands* was her debut novel and was the world's best-selling novel on Amazon in March 2008.

According to psychoanalyst and linguist Julia Kristeva (1982), the abject is an ontological state of being between subject and object, which can be both psychological and physical. Physical examples of the abject include bodily wastes such as blood, sweat, urine, pus, sperm, faeces and dismembered body parts; i.e. things that come from the body but are no longer part of it. The abject is thus neither fully of oneself (subject) nor fully something else (object).

In developmental psychology, abjection is the earliest phase in which the infant is about to separate from the mother, but in which the boundaries between child and mother are still tentative and fragile. The child rejects the mother, yet the two of them are not fully separated. This separation is associated with ambivalence, and there is a great risk of relapse into the symbiosis of the mother: "It is a violent, clumsy breaking away, with the constant risk of falling back under the sway of power as securing as it is stifling" (Kristeva, 1982, p.13). The infant wavers between separation from and fusion with the mother. The infant's "strategy" is therefore repetition; to repeatedly reject the mother until the boundary between infant and mother becomes more stable (Kristeva, 1982, p.10). With what in Lacanian terminology is called "castration", the infant enters "the symbolic order". The symbolic order is the linguistic and social norms, language and rules that construct the order and structure in a given culture (Lacan, 1977). The symbolic order establishes the infant as a subject, the mother as "another"; the abject borderline states and phenomena are ignored or pushed out of sight. The subject thus exists at the expense of the abject, which is alienated and excluded (Kristeva, 1982). Kristeva writes: "The clean and proper (in the sense of incorporated and incorporable) becomes filthy, the sought-after turns into the banished, fascination into shame" (1982, p. 8).

For the infant, abjection is thus a borderline state on its way to the infant becoming a "subject". For the castrated subject, on the other hand, the state of abjection is associated with shame, pain, disgust and anxiety. Approximation to this state emphasizes the subject's fragility and instability: "We may call it a border; abjection is above all ambiguity" (Kristeva, 1982, p.9). In the state of abjection, the subject is about to collapse and therefore constantly demarcating its borders (Kristeva, 1982, p. 8).

This article seeks to investigate the characteristics and structure of the abject as it appears in the two aforementioned novels. The two novels were selected because both have been regarded as shameless and obscene by some readers, exposing the most intimate and shameful aspects of the body. As we will see in the following, however, both novels use the abject voice to examine the identity challenges facing the modern subject. Where *Wetlands* challenges the aestheticized female ideal, but seems to affirm another female ideal, namely the neoliberal demand 'to enjoy', The Skin Is the Elastic Covering That Encases the Entire Body attempts to find a means of coping with unstable and problematized identity categories.

To be nothing

The Skin Is the Elastic Covering That Encases the Entire Body (2019) (abbrev. *The Skin*) is a story about Bjørn's troubled development from adolescent to adult. The opening describes an encounter between the grown-up Bjørn and his riding instructor and lover from his youth. This encounter gives rise to a stream of non-chronological and lyrical reflections, fantasies, memories and flashbacks to his childhood. Through a nonlinear, associative, intertextual and auto-fictional text, *The Skin* describes an unstable, ambivalent and self-destructive subject, who sometimes seems to be held together only by his skin.

Quotations from famous texts, such as *The Lover* by Margerite Duras and *The Little Prince* by Antoine de Saint-Exupéry is woven into the text. The novel is furthermore autofictional, i.e. there are details indicating a mix between fiction and the author's own memories.[3] These literary techniques provide an impression of a subject who is influenced by pre-existing cultural products, but not in a static or fixed way. Instead, the subject can be infinitely varied, modified, and adjusted without finding a stable or authentic identity. "The story of my life doesn't exist" (2019, p.9), the text states and the novel ends with an open "and", which is not followed by a full stop. The text seems to describe the ambivalent feelings of being placed into the boundaries of the symbolic order. As the text itself puts it:

> Having to be someone can be rather a depleting form of conceit. It's an immensely tiresome project, trying to rid oneself of everything one is not, as in: attach vacuum to solar plexus, locate and perform removal of foreign bodies in own body, be with you in a sec. (Rasmussen, 2019, p.38)

Bjørn hesitates to take on any of the identity categories provided by his culture: homosexual, man, manipulative, hysterical, cutter, etc. Bjørn can be anything – or nothing. Or maybe he just doesn't fit into the existing categories. As it says: "I'm lying in a cocoon. I just have to find a way to get out" (Rasmussen, 2019, p.16).

Bjørn harms himself; he pounds his head against the wall, pull out hairs from his head, hits and cuts himself. This can be understood as a desperate attempt to open "the cocoon: "I have thoughts about cutting my face, so that people can see that I'm just as ugly on the outside as I feel inside" (Rasmussen, 2019, p.61). Figuratively, the text ca be understood, as an opening of the skin which exposes his insides. However, to do this is also associated with ambivalence, since the skin is what upholds the border to his surroundings. To cut his skin is

---

[3] The main character and the author have the same name and the same hometown. Moreover, there are two pictures in the middle of the book that apparently show the author/main character and his horse/the horse in the novel as well as a score sheet from a dressage contest on which the names of the author and his horse appear.

therefore also to destroy the one thing that keeps him together and the inside of the cocoon is chaotic, vague, and undetermined:

> The frequencies of the car radio merge with my teeming thoughts, and I realize there's no difference. I'm an open shell, amenable to whatever. I'm the potholes in the gravel road, the hole for the gasoline in the car; I keep getting filled; it's a momentous discovery. (Rasmussen 2019, p.18)

Bjørn thus seems to fill the position of the abject. He is constantly in between being something and nothing (fusing with his surroundings), and he describes the existential shame of this abject position: "I'm just a bagful of bacteria myself, nothing else" (Rasmussen, 2019, p.20). Or: "Someone should put a bolt through my head, like they do with pigs, and horses too. No one will ever feel happy with me" (Rasmussen, 2019, p.26).

Bjørn struggles to find a bearable way to exist with his chaotic, fragile, and ambivalent mind. The novel can be read as an attempt to construct a story of his life in his own way. He examines other ways of creating coherence or integrity, for instance through the body:

> There's a document saved on my computer, its name is: Bjørn has a body. I use it to keep a catalogue of my body's ingestions and excretions; crispbread, avocado, black tea, urine. I note down my bodily business; enema, tooth brushing, beard trimming. I strive to archive the facts – there's nothing at all romantic about it, the idea is simply to carve a template. (Rasmussen, 2019, p.68)

This "body diary" is a means for Bjørn of defining himself as something besides the possibilities of language. The text constantly refers to the body as a kind of reference point or scaffolding, corresponding to what Kristeva says about the abject position: "Instead of sounding himself as to his 'being', he does so concerning his place: 'Where am I?' instead of 'Who am I?'" (Kristeva, 1982, p. 8).

The relationship to the riding instructor can also be read as an attempt to stabilize Bjørn's fluid subjectivity, e.g. by means of a contract providing instructions for the sexual relationship, which could be seen as a kind of replacement for the norms and rules of the symbolic order: "You don't shower without my permission, you don't give me gifts or pay me compliments, no flowers or wine, do as I say" (Rasmussen, 2019, p.14).

Another way in which Bjørn deals with the position of being abject is to fantasize about becoming an everlasting consumer object. He has a dream of this transformation in which his body becomes a product, which can be sold on the free market. This makes Bjørn almost happy:

> When Bjørn received his first paycheck at the end of the month, his wounds were healed, the fatiguing sound in his eyes was gone, and he had put on considerable mass thanks to the gym next door to the brothel. His mind had erased the Mother and his Brothers, the horses and the hounds, he remembered absolutely nothing of the rigors he had gone through on the journey toward this, his adult life. He performed his good deeds for the day and earned himself a shitload of dough. Indeed, one might be tempted to suggest that he was now happy. (Rasmussen, 2019, p.38)

Being object is in some way a relief compared to being abject. To be object is an imaginary condition pointing back to the mirror stage in which the child discovers his image in the mirror; The whole and undivided image appears at the expense of the inner fragmented and chaotic sensations. Bjørn becomes an omnipotent, everlasting, and immortal rent boy. He is pure, uncastrated body.

Through this exposure of a deeply unstable and self-doubting subject, the text gives the abject self a voice. "Write with the asshole" is what it suggests (Rasmussen, 2019, p.8), and Bjørn begins to write the day the veterinarian comes to inseminate his mare. First, the veterinarian digs out a large handful of excrement. Figuratively, these large handfuls of formless, mouldable excrement from inside the horse's body become associated with the text coming from inside of Bjørn. It is in this light that the invitation to "write with the asshole" should be understood. The anus is both genderless and one of the most intimate and shameful bodily organs. However, writing with it does not seem to be an invitation to shamelessness; instead, it involves exposing the unidentifiable and the obscure, thereby giving a voice to the alienated and the excluded. This is what the novel does: It describes the state of abjection in appropriately ambivalent, uncomfortable, frustrating, and fascinating terms, thereby seeking a means of being an 'I' in a reality of weak and problematic identity categories.

Shamelessness as resistance

"As far back as I can remember, I've had haemorrhoids." This is the opening sentence of *Wetlands*. The protagonist, 18-year-old Helen Memel, is confined to a hospital bed because of an anal lesion after an intimate shaving incident. From a first-person narrator perspective, the text takes the reader through descriptions of "ass shaving," homemade tampons, the mother's intimate hygiene and various sexual experiences. "Let it all out, that's my motto – otherwise you'll get cancer," Helen declares (Roche, 2009, p.162).

Some readers have regarded the novel as a liberating feminist manifesto, while others have seen it as pure porn. The text examines and discloses all the most intimate and private aspects of Helen's body. "I learned that from dad. To try to figure things out so thoroughly it makes you puke" (Roche, 2009, p.76). However, this is probably not what her engineer father had in mind. The object of Helen's examination is not a bridge or a machine but her body and its secretions.

In an almost infantile way Helen's sexuality binds her attention to her body. When she attempts to divert her attention to the world around her, it does not last long: "I want to look out the window.

Can't see anything. There's nothing out there. Just me and my room reflected in the glass" (Roche, 2009, p.223).

Is this a modern version of Narcissus falling in love with himself upon discovering his image in the water? Unlike Narcissus though, Helen is repelled by her image: "I don't look good. Not that I ever do. But I really look bad now" (Roche, 2009, p.223). Even though Helen is self-obsessed, she is no Narcissus. She is not the idealised and aestheticized image of a woman. She is a flesh and blood person with blackheads and greasy hair.

When Helen was a little girl, her mother made her believe that she never went to the bathroom but "held everything inside until it disintegrated" (Roche, 2009, p.72). This has made Helen embarrassed of her needs: "As if crapping is a crime" (Roche, 2009, p.73). However, this barrier is well and truly transgressed in the hospital. Helen makes a nurse take close pictures of her anus after the operation:

> It shows a photo of a bloody hole. The flash has cast light deep inside. My ass is wide open. There's nothing to suggest the closure of a sphincter (...) I'm appalled at my own asshole – or rather what's left of it. More hole than ass. (...) You can look right in. (Roche, 2009, p.42)

There is an obvious connection between this exposure of the anus and the novel's exposure of Helen's body, pleasures, and enjoyments. The reader can look right into Helen's most intimate secrets: There is no "sphincter."

Displaying the abject can seem shameless. Kristeva writes:

> The abject is perverse because it neither gives up nor assumes a prohibition, a rule, or a law; but turns them aside, misleads, corrupts; uses them, takes advantage of them, the better to deny them. (Kristeva, 1982, p.24)

When Helen shows the pictures of her to Dr Notz, who operated her, he seems disgusted, almost angry: "I see panic in his eyes: Help! My little operating room asshole can speak, ask questions. It's even taken photos of itself" (Roche, 2009, p.65).

The insistence of the shameless honesty in the novel could be an attempt to resist the standards of female beauty and hygiene presented in commercials and by Hollywood. The text challenges the female type that Helen calls "doctors' daughters": the well-groomed women who get their hair, nails, lips, feet, faces, skin and hands coloured, lengthened, painted, peeled, plucked, shaved and anointed (Roche, 2009, p.105). These women are according to Helen too prudish to follow their impulses and pleasures: "What these women don't know: the more effort they put into these little details, the more uptight they seem" (Roche, 2009, p.105). The text here then appears to represent a liberatory project, challenging the standards of the woman and take the enjoyment of the body to the extreme.

The question is whether the text through the transgression instead ends up with affirming another pre-existing ideal. Jacques-Alain Miller points out in his article *On Shame*, that the gaze of the other in the neoliberal society no longer induces shame. The subject is not prohibited from but is permitted to consume or to be consumed: to enjoy (Miller, 2006, pp.15). In fact, the text seems to take on this neoliberal demand "to enjoy".

Voices of the arseholes

The injunction "write with the asshole" presented in the novels explicit or implicit, could be an invitation to give the abject position a voice, through which the novels demonstrate some of the challenges the modern subject faces today.

In *Wetlands*, the abject voice is motivated by anger and spite against the narrow, aestheticized female ideal. Using the abject, the text point to the women ideals in the late modern society and emphasizes the unaesthetic and sexually driven aspects of the woman.

Thereby it challenges the narrow, aestheticized female ideal. However, the novel exposes this enjoyment and takes it to – and beyond – the extreme. The text thus seems to describe the radical consequences of adherence to the demand "to enjoy".

In contrast, *The Skin* is written with suffering and distress. It portrays an extremely fragile and unstable subject, who wavers between being something and being nothing. The text describes the shame of this uncertain, unstable, and self-doubting subject. Through a weakened symbolic order and an approximation to the abject, it examines and articulates new ways of being in the late modern society.

References

Kristeva, J. (1982). *Powers of horror: An essay on abjection*. Translation by L. S. Roudiez. New York: Columbia University Press.

Lacan, Jacques (1977): The four fundamental concepts of psychoanalysis, translated by Alan Sheridan in The Seminar XI, New York: W.W. Norton &Co.

Miller, J.-A. (2006). On shame. Translation by Russell Grigg. In J. Clemens and R. Grigg (ed.), *Jacques Lacan and the Other Side of Psychoanalysis*. Durham and London: Duke University Press.

Rasmussen, B. (2019). The Skin Is the Elastic Covering That Encases the Entire Body (2019). Translation of *Huden er det elastiske hylster der omgiver hele kroppen* (2011) by Martin Aitken. San Francisco: Two Lines Press.

Roche, C. (2009). *Wetlands*. Translation of *Feuchtgebiete* (2008). London: Forth Estate.

12.
Shame in Hassan's and Llambías' poetry

René Rasmussen

Shame seems to have found a new place in literature, at least if we look at Yahya Hassan's and Pablo Llambías' poems, which form the main focus of this article. But before looking more closely at shame in some of these poems, it is necessary to understand shame as something that is distinct from guilt and anxiety. Moreover, it is necessary to sketch out some of the historical reasons for this new position outside of literature. Yet, the poetry of Hassan and Llambías is very interesting in such a historical context because it expresses different versions of a shameless shame grounded in the poets' respective subjectivities and their poetry's auto-fictional form.

Hassan (1995-2020) was a young man, who was beaten, who beat others and who was threatened. His hatred of his father and Islam go hand-in-hand, but in 2103, aged just 18, he managed to write one of the bestselling Danish poetry collections (*Yahya Hassan*) ever. Since the book criticizes Islam, it led to him receiving a number of threats and to attacks being attempted against him. This is why he surrounded himself with bodyguards from PET (police intelligence service) and wore a bulletproof vest. His criticism of Islam has, however, made him a darling of Denmark's populist political party (Danish People's Party).

Hassan was a child of the urban environment, but he was first and foremost a child of the late-1980s generation of misfit war survivors from Lebanon, as the war between the Israelis and the Palestinians during the late 1980s and early 1990s sent refugees with Palestinian roots from Lebanon to Denmark. Second- and third-generation immigrants in this context grow up in a society in which everyone speaks Arabic at home, in the courtyards between the blocks of flats and in the mosque, while the children learn Danish language and Danish history at school. When they come home in the afternoon, however, they are met with the sound of Quran radio from the Middle East and parents, who, since their arrival in Denmark, have succeeded in creating a parallel society in which the local imam's demands and prohibitions matter.

Llambías (born 1964) is the son of a Danish mother and an Argentinean father. He has presented readings and participated in a variety of literary arrangements across Denmark. He has published a number of books, mostly novels, but his most recent three publications consist of sonnets (two of which are discussed below). From 2009 to 2105, he was the head of *Forfatterskolen* (The Writers' School) in Denmark.

Llambias' main character in these sonnets assumes a shameless shame, as indicated in the words: "I have cheated my way to / love, cheated my way to sex" (Llambias, 2013a, p. 105; my translation of all the citations form Llambias).[1] In contrast, the shame in Hassan's poetry is projected onto the main character's father, whereby the son seems to escape this shame, although the son's jouissance is evident, as seen here: "WITH MY MOUTH I SEEK MY COCK / STOOPED AS THE CRIPPLE I AM / WHEN I SEEK MY COCK WITH MY MOUTH" (Hassan, 2013, p.138; my translation of all the citations from Hassan).[2] Even the projection is projected and has become unknown to the son, who can thereby avoid the shadow of shame that covers his father and his enjoyment. The message is: It is not me, but the other

---

[1] "Jeg får tiltusket mig / kærlighed, jeg får tiltusket mig sex."
[2] "MED MIN MUND JEG SØGER MIN PIK / KRUMBØJET SOM DEN KRØBLING JEG ER / NÅR JEG SØGER MIN PIK MED MIN MUND."

(my father), who is to blame, though I, too, exploit violent patterns of enjoyment. This also absolves him of any kind of guilt. The two writers thus represent two important ways of handling shame and enjoyment in today's world.

The relationship between guilt and shame can scarcely be understood without considering anxiety, which appears everywhere in today's neoliberal society, apparently eliminating shame and thus rendering us shameless. In today's world, shame is abolished, and the character of shame is altered, one result of which is that anxiety enters the subject. Shame at enjoying something (a previously ill-regarded phenomenon) has, however, been replaced by shame at being unable to enjoy enough. Previously, enjoyment was connected to shame and the Other (think of Puritan dresses that completely covered women's bodies), while today, enjoyment has become shameless (think of the TV show *Paradise Hotel*, in which young men and women are more-or-less naked). Puritanism has been replaced by a regime of demands and permissions, in which the very prohibition (of enjoyment) has become forbidden (cf. Miller, 2006, p. 12). Nudity is therefore no longer a shame provoker, but a must, at least on reality TV, where it is no longer the Other who watches, but we, the TV viewers, who gaze and are watchful.[3]

Shame at not enjoying enough results in anxiety since the subject succumbs to the infinite enjoyment that is demanded of it. The *shameless* shame – to express it paradoxically – leads the subject to anxiety because the subject can never enjoy enough, according to today's norms of consumerism and enjoyment.

But it is also possible to understand this shameless shame as the release of a somewhat different factor. The issue is no longer shame

---

3 Miller makes an essential distinction here, distinguishing the Other, who judges the subject with regards to shame, from a former Other, who sees shame (cf. Miller, op. cit. 13). It is this former version of the Other who previously saw the subject's nudity and whose gaze provoked shame, while it is the latter Other who judges it today.

of enjoying but of not enjoying enough. When the subject temporarily cannot fulfil the norms of enjoying, the subject is left behind. Shame previously emerged on account of the body and its enjoyment, when these were exposed to a given other or to the Other, hereby reducing the subject to social waste, to a miserable object, to an abject, alone with its enjoyment. The subject's existence depends on the artificial objects of enjoyment that are being offered. If it cannot enjoy as much as is demanded, it not only experiences shame, but its existence also becomes worthless because this existence depends on its ability to enjoy and consume. The shame of enjoying too little is combined with the shame of existing.

The neoliberal shameless version of shame thus leads to a shame caused by not enjoying enough, anxiety caused by not enjoying sufficiently, or shame of existing because enjoyment can no longer be separated from the subject's existence. Another reason for considering anxiety is that, from a psychoanalytic perspective, both shame and anxiety are affects. Shame is an affect that concern the subject's body, just as anxiety is an affect that concerns the body outside of language.

Guilt or bad conscience, however, concern the subject's language. The subject experiences a bad conscience when, for example, an action leads to something unpleasant even though he or she does not really want this to be the result. Alternatively, he or she experiences a bad conscience when he or she is plagued by thoughts or ideas of something he or she wants to do, and yet refrains from doing. This kind of bad conscience can, for example, rely on the constrained subject that imagines it will accidently poison the food it cooks for its family every evening, even though there is no poison in the house. Furthermore, there is an Other who judges the subject. What is essential here is that the subject is plagued by a bad conscience arising from a desire or wish that is articulated through language, even though this desire or wish has an unconscious source, which the Other condemns. Shame and anxiety therefore predominantly concern enjoyment and the body, while a bad conscience pertains to language, the subject's position in language, and the signifiers it uses in its own way in language, namely the subject's desire. The difference between these two can also be described in another way: Guilt requires an excuse and a (symbolic) debt to be paid, whereas shame lacks these aspects.

The Other plays an important role in anxiety and shame. Jacques Lacan connects anxiety to Sigmund Freud's involvement with Otto Rank's idea of birth anxiety, here meaning the anxiety the baby experiences when it is born (cf. Lacan, 2004, p. 378). Birth anxiety is often understood as a separation anxiety, the anxiety of being separated from one's mother – an anxiety that stays with the subject until later in life, but Lacan points out that, in fact, it concerns something completely different. Birth anxiety is not about one's separation from one's mother, but about meeting an entirely 'Other' universe: It is about helplessness in a completely Other universe with which the subject is confronted at birth, in which it cannot orient itself and which it cannot understand by way of language (which the subject does not yet master). So, it is not the separation from, but the impossibility of being separated from, the Other or from the Other universe that is the cause of this anxiety.

Here is another example: You are about to drown in a river, and the water begins rising over your head. You are helpless and caught in the Other's universe from which you cannot escape. This is an example from physical reality, but in psychological reality the relationship is the same: In anxiety, the subject cannot be separated from the Other, but instead experiences being reduced to an object, object *a* as Lacan designates it. The paranoid subject experiences, for example, that it is being pursued by cars and that someone wants to kill it. The paranoid subject cannot escape the evil Other. It even knows that this is true but does not understand why. The subject is the object of this threatening Other's enjoyment: $ is reduced to *a*.

Regarding shame, affect relies on a different mechanism. If we look at the classic kind of shame in which the subject, for example, believes it is worthy of doing something brave – in which the subject believes it is the sublime object or seeks to incarnate the image of the sublime object: $i'(a)$. Here, the gaze plays an important role since this sublime object is seen by the Other, but if the image cracks, the Other will fail to appreciate it, and this is when shame appears. We can, for example, imagine a woman in Elizabethan times, she is beautifully dressed and walking across the floor at a court ball when something rips open her dress. Scandal and shame. Or imagine a male member of parliament on his way to address the assembly, when his trousers suddenly drop. Both cases would involve shame because of the gaze, the awareness of being observed by the Other. The subject not only knows it is being looked at, but also knows that the Other's gaze sees that it is being seen and that it is seen as an abject at the moment of shame.

The subject goes from $i'(a)$ to a, which is an abject: $i'(a) \rightarrow a$. The subject falls in front of the Other's gaze from, for example, a sublime position to the position of waste, and it exits the world stage. As abject, the subject is expelled from the world stage. That is what is meant by the expression 'to die of shame': To die of shame means that the subject no longer has a position on the world stage but is expelled and maybe even chooses to leave it for good. For example: A university professor is exposed for having committed plagiarism, is forced to withdraw her dissertation and apparently, he has no further reaction, for ex. shame. Another university professor speaks out, if he had been caught in a similar situation, he would have committed suicide (left the world stage).

In the classic kind of shame, a reduction from $i'(a)$ to a take s place, but the mechanism is somewhat different in our day and age. Now, object a, the object of enjoyment, is at the top of the agenda. There is no reduction from the sublime position to the status of waste, but the subject is more-or-less identical with the objects of enjoyment it has to enjoy. This concerns the consumer mechanism that is linked to enjoyment, to all objects of enjoyment that are imposed on us to today. Just think of all of the gadgets we are compelled to purchase. The problem with consumption of these gadgets or other consumer objects is that not only is the subject supposed to consume them, but the subject consumes, even devours, itself in the process of consuming the gadgets. When this occurs, the subject surrenders itself to the rhythm and drive of the consumption of such objects and neglects its desire and place in language. In this context, the subject consumes itself. Its identity also depends on an object *a* giving it identity and as well as its being alone in its devouring – without a partner. The subject thereby becomes an object a without another: $ \$ \rightarrow a $. Its very existence is reduced to an object outside of its position in language, to a miserable object or an abject.

"Shall I be condemned as human" – about Llambías' sonnets

In the following, I will consider shame and anxiety in *Sex Rouge*, which, like many other publications today with an auto-fictional character, attempts to subvert the common ideas that we do not accept mistakes and flaws in the subject.[4] I, however, intend to point out these mistakes and flaws. One sonnet in *Sex Rouge* expresses it in the following manner:

In my autobiography the subject is

divided, impossible to unite, inconsis-
tent. It is impossible to tell a
coherent story about the subject.
It is like light. It only lets itself be read
partially. It does not submit to ownership.
(Llambías, 2013b, p.194)[5]

---

4 Cf. for example, Asta Olivia Nordenhof: *Det nemme og det ensomme*, Bjørn Rasmussen: *Huden er det elastiske hylster der omgiver hele legemet* and Christel Winblad: *49 forelskelser.*
5 My translation of all the citations from Llamías.

I will, however, take leave of the question of auto-fiction and the divided subject and instead concentrate on the particularity of the subject's shame and anxiety.

Sex Rouge is, like Llambías' two previous sonnet collections, *Monte Lema* and *Hundstein*, the name of a mountain. The first-person narrator apparently has many similarities with the writer and narrates his life following the publication of his two earlier volumes: In the beginning of the book, he still takes medication against anxiety and often feels unhappy. Perhaps he is (as he says) psychotic and unable to cope with all of the demands he experiences, and he continues to worry about the damage done by writing and publishing these personal sonnets. At the same time, in many of his texts, he reflects upon who actually knows the truth about one's life and the extent to which texts can be honest. The first-person narrator does not believe that one can say whether a text is honest, only that the story of his life as it is expressed in the sonnets is just one of many possible versions. He also says that texts cannot be regarded as authentic:

> It does not make the text authentic, that
> inside of the reader's head arise ideas
> of authenticity. That says nothing
> about the author either. (...)
> The publications have insight in neither
> one direction nor the other.
> (Llambías, 2013b, p.335)

The text thus expresses that texts cannot be authentic, but since it is a text that claims texts cannot be authentic, this is a paradoxical statement that denies itself. Expression is authentic, however, guaranteeing that the text's sentence, at the level of what is enunciated, is inauthentic. Maybe this lack of authenticity can explain why the book consists of sonnets, given that sonnets are not normally read as autobiographical material.

This is an exceptional sonnet collection even though it only consists of sonnets of 14 verse lines within three stanzas (4, 4 and 6 lines, respectively). These verses predominantly contain breaks on the lines determined by the number of syllables per verse. It may to some extent be called a kind of 'broken' prose put into the structure of a sonnet, the topic often being everyday activity. As it says in *Hundstein*: "I break the prose down through / the shape of a sonnet" (2013a, p.118). The narrator also writes that his sonnets are not poems. They are barely literature, or, as he says in *Sex Rouge*: "The lyric shape // is a tool that allows me / to write within a certain frame, which in advance / has a fixed duration and length. It / makes me feel safe" (2013b, p. 294). These are not, however, poems with a specific lyrical appearance, in which particular compositions of words constitute the essential material. The frames are what is important and also what makes the narrator feel safe. As it says in *Hundstein*: "I must get through anxiety / to the other side. Yes, / I write, I think it is a good / idea. That is what the idea is behind / these sonnets. The therapeutic / in it. Not particularly literarily correct" (2013a, p.109).

The kind of shame that seems most obvious in *Sex Rouge* is the classic kind of shame in which the subject cannot live up to its own ideal of *i(a)* but feels reduced to waste. This is, for example, shown here:

> I am ashamed of my
> work. I am ashamed of my book.
> I am ashamed of this sonnet.
> I am ashamed of being unable to do more,
> of not being better. I am so deeply ashamed
> of myself, as one on the whole can be
> ashamed. I wish I were not forced
> to live in this body with this
> miserable soul. With this miserable soul.
> (Llambias, 2013b, p.27)

We see here how the narrator feels sad, feels in possession of a miserable soul, which makes him feel like an abject. Shame denies his existence (in language) and desire. The same goes for anxiety: "The shame of being anxious / shines out of me. Shines out of me" (2013b, p.53). Although there is no Other who fixes the subject with a gaze that reduces it to an object, we see shame combined with a self-condemnation or with the Other's judgment (cf. Miller's distinction between the two versions of the Other).

The neoliberal shame of existing is also present. It is present, for example, in *Hundstein*: "I am ashamed of being me" (2013a, p.125) and in *Sex Rouge*: "You are not worth loving. / You are worth nothing. You are poor. You / are the poorest in the world. You are shit" (2013b, p.206). Here, we do not see a subject before the Other's gaze being exposed in the midst of his villainous enjoyment; instead, we see a subject that feels inherently unworthy of existence even though judgement of this miserable existence is also delivered to the Other. However, as it says elsewhere, the subject judges himself a bad person: "Shall I be condemned as / human. Yes. Shall I be condemned as / a writer. Yes. I am a bad person" (2013b, p.309). Such a judgement can hardly be separated from the sense of guilt and the Other's judgement. Nor can shame can be disconnected from the idea of authenticity, though the text uses this idea in a slightly different way. Perhaps a text is inauthentic, a least on the level of that which is expressed, but in terms of this version of shame, a subject that is inauthentic, that has given up its desire, is struck by shame.

The shame of enjoying too little, the other version of neoliberal shame, is also expressed by the subject in his relationships with a series of younger women, approximately 20 years younger than himself. He is not ashamed of his relationships with these women, but of becoming old and looking old, as is expressed in the following sonnet from *Sex Rouge*:

> I have seen pictures of one of my ex-
> girlfriends on the internet. I am surprised
> by how old she looks. She also looks
> chubby, not to say flabby.
> (...) ... It
> is disgusting to become old.
> (Llambias, 2013b, p.161)

He is ashamed of enjoying himself too little with these young women, who are also meant to keep him young and forever joyful. In vain, he desperately seeks to capture youth through:

> young girlfriends, youthful sport and a
> stubborn insistence on being able to do
> everything that I had been doing so far, among these
> partying all the way dancing and with an un-
> conditional intake of alcohol. I mirror
> my own collapse in the collapse of the West, in
> the world's climate changes.
> I mirror my own anxiety in all that
> is anxious out there.
> (Llaambias, 2013b, p.293)

The excessive enjoyment leads to anxiety and makes the subject see himself reflected in all that is anxious in the world.

This also appears indirectly in a comparison with Jørgen Leth, who has likewise had relationships with very young women.[6] The subject in Llambías' sonnets has problems regarding his relationships with younger women while Jørgen Leth does not have such problems. But it is not the relationships as such that constitute the real problem; instead, the problem is that he cannot live with himself and feels

---

6   Jørgen Leth is a well-known Danish writer and journalist.

condemned by the Other: "I am being condemned / not because of abuse of women but because of being a pa- / thetic, pitiful, unworthy self-hater. / This is my final cross" (2013b, p.182). So, the actual relationships to these women are less problematic than the sense of guilt over being unable to accept them. The sonnet also shows the shame the narrator feels at being who he really is.

It is a bit difficult to determine the reason for the subject's anxiety. Perhaps it is caused by a psychosis, although this explanation is partly denied in *Sex Rouge* since an alternative explanation for the subject's suffering insists on him having the mind of an artist. But if we look at the psychotic version, anxiety is said to be connected to a kind of paranoia (mentioned many times in the poems), which can explain why the subject is always concerned about what others might think of him or what they want from him. This appears in a sonnet in *Hundstein*:

> ... anxiety
> of being fired because of anxiety
> of not being good enough. All this will
> happen. And I will get all those enemies that I,
> in all of my paranoia, fear to get.
> (Llambias, 2013a, p.150)

These enemies are constantly capable attacking the subject, and this may explain his paranoid imagination.

To sum up with respect to *Sex Rouge* (and *Hundstein*): The subject feels himself in constant conflict with what other people might think of him and he fears that the others (or the Other) are his enemy. There is a clearly paranoid element connected to this fear, albeit without making it possible to claim that the subject in the text is as such paranoid (even if this is what he says about himself). The question is, of course, whether one can use the term 'paranoid' about a fictional character, but apart from this, there is barely enough material in the two sonnet collections to conclude that the subject is paranoid. Nevertheless, it is clear that anxiety is associated with what the Other thinks or wants to do to the subject. It is correlated with a form of shame, which also has a shameless side: Enjoying too little, being unable to enjoy himself enough with all these young women without being ashamed of his limited enjoyment with them. The idea of enjoying too little echoes our time's demand for consumption, in which the subject is forced to enjoy more and more, with the result that its place in language and its desire disappear.

The shameless shame furthermore correlates to the shame of existing, with the subject's idea of being alive and the shame of just existing. It is a neoliberal shame, in which enjoyment as such is no longer shameful and in which exposure of the abject behind the ideal picture, behind $i(a)$, is no longer central. On the contrary, this is a shame connected to the experience of being reduced to a self-destructive being, which – together with other objects (mostly younger women and alcohol) that are being used and constantly consumed in *Sex Rouge* – is an image of the subject. The subject is an object, turns itself into an object in its obeying the demands of consumerism. The anxiety that strikes the subject should thus be related not only to a possible form of paranoia but also to this reduction of the subject to an object that devours itself. The shame of existence is a shame of desire, which goes further than any immediate satisfaction of enjoyment. The shame of desire, which cannot be satisfied, represents an accusation directed at the desire, but the subject, which gives up its desire and surrenders itself to enjoyment, is as a consequence struck by anxiety. The shameless shame represents just such a capitulation, and this explains the intimate relationship between shame and anxiety.

The absence of shame – about Hassan: Yahya Hassan

Shame and guilt look different in relation to Hassan: *Yahya Hassan* has mainly a narrative form and a first-person narrator (the main character). Guilt is barely perceptible in the narrator. In contrast, shame – or rather its apparent absence – corresponds to the father's position. The father is violent and hypocritical: He shows tenderness and love while at the mosque (Hassan, 2013, p.13), but is extremely aggressive (just like his son, the main character) at home and everywhere else.

If a father has a socially defined role, it is by virtue of the laws and rules set by the social field. In this manner, a father does not grant authority to the social area but gains authority from it. A father gains authority from the social area that Lacan calls the symbolic, which is essentially determined by two prohibitions: 1) You must not kill, and 2) you must not commit incest. These prohibitions are to be understood literally and in a general context, such as: We must not subject our children or anyone else to violence or sexual assault. However, in Hassan's poems, these kinds of assaults are presented all of the time, including violent actions committed by the father and the main character as well as degrading treatment of women, whether the father's wives or the narrator's sexual partners.

The single subject is kept within the bounds of the symbolic and the hitherto combined prohibitions by various social rules, which vary across countries and cultures, for example regarding age of consent and homosexual behaviour. Desire likewise keeps the single subject within the bounds of the symbolic. Desire is articulated indirectly through language, always bringing us forward, on to something different, onward to something new. Desire constitutes a protection against enjoyment (read: suffering) in violence and sexual assault. In accordance with this understanding, the law supports desire while seeking to regulate enjoyment.

In Hassan's book, enjoyment is central, and desire is overruled most of the time. For the main character, desire is limited to writing poems, while sexual enjoyment, violence, drugs and crime are central, and the father apparently has no desire apart from his religious faith. The father constitutes a version of what Freud in his myths calls a primordial father, who seems to have the right to infinite enjoyment, which not only includes having several wives but also the pleasure of being violent:

> HE SAID THE HANDS OR THE FEET
> AND BROKE OFF A WOODEN SLAT FROM THE BED
> (...)
> THE SCREAMS OF MY SIBLINGS FROM THE ROOM NEXT DOOR
> DROWNED MY OWN
>
> (Hassan, 2013, p.17)
>
> THE NIGHT BEFORE WE WERE SENT INTO THE LIVING ROOM
> THE DOOR TO THE BEDROOM WAS CLOSED
> SOUNDS BEHIND THE DOOR AND A PEEK THROUGH THE KEYHOLE
> MOTHER WITH A WIRE AROUND HER NECK
> I TORE THE DOOR OPEN, AND HE TOOK OF HIS BELT
> I HAD ALREADY BEEN TOLD TO STAY IN THE LIVING ROOM
>
> (Hassan, 2013, p.25)

This father emerges as a violent version of Freud's primordial father, but from my perspective, it is equally important that the father (and not the son) appears to be the one who should be ashamed of his behaviour. It is not the subject but the Other (the father) who has a shameful way of being and behaving. The son's own enjoyment is unproblematic, but the father's is not.

Freud saw the ideal father in relation to the Oedipal complex to the extent that Oedipus realised what the symbolic excludes: incest and killing the father. The Oedipal complex's father is, in contrast, the one who must prevent negligence of the Oedipal law. The father must thus manage to separate his sons (and daughters) from their origins, the maternal body, and the enjoyment that is attached to it. Freud connected the Oedipal complex to neurosis since the subject, who suffers from the psychosis, never really separates from his or her mother and often experiences his or her father as an overwhelming and threatening figure – a bit like Hassan's father. To Freud, neurosis was the right reaction even though neurosis also included suffering. Neurosis was, like the Oedipal complex was to Freud, an ideal while psychosis was something distinct from this ideal.

However, as Lacan has emphasised, this accentuation of the ideal father in the Oedipal complex is a mistake. This so-called ideal father is not a necessity in terms of separation from the mother's enjoyment. Actually, there does not need to be any father at all to assure such a separation. It is sufficient that the mother refers to something outside of herself to ensure the symbolic and the prohibition against incest. Even in cases in which separation never really occurs, as in psychosis, other phenomena can temporarily assure separation. The separation from an original enjoyment connected to the mother, an enjoyment that seemed unlimited, can thus be ensured in a number of other ways in the subject's life.

Certain psychotic subjects sustain their desire through submission to art, including being a writer, maintaining a religious faith or participating in social movements or special activities. Such activities ensure a distance to infinite enjoyment that is meant to have existed since the start of one's time with the mother, even though the idea of such infinite enjoyment is, of course, only an illusion. Such activities can offer an alternative to motherly enjoyment and therefore they represent the Name of the Father which is a symbolic position not necessarily connected to a specific or idealised father, but simply to a symbolic alternative to the mother fixation. Infinite enjoyment is a fantasy, although this is the fantasy we are being offered today, with the father's symbolic position, the Name of the Father, having been more or less suspended.

The father-son relationship in Hassan's *Yahya Hassan* reminds us of Oedipus' relationship to his father, but with the essential difference that Oedipus does not know that he kills his father and marries his own mother. Although Oedipus reacts with spectacular guilt and he tears out his eyes when he realises what he has done, he also reacts with shame and condemns himself to exile. The main character in Hassan's work does not have a sexual relationship with his mother, but nor does he avoid enjoyment of or fascination with women, as his hypocritical father says he must. It is not just because he has seen through the hypocrisy dominating his father's universe; it is also because the Name of the Father does not work for him. The threats he makes against his father, which suggest patricide, are also essentially different from Oedipus' reaction, since he feels neither shame nor guilt:

> I SAID NEXT TIME YOU TOUCH MY SIBLINGS
> I WILL BURN YOUR CAR
> I COULD BEAT HIM IF I wanted to
> A COUPLE ON THE HEAD TILL HE LAY DOWN
> STAMP ON HIM AGAIN AND AGAIN
> STAMP HIM TO DEATH
> HE WAS DEFENCELESS AGAINST THE PERSON
> HE HAD BROUGHT TO LIFE
> (Hassan, 2013, p.97)

The narrator has no shame or guilt. He instead heaps guilt upon his father when the father enjoys something that he himself does not. The father (the Other) is the place where shame is located (cf. David Bernard's description of shame in *Lacan et la honte. De la honte à l'hontologie*; Bernard, 2011, p.238). He implements what Oedipus sought so strenuously to avoid: a violent revolt against his father and a search for infinite enjoyment. He does not have an Oedipus complex. Freud rightly connects the Oedipus complex with neurosis, but no such neurosis is present in the poems. What we find instead is a kind of free-flowing paranoia, as the main character also states on several occasions (cf. 2013, p.118 & p.128). This paranoia can perhaps explain why shame is projected onto the father.

In contrast to what we see in Llambías, Hassan's main character has no shame, neither the shameless shame nor the shame of existing. From the son's perspective, however, the father's enjoyment is shameful even though the son does not refrain from enjoyment himself. It is not the son but the father who is to be ashamed or who appears as a shameful person.

Conclusion

Both Hassan's and Llambías' books claim to be written in the genre known as auto-fiction. Auto-fiction constitutes a special deconstruction of autobiography, since autobiography is a veritable representation of a larger or smaller portion of a life story – which is expected to be referentially correct. Auto-fiction is, instead, a fictional representation of a possible life story, often fragmented, as is the case in Hassan's and Llambías' books. Because it emphasises the fictional elements, auto-fiction differs not only from autobiography as a special literary genre, but also from other forms of 'autobiography' that we present in everyday life: in job applications, at the job centre and so on. The difference between our public lives and private lives are more-or-less suspended in these autobiographical presentations or performances. What was private has become public, especially because we ourselves – in accordance with neoliberal ideology – are responsible for our work and school lives. If you do not have a job, it is your own fault. If you do not have an education, it is because you are weak. It is not due to circumstances of the labour market, the crisis of capitalism or an ever-more disciplined and unidirectional school system.

This ideology individualises us, paradoxically claiming that everything can be measured by means of general standards taken from so many tests, evaluations, notes, questionnaires, etc. The logic of capital is paradoxical because it, on the one hand, understands our behaviour in accordance with quantitative norms and measures, yet, on the other hand, it states that we are masters in our own house. If we are not master in our own house, we must become so through various kinds of therapy – for example, coaching and cognitive therapy – and related techniques that make it possible for us to understand ourselves.

Privatisation of publicity and publication of the private have caused the dissolution, or at least radical transformation, of the family, as is evident in the two books we have considered. Just as auto-fiction breaks away from the idea of transparency that underlies the privatisation of publicity, these books represent places without transparency, no matter how close they are to the writers' lives. This also means that the cause of shame and guilt can be exposed in a way that emphasises the connection between capital logic, consumerism and different kinds of enjoyment.

Whereas Llambías' narrator provisionally assumes and presents his anxiety, the shame in Hassan's text is projected onto the Other (the father), who represents the bad kind of enjoyment, the kind that is shameful in a traditional sense. Whereas Llambías assumes shameless shame and anxiety, the shame in Hassan's poetry is projected onto the father, whereby the son escapes shame. Even this projection is projected and has become unknown to him, allowing the narrator to manoeuvre in the shadow of shame that falls upon his father's enjoyment. The subject does not have shameless enjoyment, but the other does. I am good; the other is not: This is the secret message of this projection. Guilt is not an issue here, though we still encounter it in Llambías.

References

Bernard, D. (2011), *Lacan et la honte. De la honte à l'hontologie*. Paris: Éditions du Champ lacanien.
Hassan, Y. (2013). *Yahya Hassan*. Copenhagen: Gyldendal.
Lacan, J. (2004). *L'angoisse*. Paris: Seuil.
Llambías, p. (2013a): *Hundstein*. Copenhagen: Gyldendal.
Llambías, P. (2013b): *Sex Rouge*. Copenhagen: Gyldendal.

Miller, J.-A. (2006). "On Shame". In J. Clemens and R. Grigg (Eds.), *Jacques Lacan and the Other side of Psychoanalysis*. Durham and London: Duke University Press., 2006.

Nordenhof, A. O. (2013). *Det nemme og det ensomme*, Copenhagen: Forlaget Basilisk.

Rasmussen, B. (2011). *Huden er det elastiske hylster der omgiver hele legemet*. Copenhagen: Gyldendal.

Winblad, C. (2008). *49 forelskelser*. Copenhagen: Athene, 2008.

Personal information

Lone Elmstedt Bild, Master in Modern Culture, University of Copenhagen. Publication:
(2014). Fra ord til kød. [From words to flesh]. *Kritik, 46*(210). Copenhagen: Gyldendal.

Anna-Klara Bojö, Ph.D. student at the Department for Literature, History of Ideas and Religion, University of Gothenburg, Sweden. Previous publications:
(2012). With and beyond the concept 'woman'. In *Anthology on Nordic feminism and gender research*. Karlstad University Press, Karlstad.
(2016). Topos: Taxi. Michel Foucault and Virginia Woolf on two modern grammars of love. *Feminist Theory, 17*(3).

Anna Smedberg Bondesson, Ph.D., Associate Professor in Comparative Literature at Kristianstad University. Place and emotion in literature are research interests of hers. Selected publications:
(2004). *Anna i världen. Om Anna Rydstedts diktkonst*. [Anna in the World. On Anna Rydstedt's poetry]. Lund: Ellerströms.
(2011). Italy seen from Sweden and Sweden seen from Italy. Selma Lagerlöf's Sicilian novel and Italian translations. *Scandinavian Studies, 2*.
(2014). *Ditt språk i min mun. Grannspråkets glädje och gagn*. [Your language in my mouth. On the joys and benefits of neighbouring languages]. Gothenburg & Stockholm: Makadam.
(2017). Through the land of Lagom in literature. Passing small towns in Middle Sweden. In S. P. Sondrup, M. B. Sandberg, T. A. DuBois & D. Ringgaard (Eds.), *Nordic Literature. A Comparative History. Volume 1: Spatial Nodes*. Amsterdam: John Benjamins Publishing Company.

(2018). *Gösta Berling på La Scala. Selma Lagerlöf och Italien.* [Gösta Berling at La Scala. Selma Lagerlöf and Italy]. Gothenburg & Stockholm: Makadam.

(2019). Maggioland. Tröskelns kronotopi, minnets heterotopi och kreativ nostalgi. [Maggioland. The chronotopia of threshold, the heterotopia of memory and creative nostalgia]. In H. Oftedal Andersen & C. K. Madsen (Eds.), *Nye posisjoner i poplyrikken.* Modernisme i nordisk lyrikk 11. Bergen: Alveim & Eide Akademisk Forlag.

Alexander Carnera, D.Phil. and Ph.D., Lecturer in Philosophy, Aesthetics and Social Economy at Copenhagen Business School. Permanent critic at the Scandinavian version of Le Monde Diplomatique and Ny Tid. Independent author and essayist. Several book publications and international journals.

(2009). *Engagementets ABC.* Essays [*Engagement ABC. Essays*] Hellerup: Forlaget Spring.

(2010). *Magten over livet og livet som magt. Studier i den biopolitiske ambivalens* [*Power over life and Life as Power. A Study of the ambivalence of biopolitics*]. Doctoral thesis in philosophy. Copenhagen: Handelshøjskolens forlag.

(2014). Opfindelsen af lediggang. Eller kunsten at fare vild. En essayroman. [*The invention of idleness. Or, the art of getting lost.* Novel]. Hellerup: Forlaget Spring.

(2016). *Erfaringer på kanten.* Essays [*Experience on the edge. Essays*]. Hellerup: Forlaget Spring.

(2021). *Jordens drejebænk* [*The turning lath of the earth*]. Århus: Antipyrine.

Carin Franzén, Professor of Comparative Literature at Stockholm University. She has published various articles and books on literature and psychoanalysis as well as on literary history, most recently:

(2018). Subjects of Sovereign Control and the Art of Critique in the Early Modern Period. In F. Beckman (Ed.), *Control Culture: Foucault and Deleuze after Discipline*. Edinburgh: Edinburgh University Press.

(2020). An Antidote to the Crisis of Contemporary Culture: Rereading Kristeva on Duras. In S. G. Beardsworth (Ed.), *The Philosophy of Julia Kristeva*. Chicago: Open Court Publishing.

(2020). Queen Christina's Coolness. In G. Hermansson & J. Lohfert Jørgensen. (Eds.), *Exploring Nordic Cool in Literary History*. Amsterdam: John Benjamins.

(2020). Lacan and the Archeology of the Subject. In M. Rösing et al. (Eds.), *Analysing the Cultural Unconscious: Science of the Signifier*. London: Bloomsbury Academic.

Gorm Larsen, Ph.D., Associate Professor at Department of Communication, Aalborg University, Copenhagen; Head of the research group *Communication Dynamics*. He has for years studied and written about narratology and especially the act of narration in fiction in light of Bakhtin. Currently, he is doing research on shame and guilt in media and literature from a philosophical and social psychological point of view. He is author, theme-editor as well as co-editor-in-chief of the Danish online encyclopaedia of literature:

(2005). The question of the addressee and the structure of enunciation in Andersen's tales. Or: why the fairy tales are not told for children. In P. K. Hansen and M. Wolff Lundholt (Eds.), *When we get to the end.... Towards a Narratology of the Fairy Tales of Hans Christian Andersen*. Odense: University Press of Southen Denmark.

(2014). Fortællende elementer – altid ufatteligt muligt. Narratologi [Narrative elements – always unbelievably possible. Narratology]. In G. Larsen & R. Rasmussen (Eds.), *Blink. Litterær analyse og metode* [Blink. Literary analysis and method]. Aalborg: Aalborg University Press.

(2015). Genre and the novelistic. In S. Auken, P.S. Lauridsen and A.J. Rasmussen (Eds.). *Genre and…*. Valby: Ekbátana. (Copenhagen Studies in Genre 2).

(2019). Aesthetic and Aestheticization. With P. Allingham. *Academic Quarter*, Vol 19.

(2020f). Hejlsted, A., Larsen, G. and Svendsen, E. (Eds.), *Litteraturleksikon* [*Literature encyclopedia*] (*https://www.sllitteraturleksikon.dk*). Copenhagen: Samfundslitteratur.

Magnus Bøe Michelsen, Ph.D., Teacher at Akademiet Bergen, Norway. Topics of interests include theories of the subject, radical philosophy, psychoanalytic theory and modernist literature. Defended his doctoral thesis at the University of Bergen (2018): *Tarrying with Sexual Matters; Thinking Change from Lacan to Badiou*.

Lars Nylander, Professor of General Literature at NTNU, Trondheim. Earlier publications include:

(1986). Litteratur och psykoanalys—den dubbla utmaningen [Literature and psychoanalysis—the double challenge]. In L. Nylander (Ed.), *Litteratur och psykoanalys*. Stockholm: Norstedts.

(1990). *Prosadikt och modernitet* [*Prose poetry and modernity*]. Stockholm: Stehag, Symposion.

(1998). *Den långa vägen hem. Lars Noréns författarskap från poesi till dramatik* [*The long way home. Lars Norén's writing from poetry to drama*]. Stockholm: Albert Bonniers förlag.

(2010). *Litteraturen, könet och konsten att begära i antiken* [*Literature, gender and the art of desiring in antiquity*]. Oslo: Tapir akademisk forlag.

René Rasmussen, Ph.D., Associate Professor Emeritus, in Danish literature at the Department of Nordic Studies and Linguistics, University of Copenhagen. Selected book publications:

(2000). *Bjelke lige i øjet—om Henrik Bjelkes forfatterskab* [Bjelke Bull's-eye—on the authorship of Henrik Bjelke]. Copenhagen: Forlaget Politisk Revy.

(2004). *Litteratur og repræsentation* [Literature and representation]. Copenhagen: Forlaget Politisk Revy.

(2004). *Kognition—en liberalistisk ideologi* [Cognition—a liberalistic ideology]. Copenhagen: Forlaget Drift.

(2007). *Moderne litteraturteori 1-2* [Modern theory of literature 1-2]. Hellerup: Forlaget Spring.

(2009). *Lacan, sprog og seksualitet* [Lacan, Language and Sexuality]. Hellerup: Forlaget Spring.

(2010). *Psykoanalyse—et videnskabsteoretisk perspektiv* [Psychoanalysis—an epistemological perspective]. Copenhagen: Forlaget Drift.

(2012). *Angst hos Lacan og Kierkegaard og i kognitiv terapi* [Anxiety in Lacan and Kierkegaard and in cognitive therapy]. Hellerup: Forlaget Spring.

(2017) *Kærligheden til det uden navn. Om samtidslyrik.* [Love to that which has no name. About contemporary poetry]. Hellerup: Forlaget Spring.

(2020) *Psykiatri og diagnoser.* [Psychiatry and diagnoses]. Copenhagen: Forlaget Politisk Revy.

François Sauvagnat, (1951-2020) Ph.D. Until his death: Professor at the Psychology Department of the Université de Rennes-II, France; Research Director at the University of Paris VII; directs a seminar at the Ecole Normale Supérieure (Paris). He has mainly developed a comparative viewpoint, studying the mutual influences between the various psychoanalytic trends and their relationships with psychiatry. His publications include ten books and more than 300 articles in seven languages. A good introduction to his approach could be that given in his paper from 2010.

(2004). *Fundamentos de psicopatologia psicoanalitica.* Madrid: Editorial Sintesis.

(2008). (Ed.) *Le trauma psychique*. Paris: Editions L'Harmattan

(2010). A historical perspective on the collaboration between psychoanalysis and the neurosciences. *Journal of Physiology, 104,* 288-295.

Kjell R. Soleim, Professor Emeritus at the University of Bergen. Doctor of Art of Philosophy and Gender Research. Directed courses in psychoanalysis at the University of Bergen, 2005-2013. Member of the New Lacanian School and the World Association of Psychoanalysis. Translator of a selection of texts from Lacan's *Écrits* into Norwegian. Examples of psychoanalytical writing:

(1990). Knut Hamsun et la fin de La Faim. *Information sur les sciences sociales,* SAGE, London, nr. 29,3.

(2012). Who comes after the act? In J. Ayerza (Ed.), *The Symptom,* 13. New York.